(6-27-69) 7days Suored 68-7302

A LINGUISTIC HISTORY

OF ENGLISH

A Linguistic

Robert A. Peters

WESTERN WASHINGTON STATE COLLEGE

History of English

HOUGHTON MIFFLIN COMPANY • BOSTON

New York   Atlanta   Geneva, Ill.   Dallas   Palo Alto

The script on the cover and the title page

is derived from a Secretary hand of 1591.

To my parents,

Dr. and Mrs. L. J. Peters

Preface

This textbook is intended for the first undergraduate course in the history of the English language, the introductory survey of the development of the language from Old English to American English. As such courses are generally either one quarter or one semester in length, the material herein has been tailored to fit that time span. Similarly, the descriptions, definitions, and discussions have been tailored to the level of the course and the audience, primarily English and secondary-education majors, the majority of whom have not had a course in linguistic methods. As a supplementary teaching device for such students, the exercises in the accompanying workbook have been designed to help them retain basic data and to permit them to explore historical material further.

This textbook was written to supply the need for a more modern introductory text and systematic description of the history of the language than is currently available. The brief descriptions of the phoneme, morpheme, etc. offered in this work are not intended to constitute a complete course in the methods and terminology of descriptive linguistics. That is the job of other texts and courses. Similarly, in keeping with the elementary nature of this text, the more intricate linguistic details, dialectal characteristics, and special problems of the various periods have been reserved for those advanced texts and course sequences that describe Old English, Middle English, and Modern English. There is a limit to what can be adequately covered in a one-term introductory course. Suggestions for supplementary reading may be found in the footnotes and the Selected Bibliography.

For convenience in reading, footnotes have been kept to a minimum.

For materials and for permission to reprint, the writer wishes to thank the Oxford and Cambridge University Presses, The John Rylands Library, the Bodleian Library, the University of Michigan Press, the British Museum, the Public Record Office, the G. & C. Merriam Co., and The National Council of Teachers of English.

The author also wishes to thank Professors Harold Allen, Henry Hoenigswald, William Hunter, Helge Kökeritz (deceased), Hans Kurath, Jean Malmstrom, Albert Marckwardt, Raven McDavid, Jr., William Moulton, Carroll Reed, James Sledd, and Robert Van Riper.

The author especially wishes to thank his colleague, Professor Elizabeth Bowman, for aid in proofreading and various suggestions that have contributed to the improvement of the text.

ROBERT A. PETERS

Bellingham, Washington

Contents

Illustrations

Language

This is a book about the history of the English language. Its subject matter is the historical phonology, morphology, syntax, and vocabulary of the language from Old English to American English. This work also includes such related matters as the history of English dictionaries and grammars, the alphabet, and other topics (see table of contents). However, the basic matter is language. Let us begin, therefore, with a discussion of language.

The Nature of Language

Language has been defined in various ways. One definition cited by linguists is that

Language is an arbitrary system of articulated sounds used by human beings to carry on the social affairs of their society.

On the basis of this definition, these ten statements may be made about language:

1. *Language is speech.* It is oral communication. Writing, in contrast, consists of symbols or marks made with a writing instrument on a writing surface such as paper, wood, sand, stone, papyrus, or animal skin. These illustrations are over-simplified, but they illustrate that speech (oral communication) and writing (graphic communication) are not the same.

2. *Language is a human activity.* Animals communicate through various systems of calls and cries, but such forms of communication are not speech. Speech consists of articulate vocal sounds arranged in coherent, interrelated segments. Although animals

I

lack articulate speech, they have the physical capacity to adapt certain organs to produce speech, as man did. But, it is a fact that animals do not speak. A parrot may learn a few words through mimicry, but you cannot carry on a conversation with a parrot about philosophy, politics, religion, or the weather. Man can talk only with his fellow human beings because only human beings speak.

3. *Language is a form of communication.* Through language we express our desires, directives, ideas, and emotions to each other. Speech, therefore, is a medium for giving and receiving information. It is a process by which meanings are transmitted or exchanged between individuals through oral communication. Indeed, if we could not communicate through speech, we would be limited to non-oral forms of communication, such as writing, hand signals, gestures, or the telegraph.

4. *Language is a system.* If it were not, each of us would utter a babble of random noises devoid of common meaning and order of arrangement. We do not do so because the English language consists of a subsystem of sounds (phonology), a subsystem of words (morphology), and a subsystem of word order and word relationships (syntax). Thus language is a complex and inter-locking system of subsystems that may be observed and described.

5. *Language is an arbitrary system.* The number of speech sounds that a human being may produce and distinguish is theoretically unlimited. So many, however, would be impractical for speakers to manage; therefore each language consists of a limited number of speech sounds arbitrarily selected from a number of possibilities. Similar arbitrary selection extends to words, their meanings, and the arrangement or order of words in a language. Hence, the system of a language (phonology, morphology, syntax) is an arbitrary selection by the speakers of that language, and they, as a social group, may arbitrarily change any aspect of their language system whenever they collectively desire to do so.

6. *Language is non-instinctive.* A child does not speak at birth. Speech is something a child learns by imitating the vocal habits of his parents and peer-group members. A child that never heard human speech would have no speech pattern to imitate. Consequently, he would not speak a language. In

order to speak, he would have to learn a set of vocal habits from another human being because language is non-instinctive.

7. *Language is a form of social behavior.* Through language we conduct the innumerable daily affairs of our society. They include telephone conversations, talks with neighbors and friends, gossip over coffee, communications between parents and children, college lectures, and so on. Such verbal conduct is a form of social behavior, and, like our other herd activities, it has commonly accepted norms or standards of behavior. The norms of verbal behavior may vary from one social-economic class to another, but those norms may be measured and described, as may other forms of group behavior, such as dress, etiquette, and ceremonies.

8. *Language is subject to change.* We may not realize it, but we make small sound changes in our language every day. In fact, it is rather difficult for one to pronounce the same word twice in precisely the same way. The tongue may be a millionth of an inch higher or lower, the lips may be a fraction of an inch more open or closed, a speech sound may be pronounced a thousandth of a second longer or shorter, and so on. Normally we are not aware of such variations or changes because they are minute, because they have a short life, and because they are generally meaningless. But, if a change persists and is adopted by a majority of the speakers of a language, a change in that language will have occurred. Actually, all languages change over the centuries as a result of gradual changes in the vocal habits of their speakers. Languages stop changing only when they are no longer spoken, as in the case of a "dead" language such as Gothic, a once "living" cousin of English. As you will learn, many changes have occurred in the English language during its long history.

9. *Language is adequate to its culture.* Each language is a form of communication developed by a particular culture to meet its social needs. For example, if an arctic society needs twenty different words to describe twenty different kinds of snow, the language of that society will have twenty such words; if a tropical society has no need of a word for snow, the language of that society will lack such a word. If any society wants to add or drop words, or to change the meanings of words, or to change

the phonology or syntax of its language, it does so. As a result, no language or dialect is better or worse than another. Each is adequate to its culture.

10. *There is no universal language.* Languages are arbitrary creations of social groups. They are not acts of discovery. Therefore, there is no universal language that all men speak. Rather, the converse is true. Many thousands of languages are spoken around the world.

Origin of Language

How and when did language originate? Over the centuries many men have asked this question, and many have attempted to supply an answer. Some speculations are that language developed from man's attempt to imitate noises (the so-called bow-wow theory), that it arose from cries and exclamations (the pooh-pooh theory), from natural vocal responses (the ding-dong theory), and from imitation of natural sounds (the echoic theory). But these and other philosophic guesses about the origin of language are futile, because we simply do not know how language originated. Man began speaking a long time ago, but we do not know when or at just what stage in his development. Estimates range from twenty-thousand years to a million-and-a-half years ago.

Grammar and Usage

The grammar of a language is its morphology and its syntax, and for convenience some analysts also include phonology. We shall do the same. In this book, therefore, grammar means the phonology, morphology, and syntax of a language. In describing these three subsystems of English, we describe its structure or grammar.

Usage means linguistic behavior, and refers to customary or habitual linguistic practice. For example, we may elect to say either *I do not have a book* or *I ain't got a book*. Our selection of the one construction or the other is a matter of linguistic usage. If we elect *I do not have a book*, we may do so from knowledge that the construction is in accordance with standard usage or the linguistic norm of our society, whereas *I ain't got a book* reflects nonstandard usage or a deviation from the accepted norm of linguistic behavior. In short, our decision involves language etiquette. Although *I do not have a book* is standard and *I ain't got a book* is nonstandard, both constructions are identical in structure, namely pronoun-verb phrase-noun. Thus, grammar and usage mean two different things. Grammar is linguistic structure, and usage is linguistic behavior.

It is helpful to remember the analogy that grammar is to language as anatomy is to the human body. Anatomical analysis provides us with a description or catalogue of the bones, muscles, and organs of the body. Grammatical analysis provides us with a description or catalogue of the bones, muscles, and organs of a language, namely its phonology, morphology, and syntax.

In contrast, usage is to language as hygiene is to the human body. Hygiene tells us how to maintain the health of our bodies. It provides us with a pattern of standard physical behavior. In similar fashion the measurement of linguistic usage provides us with a norm of verbal behavior against which we can evaluate the status of our own linguistic practices. Whereas the study of anatomy and grammar provides us with a classification of parts, hygiene and usage provide us with a norm of behavior.

Levels of Usage

Two labels applied to verbal behavior are standard usage and nonstandard usage. Standard usage is the usage of standard speakers, whose speech practices constitute the linguistic norm. In America standard speakers are primarily educated and urbanized and constitute the upper and most of the middle social-economic classes in America.

Nonstandard usage is the usage of nonstandard speakers, whose speech practices do not conform to the norm. In America nonstandard speakers are generally uneducated.

Standard English is a purely arbitrary set of speech habits that standard speakers employ. For example, the fact that *is not* is standard and *ain't* is nonstandard is little more than a caprice of social history. There is, after all, no divine law which states that *is not* is standard and *ain't* is nonstandard. Perhaps in one or two hundred years the opposite may be true: *is not* may become nonstandard and *ain't* standard. This does not mean that the change actually will occur, but only that there is nothing to prevent society from making the change if it desires to do so. At one time "me thinks" and "thou art" were standard English, but they are not so today because standard speakers stopped using those constructions. No linguistic congress or divine command told them to do so. They simply stopped, quite arbitrarily.

Standard English is important because it is the language of our churches, our law courts, our legislative assemblies, our entire official community. Our writing is also based on standard English, and standard is the form of English taught in our schools, recorded in handbooks and dictionaries, and taught to foreign speakers. As the linguistic norm of society, standard English is essential for success in school and in business, as well as for social advancement. The speaker of nonstandard English has a linguistic handicap in "getting ahead."

Every native speaker of English acquires either standard English or nonstandard English very early in his life, and which it will be is essentially a matter of environment. Those who grow up in an environment where standard English is spoken soon acquire the use of it through imitation of the speech habits of their parents and peer-group members. In similar fashion, those raised in an environment where nonstandard English is spoken acquire it through imitation of the speech habits of those about them.

But by the time these two groups reach school, the group that speaks standard English has the advantage over the one that does not. The latter discover that for success in school they must adopt the speech and writing habits associated with standard usage. Thus we are rewarded or penalized in school by our early linguistic environment.

The Doctrine of Usage

What is or is not standard English is determined from the actual practices of speakers of standard English. Some persons, however, are reluctant to accept that fact. For example, they may insist that the language etiquette of standard English dictates that one should always say "It is I," never "It is me." It is true that "It is I" is standard, but so is "It is me." How do we know? We know from measuring the actual usage of standard speakers. To maintain, therefore, that only "It is I" is standard is to bend the truth somewhat.

Many standard speakers admit that "It is me" is standard or acceptable in conversational or informal situations, but not in a formal situation, such as a public address. In other words, they maintain that there are social situations in which some linguistic constructions are acceptable and others are not, just as they would feel that bluejeans may be worn on a camping trip but are not appropriate at a formal dance.

Other Usage Labels

In addition to standard and nonstandard, there are other labels of linguistic usage. *Colloquial*, for example, simply means conversational, and has no implication of faultiness, although many people think it has. *Folkspeech* refers to isolated rural speech; *vernacular* means the everyday speech of the people, frequently in contrast to *cultured speech*, or that which is cultivated or refined. And *common speech* designates the speech of the great majority of the community, those whose position is neither too high nor too low

Another usage label, *jargon*, refers to the technical or private language of persons engaged in a particular trade or profession or who share a way of life, such as circus performers, monks, reporters, or medical workers. Closely related to jargon is *argot*, or the special vocabulary employed by an underworld group, such as thieves. *Cant* is a derogatory term which implies that the language of a group or clique is lacking in clarity or precision. *Lingo* refers to outlandish usage or language.

Taboo, another label of usage, indicates that which is prohibited or sacred. *Slang* designates coinages and usually short-lived words and expressions in the informal vocabulary which are or once were characterized by novelty, vogue, or force. *Vulgar* describes language practices lacking in culture, refinement, or taste.

7

Although lower levels of usage may sometimes be interesting as items of linguistic curiosity, it is well to remember that social success in life is determined linguistically by standard English. Common sense, therefore, tells us not to use taboo words, vulgar words, slang, cant, argot, and so on. Socially it does not pay.

Dialect

A *dialect* is a regional or class variety of a language that differs from the standard language in features of phonology, morphology, syntax, and vocabulary. As a variety of a language, each dialect differs from every other in some linguistic features. For example, the Southern dialect of American English differs from the Northern dialect of American English in various linguistic features. The Southern, Northern, and other regional American dialects, however, together make up or constitute American English. Although the dialects of a language differ from each other, each contains features of the linguistic core or structure of the language. If this were not so, speakers of different dialects would be unable to communicate with each other. But, as we know, speakers of the different American dialects are able to communicate with each other, because each American dialect shares a sufficient number of common linguistic features intelligible to speakers of the other dialects. For example, a Northerner may have some difficulty in understanding every phrase and expression a Southerner uses, but the linguistic difficulties he encounters are not so great as to make communication between the two speakers impossible.

Isogloss

Dialects are determined by (1) recording the speech habits of the inhabitants of a region, (2) charting those linguistic features on a map of the region, and (3) determining the geographical distribution of those linguistic features. When such regional maps are put together to form a composite map, they give a linguistic portrait of a large area.

The line which the linguistic geographer draws to mark the edge of an area in which a linguistic feature occurs is called an isogloss. Often several isoglosses more or less converge into a bundle of isoglosses. When they do, that bundle of isoglosses usually marks a dialect boundary that separates one dialect area from another.

Regional Dialect

There are many kinds of dialects, of which one kind is the regional dialect, characteristic of a particular region, such as the North or the South.

Class Dialect

Another kind of dialect is the class dialect, used by a certain social class within a speech community. The linguistic differences between one class dialect and another reflect social differences, such as those associated with education and family tradition. Thus in a speech community the speech habits of the upper class of area x may differ from those of the middle class of area x.

Prestige Dialect

Yet a third kind of dialect is the prestige dialect, which is preferred over the class dialects in an area for reasons of prestige. For example, if the upper-class dialect of, say, Charleston, South Carolina, came to be regarded as the dialect socially preferred over all other South Carolina speech, that dialect would be a prestige dialect.

It is well to bear in mind, however, that the social preference given one dialect over another in an area has nothing whatever to do with its linguistic merit as a form of communication, but only with notions of herd prestige associated with a particular set of verbal habits. Prestige, as such, is an odd business involving social aspirations and the need for marks of social distinction. But whether we like it or not, we will be wise to accept the fact that human beings are what they are, and that although the marks of prestige may be inconsequential or trivial, they are no less potent socially and psychologically.

Focal Area

Within a regional dialect area there may be a focal region, containing a major cultural center from which linguistic forms appear to radiate. Such a situation is suggested when the isoglosses surrounding a focal area appear to be expanding outward. For example, in the South, New Orleans is a focal area from which linguistic forms characteristic of the speakers of that city appear to be spreading out to southern Louisiana and southwestern Mississippi.

Relic Area

The opposite of a focal area is a relic area, one in which local speech forms appear to be in recession. The relic area lacks a major cultural center, such as a large city or a group of interdependent cities, and the isoglosses surrounding it seem to be receding inward. Thus a relic area is one that tends to be out of the linguistic main stream of the regional dialect area in which it is located. Cape Cod, for example, is a relic area.

Transition Area

Finally, between regional dialects there may be a transition area which lacks sharply defined characteristics of its own and shares the linguistic features of neighboring areas. Oklahoma, for example, appears to be a transition area, one that shows a mixture of Southern and Midland features.

SUMMARY

In summary, the chief topics discussed in this chapter are:
Language — its characteristics, origin, and age.
Grammar.
Usage — standard, nonstandard, folkspeech, vernacular speech, cultured speech, common speech, jargon, argot, cant, lingo, taboo, vulgar speech, slang.
Dialect — isogloss, regional dialect, class dialect, prestige dialect, focal area, relic area, transition area.

Writing and Printing

This chapter discusses several topics as a unit: writing; the origin of the alphabet; its extension to Britain; the Germanic runic alphabet; manuscripts; and printing.

Writing

We have said that man has perhaps been speaking for a million years, although we are not certain about it. But, man has been writing for a relatively short period of time. For example, Sumerian cuneiform writing in Mesopotamia and Egyptian hieroglyphic writing both date from about 3000 B.C. Writing, therefore, is about 5000 years old; it is much younger than speech.

We have also said that language and writing differ. We equated language with human speech and called writing a system of visible signs. Although both speech and writing are forms of human communication, the former is an oral system of signs, the latter a visual one. We hear speech, but we see writing.

Writing Systems

Tens of thousands of years ago in the oldest paleolithic, or Stone-Age, period, primitive man depicted life in rock drawings, paintings, and carvings. Such petrograms, petroglyphs, and other representational forms of communication, like Indian drawings, are called the forerunners of writing because they lack signs to express linguistic elements. True systems of writing represent utterances in speech, such as logography or word writing (sign = one or more words), syllabary or syllabic writing (sign = one or more syllables), and logosyllabic writing, which employs logographic and syllabic signs.

We have mentioned these matters briefly to illustrate that there are forms of writing other than alphabetic writing, which is a system of graphemes (letters) used to represent the distinctive sound units (phonemes) of a language. The correspondence between sound and symbol is not always perfect; for example, $b = $ /b/ as in *bat*, but $c = $ /k/ as in *cat* or /s/ as in *city*.

The Alphabet

Despite various attempts in the second millenium B.C., none of the Egyptian-Semitic syllabaries succeeded in fully developing a means of indicating vowels. Therefore, none of those writing systems was a true alphabet because each lacked a full system of vowel signs.

The first true alphabet expressing the sounds of a language by consonant and vowel signs was the Greek alphabet. The prototype of that alphabet was introduced to the Greeks in the ninth century B.C. by the Phoenicians, a seafaring Semitic people who lived on the eastern coast of the Mediterranean Sea and traded with the Greeks. The latter made methodical application of vowel signs irregularly used by the Phonecians and thereby developed a full alphabetic system of writing.[1] The Romans later derived their Latin or Roman alphabet from the Greeks. The Romans brought that alphabet to Celtic Britain during their occupation of Britain from 43 A.D. to c. 410.

Runic Alphabet

Germanic warriors from northwestern Europe, the so-called Anglo-Saxons, invaded Romano-Celtic Britain in the fifth century and subsequently conquered that land. The Anglo-Saxons, whose dialects evolved into what we today call Old English, brought with them from the Continent a form of writing based on the runic alphabet or *futhark*. The latter name is derived from the phonetic equivalents of the first six letters of the runic alphabet.

The letters or graphemes of the runic alphabet are called runes, and they consist of vertical and diagonal strokes like those formed in carvings. Plate 1 depicts the forms of some runes.

The origin of the runic alphabet is not known, but it may have been derived from a North Italic source, and developed in part in Denmark by a people called the Eruli. The oldest runic inscriptions, at any rate, come from Denmark and probably date from c. 300 A.D. Thereafter runic writing apparently spread south to Hungary, the land once occupied by the Germanic Goths, and west to northwestern Europe, from which the Anglo-Saxons migrated to Britain.

The name *rune* is derived from Old English *rūn* 'secret, mystery, secret discussion.' In the Old English period, runes were used as magic symbols on weapons and ornaments, and also for messages, inscriptions, and signatures. Runes were used in England for about five centuries, including the period when runic writing was being superseded by the Irish-Roman system of writing.

Plate 1. Anglo-Saxon runes (Thames Scramasax).

f u þ o r c g w h n

p x s t d m æ y b j l

Insular Script

Following the conversion of Ireland to Christianity by St. Patrick in the fifth century A.D., the Irish came to use a half-uncial script which developed from models carried over from the Continent. That script or hand was a lower-case or minuscule script, as distinguished from capital-letter or majuscule script. The graphemes of that minuscule script were round, but they were not normally linked together.

In the early seventh century, Irish monks at monasteries in northern England introduced their half-uncial script to the Anglo-Saxons, who subsequently developed a characteristic variety known as Insular script, which displaced runic writing. Plate 2 illustrates some forms of Old English Insular script.

In the late tenth and early twelfth centuries, insular script was replaced by another script called Caroline minuscule. In later centuries other scripts such as Gothic script, various Court scripts, Secretary script, and Italic were used. We cannot examine these in detail here, but for the purposes of comparison and contrast, Plate 3 depicts one of those later scripts (EModE) Secretary.[2]

Plate 2. OE Insular minuscule script (c. 900).

a   b   c   d   e   f   g   h   i   k   l   m

n   o   p   q   r   s   t   u   v   w   x   y   z

Plate 3. EModE Secretary minuscule hand (1591).

Manuscripts

Before the introduction of printing to England in the late fifteenth century, poems, wills, sermons, and official reports were handwritten by scribes. They wrote with a reed or quill pen, frequently on parchment made from the skin of a sheep or goat. Vellum, a superior grade of parchment, was made from the skin of a kid, calf, or lamb. Many of the handwritten documents or manuscripts of the Old English period were produced in the scriptoria or writing rooms of monasteries and monastic schools.

The production of manuscripts required many hours of work. First the hide was prepared by bleaching, pounding, and rubbing. Then the scribe began his task of writing. The production of a codex or manuscript volume required months of work, but, despite the amount of drudgery involved in such work, many Old English and later Middle English manuscripts show exceptionally fine penmanship. Many are also beautifully decorated with highly ornamented capital letters of various colors — red, blue, green, purple, brown, gold, and silver.

Parchment was costly and difficult to prepare, and therefore scribes made economical use of space in manuscripts. For example, in Old English manuscripts the spacing between sentences and words was frequently the same as that between letters, and lines of verse were written together as lines of prose. Abbreviations and graphemic substitutes were common. Some examples are $7 =$ 'and,' $l =$ Latin *uel* 'or,' $\not{p} = \not{p}æt$ 'that,' and $o\bar{f} =$ *ofer* 'over.'

In the Middle English period a few changes in manuscript practice occurred. Sometimes paragraphs were begun on a new line, and words generally were separated from each other by space, as in Modern English. Toward the end of the Middle English period, capitals or majuscules came to be used freely in names, for words of importance, and for emphasis although capitals generally were not used to indicate the beginning of a sentence.

Following the introduction of printing to England in the fifteenth century, handwritten documents eventually gave way to printed books, except in private and government accounts.

Printing

The art of making paper, invented by the Chinese about 100 A.D., was carried by the Moslems to Spain in the tenth century. Subsequently that art spread to Sicily, Italy, and France, as well as to other countries. At first paper was expensive; it was rarely used in Europe as material for printed books until the fourteenth century, when a reduction in the manufacturing cost of paper was effected through the use of cheap linen rags.

The Chinese also invented printing, using wood blocks in the eighth century A.D., and movable clay type in the eleventh century. But the complete manufacturing process of modern printing was a European invention. Johann Gutenberg (?1398–1468), a German, is reputed to have been the first modern printer, although we do not know whether he or someone before him invented the process of modern printing. At any rate, a letter of indulgence, probably printed by Gutenberg, bears the oldest printed date, 1454. By the end of the fifteenth century the new process of printing spread throughout Europe, replacing older methods of printing with fixed molds as well as the costly and laborious production of books by hand.

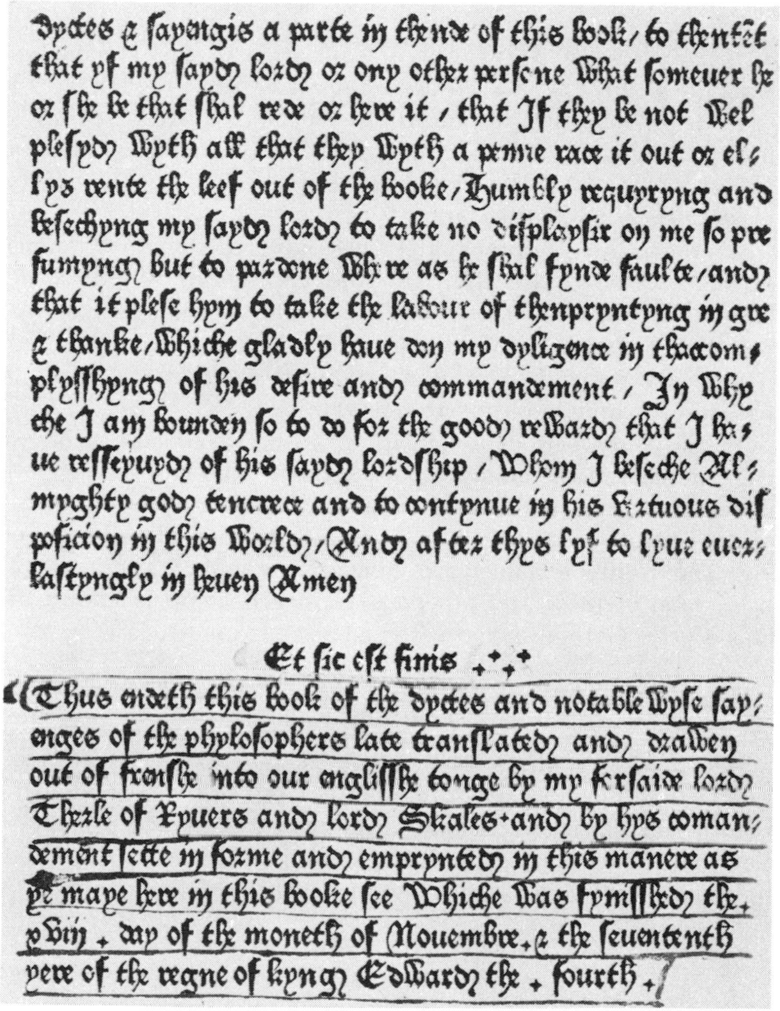

Dyctes & sayengis a parte in thende of this book, to thentent
that yf my sayd lord or ony other persone what someuer he
or she be that shal rede or here it, that If they be not wel
plesyd wyth all that they wyth a penne race it out or el
lys rente the leef out of the booke, Humbly requyryng and
besechyng my sayd lord to take no displaysir on me so pre
sumyng but to pardone whre as he shal fynde faulte, and
that it plese hym to take the labour of thenpryntyng in gre
& thanke, Whiche gladly haue don my dylygence in thaccom
plysshyng of his desire and commandement, In why
che I am bounden so to do for the good rewarde that I ha
ue resseyued of his sayd lordship, Whom I beseche Al
myghty god tencrece and to contynue in his vertuous dis
posicion in this world, And after thys lyf to lyue euer
lastyngly in heuen Amen

Et sic est finis

Thus endeth this book of the dyctes and notable wyse say
enges of the phylosophers late translated and drawen
out of frensshe into our englisshe tonge by my forsaide lord
Therle of Ryuers and lord Skales, and by hys coman
dement sette in forme and emprynted in this manere as
ye maye here in this booke see Whiche was fynysshed the
xviij day of the moneth of Nouembre & the seuententh
yere of the regne of kyng Edward the fourth

Plate 4. Last page with colophon of William Caxton's *Dictes or Sayengis
of the Philosophers*. The John Rylands Library; reproduced by permission.

Caxton

In 1475 William Caxton, an Englishman living in Belgium, printed the first book in English. This book, called *The recuyell of the historyes of Troye*, was a translation of the Frenchman Raoul le Fèvre's *Le Recueil des Histoires de Troie* (1464).

In 1476, following his return to England, Caxton set up a press "at the sign of the Red Pale" in Westminster, then a suburb of London. His first dated book (1477) was *The dictes or sayengis of the philosophres*.

Caxton printed approximately one hundred items. After his death, Caxton's associate, an Alsatian named Wynkyn de Worde, moved to London "in Flete-strete, at the sygne of the Sonne." There, by 1535, he had printed almost eight hundred items.[3] By the end of the century the art of modern printing had spread throughout most of Britain.

In the early period of modern printing in Britain, printers were influenced by manuscript practices. The earliest printed books, for example, lacked title pages. These early books, printed before 1501, which lack date of printing, place of printing, and printer's name, are called incunabula. The type of print used in these and other early printed books is known as black letter Gothic; modern Roman type is used today.

SUMMARY

Age of writing, Greek development of the alphabet, transmission of the Roman alphabet to Britain, Germanic runic alphabet, OE Insular script, production of manuscripts, manuscript practices, the invention of modern printing, William Caxton, the first book printed in English, Wynkyn de Worde, incunabula.

NOTES

[1] I. J. Gelb, *A Study of Writing* (Chicago, 1952), pp. 178, 181, 184, 197.

[2] For a brief history of the development of English scripts and hands, see N. Denholm-Young, *Handwriting in England and Wales* (Cardiff, 1954).

[3] The stalls and shops of most early English booksellers in London were concentrated around the vicinity of St. Paul's churchyard, and each trader had his own sign to identify his premises.

Speech Production

In this chapter we shall consider how speech is produced and which organs are involved in speech production. Our discussion, however, will not include an examination of certain vocal qualities like the whining tone, scolding tone, cheerful tone, tone of contempt, and so on. Neither shall we examine varieties of voice, such as murmur, whisper, and falsetto.

Vocal Tract

The organs involved in the production of speech are located in the head, throat, and chest. The primary functions of these organs are physiological: breathing, chewing, and swallowing. Speech is a secondary function to which man has adapted them.

To obtain a comprehensive view of the vocal tract and the names of its parts, let us follow the path of the airstream exhaled from the *lungs*. After leaving the lungs, the airstream travels upward through the windpipe or *trachea* (see diagram of vocal tract). At the top of the trachea the airstream passes through a functional group of structures collectively called the *larynx*, inside of which are two elastic bands or folds called the *vocal cords*. The opening between them is called the *glottis*. After the airstream leaves the larynx it passes to the upper throat or *pharynx*, from which it may travel in one of two directions. If the *velic* or nasal side of the velum (the soft rear roof of the mouth) is retracted against the rear wall of the pharynx or upper throat, the airstream is shunted through the mouth or *oral*

Plate 5. Cross section of the vocal tract.

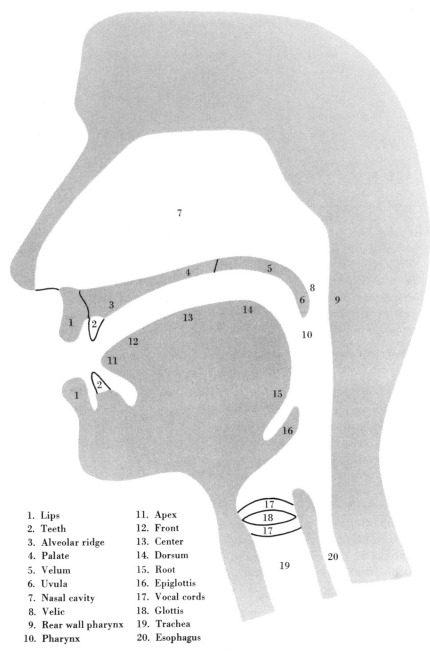

1. Lips	11. Apex
2. Teeth	12. Front
3. Alveolar ridge	13. Center
4. Palate	14. Dorsum
5. Velum	15. Root
6. Uvula	16. Epiglottis
7. Nasal cavity	17. Vocal cords
8. Velic	18. Glottis
9. Rear wall pharynx	19. Trachea
10. Pharynx	20. Esophagus

cavity, as in [s] in *sit*. The closure made by the velic against the rear wall of the pharynx resembles the action of a valve. If, however, the velum is lowered slightly and the airstream is blocked at some point in the mouth, the airstream is shunted through the *nasal cavity* and then out through the nose, as in [m] in *met*. Nasalization refers to nasal sounds as well as oral-nasal sounds. The latter are marked [~], as [ẽ] in Portuguese *bem* [bẽ] 'well.'

Airstreams

Speech sounds require the movement of an airstream in or out of the human head. The lungs, which are the most important organs for originating airstreams, initiate an egressive or out-going airstream from which all normal English sounds are produced. An ingressive or ingoing airstream results when a partial vacuum is created through release of a tongue-mouth roof formation, as in the clicks or mouth-air sounds used in urging a horse forward. Clicks are common in some African languages in southern Africa.

Vocal Cords

In normal breathing the vocal cords are wide apart and relaxed. The airstream passes freely through the glottis or opening between them. When the vocal cords are tightly drawn together so that the glottis is completely shut, the air stream is blocked. This happens when we hold our breath, or strain to lift a heavy object. Closure of the glottis during the act of speech produces a slight catch or choke in breath called a glottal stop. It is written [ʔ] as in [ʔʌ̃ʔʌ̃] for *unh-unh*, meaning "no."

The airstream may be partially obstructed by the vocal cords as it passes through the glottis, and varying degrees of audible turbulence or friction may result. Such glottal friction may occur when we pronounce [h] in *hit*. However, sometimes [h] is nothing more than momentary voicelessness without friction, and sometimes it is characterized by slight friction in the pharynx called pharyngeal friction, but for convenience [h] usually is labeled a glottal fricative, as we shall call it in this book.

| 2a Open | 2b Voice | 2c Closed |

Plate 6. Positions of the vocal chords.

The quasi-periodic opening and closing of the vocal cords modulates the airstream from the lungs.[1] The result is a pulsating air flow, which also has vocal resonances. A sound so characterized is called a voiced sound, and one not so characterized is called a voiceless sound. If you place your fingers on your Adam's apple, which is the prominence made by the thyroid cartilage that forms the front of the larynx, you should be able to detect the modulation of voice when you pronounce voiced [z] as in *zip*, but not when you pronounce voiceless [s] as in *sip*.

Sources and Filters

The source of a speech wave may be a voice source, as in voiced sounds, or it may be one or more noise sources, which are primary acoustic disturbances in the vocal tract, such as those that characterize stop, fricative, and aspirated sounds.[2] The source also may be a mixture of voice sound and noise sources, as in the case of voiced stops, as [d] in *din*.

The vocal tract acts as an acoustic filter that allows sound energy to pass through at frequencies at which it resonates. The pharynx and oral cavities act as acoustic filters for sounds with a voice source and an oral output. In the case of a nasal output, the filtering process involves the pharynx and nasal cavities.

Articulators

The vocal tract filter system is dependent upon the position of the articulators. An articulator is a movable speech organ that impedes or directs the airstream.

In the mouth the principal articulators are, from front to rear, the *lips*, especially the lower lip, the *tongue*, and the *velum* or soft rear roof of the mouth. A subpart of the velum is the *uvula* or small cone-shaped appendage hanging down above the back of the tongue.[3] A second subpart of the velum is the *velic* or nasal side of the velum.

Subparts of the tongue are the *apex* or tip of the tongue, the *front* of the tongue or area directly in back of the apex, the *center* of the tongue, the *dorsum* or back of the tongue, and the *root* of the tongue, which is attached to the rear floor of the mouth.

In the throat the principal articulators are the *vocal cords*, which are situated in the larynx. One vocal cord is attached to each side of the larynx from front to rear. At the front of the larynx the two cords are attached together. At the rear each cord is attached to a movable piece of cartilage. The view from the top is that of ʌ.

Point of Articulation

In the production of speech a juncture or near juncture may take place between a movable speech organ (articulator) and a relatively stationary part of the vocal tract. The position of that juncture or near juncture is called a point of articulation.

The tongue is a movable speech organ or articulator, and the *alveolar ridge* or upper gum is a stationary part of the vocal tract. In describing [d] as in *debt*, we say that the meeting of the apex or tip of the tongue and the alveolar ridge constitutes the articulation of that sound.

Other principal stationary, or nearly stationary, parts of the vocal tract are the *teeth*, the *palate* or hard roof of the mouth behind the alveolar ridge, and the *rear wall of the pharynx* or upper throat. The last is involved, you will remember, in velic closure.

Articulation may also involve a juncture or near juncture between two articulators. The two vocal cords are movable speech organs or articulators. The near juncture between the two, as in [h] in *hit*, constitutes glottal articulation.

Description of Articulation

Speech sounds may be described as either voiced or voiceless, and according to their articulation. To describe their articulation we name the *articulator(s)* at the *point of articulation*. For example, [f] as in *fit* is a *labio-dental* sound. The articulation involves the lower lip (labial) and the upper teeth (dental). On the other hand, [p] as in *pit* is *bilabial* (both lips), [t] as in *tip* is *apico-alveolar* (apex and alveolar ridge), [š] as initially in *she* is *fronto-palatal* (front of tongue and palate), [g] as in *get* is *dorso-velar* (dorsum and velum), and [h] as in *hit* is *glottal*.

Plate 7.   English articulations.

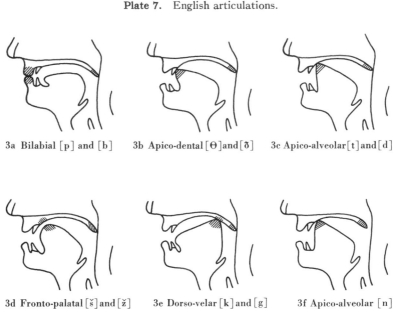

3a Bilabial [p] and [b]   3b Apico-dental [Θ] and [ð]   3c Apico-alveolar [t] and [d]

3d Fronto-palatal [š] and [ž]   3e Dorso-velar [k] and [g]   3f Apico-alveolar [n]

SUMMARY

Airstreams — egressive, ingressive.

Sounds — voiced, voiceless, glottal fricative, glottal stop.

Sources — voice, noise, mixed voice-noise.

Filters — pharynx, oral, nasal cavities.

Vocal tract — lungs, trachea (windpipe), larynx, glottis (opening between the vocal cords), pharynx (upper throat), oral cavity, nasal cavity.

Articulators — vocal cords, lips, velum (uvula and velic), and tip (apex), front, center, and back (dorsum) of the tongue.

Stationary parts — alveolar ridge (upper gum), teeth, palate (hard roof of the mouth), rear wall of the pharynx (upper throat).

Articulation — labio-dental (lip-teeth), bilabial (two lips), apico-alveolar (tongue tip-upper gum), apico-dental (tongue tip-teeth), fronto-palatal (tongue front-hard roof of the mouth), dorso-velar (tongue back-rear roof of the mouth), glottal (glottis).

NOTES

[1] Gunnar Fant, *Acoustic Theory of Speech Production* ('s-Gravenhage, 1960), pp. 17–18, 265–266. The conventional view that voiced sounds "are emitted with concomitant periodic vibrations of the vocal bands," and voiceless sounds "without such vibrations" is stated in Roman Jakobson, Fant, and Morris Halle, *Preliminaries to Speech Analysis* (Cambridge, Mass., 1951; sixth printing, 1965), p. 26.

[2] Fant, *Acoustic Theory of Speech Production*, pp. 16–18. A stop is a speech sound in which there is complete stoppage and then release of the airstream, as [p] in *spin*. A fricative is a speech sound with audible turbulence or friction as a result of passage of the airstream through a relatively small opening, as [f] in *fin*. An aspirated sound is one made by expelling the airstream with a slight constriction of the pharynx or oral cavities; the compressed airstream is released in an audible puff, as in the articulation of English stops initially before a vowel, as the initial sound of *pit*. Aspirated sounds are variously marked ['], [ʰ], or [h], as in *pit* [p'ɪt] or [pʰɪt] or [phɪt]. [h] as in *pit* [phɪt] usually marks heavy aspiration.

[3] The uvula is a minor articulator. A uvular sound is one produced with vibration of the uvula or with the dorsum near or contacting the uvula. A uvular trill, sometimes called uvular *r*, may be heard in the speech of some foreigners who have learned English. A trill is defined in Chapter 4 of this book.

Phone-Types: List I

We have discussed language in general, speech production, and articulation. In this chapter we shall examine the first of two lists of phonetic symbols used in this book.

Phonetic Alphabet

For the purpose of analysis, it is convenient to regard the stream of speech as a sequence of speech segments. To symbolize such speech segments or phone-types, we employ a phonetic alphabet. This is a series of phonetic symbols used to represent phone-types in a one-to-one correspondence of symbol to phone-type. For example, a pronunciation of *sit* is symbolized by the phone-types [s], [ɪ], and [t], as in *sit* [sít]. ['] indicates principal stress.

Syllable

A syllable is a unit of pronunciation. *Sit*, for example, is one syllable, *sitting* is two; and *sitting room* is three.

A syllable consists of either a syllabic peak alone or a syllabic peak with one or more syllabic margins. A syllabic peak, also called a syllabic nucleus, forms the most prominent part of a syllable. It is that part of a syllable which is the domain of stress as [ɪ] in *sit* [sít]. A syllabic margin forms the boundary or margin of a syllable, as [s] and [t] in *sit* [sít]. A syllabic margin is not under the domain of stress.

LIST I

We now turn to our first list of phonetic symbols. They represent phone-types which have regularly occurred as syllabic margins in the history of the English language. We do not include all such phone-types, only those cited in our elementary survey to describe the principal sounds of the various historical periods of English. In describing these phone-types, we shall specify (1) whether they are voiced or voiceless, (2) their articulator and general point of articulation, and (3) their sound-type: glide, stop, fricative, sibilant, affricate, nasal, lateral, or trill. We begin with glides.

Glides

A glide is a speech sound in which there is an uninterrupted movement or glide of the speech mechanism from the position of one speech sound to that of another.

The three glides we shall examine are [w], [y], and [r]. In initial positions they are on-glides, which means they are glides that move to the position of a following sound, as in *wet*, *yet*, and *red*.

1. Voiced labio-velar glide [w] as in *wet* [wɛt].

In [w] the tongue moves in an uninterrupted glide from a generally higher back position in the mouth to the position of the following speech sound. The lips are in a rounded and protruded position at the start but change as the glide occurs. Sometimes the glide movement of [w] is minimal, as in *woo*, but in other instances it is more pronounced, as in *wash*.

[hw] symbolizes the glottal variety of [w]. It is an [h]-approach to a [w]-glide. [hw] differs from [h] in that the speech mechanism is in motion, whereas for [h] the speech mechanism is relatively stationary. Some persons use [hw] in *which* and [w] in *witch*. Others use [w] in both.

2. Voiced fronto-palatal glide [y] as in *yet* [yɛt].

The glide [y] is similar to glide [w], except that the lips are usually more lax and open, and the tongue moves from a generally higher *front* position in the mouth. In contrast, in [w] the movement is from a generally higher *back* position. Sometimes the glide movement of [y] is minimal, as in *ye*, but frequently it is distinct, as in *yaw*.

[hy] is the glottal variety of [y]. We have already described [hw] as an [h]-approach to a [w]-glide. We also describe [hy] as an [h]-approach to a [y]-glide. [hy] is regularly heard instead of [h] in such words as *human* and *huge*.

3. Voiced apico-alveolar glide [r] as in *red* [réd].

There are several varieties of [r] in English, but the one we have described is generally voiced and apico-alveolar, that is, with the tongue tip pointed toward the upper gum.

Stops

A stop is a speech sound in which there is complete stoppage and then release of the air stream. In [p], for example, there is bilabial closure followed by sudden release. The six stops we shall encounter are:

4. Voiceless bilabial stop [p] as in *pin* [pín].
5. Voiced bilabial stop [b] as in *bin* [bín].
6. Voiceless apico-alveolar stop [t] as in *tin* [tín].
7. Voiced apico-alveolar stop [d] as in *din* [dín].
8. Voiceless dorso-velar stop [k] as in *cap* [kǽp].
9. Voiced dorso-velar stop [g] as in *gap* [gǽp].

Fricatives

A fricative is a speech sound with audible turbulence or friction produced as a result of passage of the air stream through a relatively small opening. The four fricatives below are called slit fricatives because the air-stream passes through a horizontal slit in the mouth.

10. Voiceless labio-dental fricative [f] as in *fat* [fǽt].
11. Voiced labio-dental fricative [v] as in *vat* [vǽt].
12. Voiceless apico-dental fricative [θ] as in *thigh* [θái].
13. Voiced apico-dental fricative [ð] as in *thy* [ðái].

Sibilants

In addition to slit fricatives, there are also groove fricatives, so named because the air stream passes through a groove-like opening centered along the length of the tongue. Groove fricatives or [s]-like fricatives are often called sibilants, a convenient term which we shall use in this book.

14. Voiceless apico-alveolar sibilant [s] as in *sip* [síp].

15. Voiced apico-alveolar sibilant [z] as in *zip* [zíp].

16. Voiceless fronto-palatal sibilant [š] as *sh* in *ship* [šíp].

17. Voiced fronto-palatal sibilant [ž] as medially (in the middle) in *vision* [vížən].

In addition to the slit fricatives [f], [v], [θ], and [ð] and the [s]-like fricatives or sibilants [s], [z], [š], and [ž], there are four more fricatives:

18. Voiceless glottal fricative [h] as in *hit* [hít].

In the last chapter we described [h] as being voiceless and produced by glottal narrowing. We also said that [h] may represent either pharyngeal friction or momentary voicelessness.

19. Voiced apico-alveolar fricative [ɹ]. Fricative [ɹ], written as an upside-down *r*, has audible turbulence or friction, but [r] as in *red* [rɛd] does not.

In fricative [ɹ] the tongue tip generally is pointed toward the upper gum, and frequently the middle of the tongue is somewhat arched toward the roof of the mouth. [ɹ] may be voiced, as after voiced [d] in *dream*, but a nearly voiceless variety may be heard after voiceless [t] as in *tree*. For our purposes, however, we shall write [ɹ] for both varieties. Instead of [ɹ] in *dream* and *tree*, some speakers may have [r].

20. Voiceless dorso velar fricative [x] as *ch* in German *ach* [áx].

Note that the final sound in German *ach* is not [k] but [x]. They are similar except that [x] has strong friction.[1] [x] also occurs finally in German *ich* [íx]. Some analysts distinguish the slight difference in quality between the final sounds of German *ach* and *ich* by writing final [x] in German *ach* and final [ç] in *ich*. But the slight qualitative difference between [x] in German *ach* and [ç] in German *ich* is conditioned by the position of the tongue for the sound that precedes the final segment in each word. We shall therefore write [x] for both variants.

[x] occurred in earlier periods of English but is now not normally heard in American English, although it occurs in Scottish English *loch* [lɔx] as in *Loch Lomond*.

21. Voiced dorso-velar fricative [γ] as *g* medially in Spanish *rogar*.

If you do not speak Spanish or do not know someone who does, it may be helpful to point out that [γ] is similar to [g] except that [γ] has friction.[2] Because [γ] is not a normal American English sound, we have to use an illustrative word from Spanish. As in the case of [x], however, [γ] occurred in English in the past.

Affricates

An affricate may be described as a stop with fricative release, or one producing friction. In the two affricates listed next, the tongue begins with an almost fronto-palatal closure. There is a relatively slow release, and friction occurs as the air stream passes through the widening aperture.

22. Voiceless fronto-palatal affricate [č] as ch in chip [číp].
23. Voiced fronto-palatal affricate [ǰ] as g in gem [ǰɛm].

Nasals

A nasal is a speech sound in which all or part of the air stream is stopped in the mouth but continues through the nasal passage, when there is no velic closure. For example, in [m] the air stream is blocked by closure of both lips. The velum is lowered so that the passage to the nasal cavity is open. The air stream enters the nasal cavity through the naso-pharynx, and is released through the nasal passage.

There are several varieties of nasals, but we shall only consider these three in our survey:

24. Voiced bilabial nasal [m] as in met [mɛt].
25. Voiced apico-alveolar nasal [n] as in net [nɛt] and sin [sín].
26. Voiced dorso-velar [ŋ] as ng in sing [síŋ].

Lateral

A lateral is a speech sound in which there is lateral escape of the air stream over one or both sides of the tongue. In [l], for example, there is apico-alveolar blockage of the air stream, which escapes through an opening over one or both sides of the tongue. Although several varieties of laterals occur in English, we shall describe only one variety in our elementary survey:

27. Voiced apico-alveolar lateral [l] as in let [lɛt].

Trill

A trill is a speech sound produced by the rapid vibration of an articulator. A trill may involve rapid vibration of the tip of the tongue against the alveolar ridge, as in the articulation of *r* in Spanish, or it may involve the rapid vibration of the uvula against the back of the tongue, as in the articulation of *r* in some varieties of German. We are concerned with the former variety, which we describe as:

28. Voiced apico-alveolar trill [r̈] as initially in Spanish *rogar* [r̈oɣár].

Trill [r̈] is written as *r* with two dots above it. The tongue, set in motion by a strong air stream, vibrates rapidly under tension, and there is a rapid succession of tongue-tip taps, generally against the lower edge of the gum behind the front teeth.

Tongue-tip trill [r̈] is not usually heard in modern English, at least in American English, but it formerly occurred in English.

Chart

This chart will help to differentiate the phone-types we have described. The abbreviation *vl* = voiceless, and *v* = voiced. The glottal varieties of [w] and [y] are not included.

		Bilabial	Labio-dental	Labio-velar	Apico-dental	Apico-alveolar	Fronto-palatal	Dorso-velar	Glottal
Stops	vl	[p				t		k	
	v	b				d		g	
Fricatives	vl		f		θ			x	h
	v		v		ð	ɹ		ɣ	
Sibilants	vl					s	š		
	v					z	ž		
Affricates	vl						č		
	v						ǰ		
Nasals	v	m				n		ŋ	
Lateral	v					l			
Trill	v					r̈			
Glides	v			w		r	y]		

31

SUMMARY

Phonetic alphabet, syllable, syllabic peak or nucleus, syllabic margin, glide, stop, fricative, sibilant, affricate, nasal, lateral, trill.
Stops [p t k b d g]
Fricatives [f θ x h v ð ɹ γ]
Sibilants [s š z ž]
Affricates [č ǰ]
Nasals [m n ŋ]
Lateral [l]
Trill [r̊]
Glides [w y r]

NOTES

[1] Namely, both are voiceless and dorso-velar, except that [k] is a stop and [x] is a fricative.

[2] That is, both are voiced and dorso-velar, except [g] is a stop and [γ] is a fricative.

Phone-Types: List II

In this chapter we present the second and final list of phonetic symbols used in this book. They represent phone-types that have regularly occurred as syllabic nuclei during the history of the English language. They are normally voiced, and in their production the air stream passes through the mouth over the center of the tongue without appreciable friction. The quality of the nuclei varies with the size, shape, and condition of the mouth.

Height and Position

Nuclei are described according to the height and lengthwise position of the tongue in the mouth. The height of the tongue may be high, mid, or low, and the position of the tongue may be front, central, or back. For example, the height of the tongue is high and its position is front for [i] in *beet* [bít], but low and central for [ɑ] in *father* [fɑ́ðər], as in this front-to-back profile view of the oral cavity:

	Front	Central	Back
High	i		
Mid			
Low		ɑ	

Tenseness

A nucleus is described as tense if the muscles of the tongue and accompanying muscles of the vocal tract are tense, as in [i] in *beet* [bít]. A nucleus is lax if the muscles are lax, as in [ɪ] in *bit* [bít].

Rounding

A nucleus is described as rounded if the lips are rounded and protruded, as in [u] in *pool* [púl]. A nucleus is unrounded if the lips are spread, as in [i] in *beet* [bít].

Key Words

To illustrate nuclei we shall use key words, although they represent a compromise. Some speakers will have nuclei other than those indicated in key words, because of variations in American English dialects. In order to distinguish the various nuclei, therefore, the reader should pay close attention to the descriptions given and should consult the nucleus chart on page 36.

Front Nuclei

These front nuclei are all unrounded:
1. High front tense [i] as in *beet* [bít].

In the reader's pronunciation there may be a slight off-glide or movement of the tongue from the position for [i] in *be* [bí] and *beet* [bít], and also with regard to [e], [o], and [u]. Nevertheless, in this book we shall represent all these varieties by the single symbols [i], [e], [o], and [u].
2. Lower high front lax [ɪ] as in *bit* [bít].
3. Higher mid front tense [e] as in *bait* [bét].
4. Lower mid front lax [ɛ] as in *bet* [bɛ́t].
5. Higher low front tense [æ] as in *bat* [bǽt].
6. Low front lax [a] as in Eastern New England *ask* [ásk], *aunt* [ánt], and *half* [háf] in contrast to [ǽsk], [ǽnt], and [hǽf] in several other areas.

34

Pronounce *beet, bit, bait, bet, bat,* (ENE) *bask.* Notice that the tongue is front but that it goes from high in *beet* to low in (ENE) *bask.* Notice also that the lower jaw drops and that the mouth opens wider.

Central Nuclei

These central nuclei are also unrounded:

7. Higher mid-central [ɜ] as in Eastern New England pronunciations of *r*-less *bird* [bɜ́d], and both *heard* and *herd* [hɜ́d].

8. Mean mid central [ə], called schwa, which commonly occurs in unstressed syllables as in *again* [əgɛ́n], *even* [ívən], and *sofa* [sófə]. Unstressed means that it does not bear a principal stress.

9. Lower mid central [ʌ] as in *cut* [kʌ́t], *bud* [bʌ́d], and *rough* [rʌ́f]. The tongue position for [ʌ] is slightly back of that for [ə].

10. Low central [ɑ] as frequently in *father* [fɑ́ðər], *not* [nɑ́t], and *palm* [pɑ́m], but see 16 below.

Back Nuclei

These back nuclei are rounded:

11. High back tense [u] as in *pool* [púl].

12. Lower high back lax [ʊ] as in *put* [pʊ́t].

13. Higher mid back [o] as in *open* [ópən] or [ópɪn] and *so* [só].

14. Lower mid back [ɔ] as often in *law* [lɔ́] and *dog* [dɔ́g] outside of Eastern New England and Western Pennsylvania.

15. Low back [ɒ] as in Eastern New England and Western Pennsylvania *law* [lɒ́] and *dog* [dɒ́g].

This back nucleus is unrounded:

16. Low back [ɑ̈] as in metropolitan New York and Southern *r*-less *car* [kɑ̈́] and *father* [fɑ̈́ðə], but [ká], [fáðə] in Eastern New England and [kár], [fáðər] in several other areas.

More Front Nuclei

These front nuclei are rounded:

17. High front tense [ü] as in German *kühn* [kǘn], or in French *tu* [tǘ]. You will come close to pronouncing [ü] if you round the lips and pronounce [i].

18. Lower high front lax [ü] as in German *müssen* [mǘsən]. Round the lips and pronounce [ɪ].

This chart illustrates the relative tongue height, tongue position, and rounding (R) or unrounding (U) in the nuclei described above.

	Front		Central	Back	
	U	R	U	U	R
High	i	ü			u
Lower high	ɪ	ü̈			ʊ
Higher mid	e		ɜ		o
Mean mid			ə		
Lower mid	ɛ		ʌ		ɔ
Higher low	æ				
Low	a		ɑ	ɷ	ɒ

Complex Nuclei

The nuclei listed above are called simple nuclei. There are also complex nuclei that differ phonetically from simple nuclei. Complex nuclei are characterized by a single continuous glide from the position for one nucleus to that for another within the same syllable.

The difference between the two types of nuclei may be noted by comparing the articulation of the simple nucleus [ɑ], as often in *baa* [bɑ], with the articulation of the complex nucleus [ɑɪ], as often in *buy* [bɑ́ɪ]. In the latter the tongue and lips are in position for [ɑ́] at the beginning. Then, in one continuous glide within the same syllable, they change through intermediate positions and end in the position approximately that for [ɪ]. This does not happen with simple nuclei.[1]

We symbolize complex nuclei with two phonetic symbols, but they do not represent two separate nuclei, for complex nuclei are single sounds. The first phonetic symbol marks the starting position of the glide and the second marks the end position of the glide, as in [aɪ] in *buy* [báɪ], and as in [aʊ] in *bough* [báʊ].

The sonorous quality of a complex nucleus may be strongest at the beginning of the glide, after which it uniformly decreases, as in [áɪ] in *buy* [báɪ]. In other complex nuclei a reverse pattern of sonority may occur. The sonorous quality may be weakest at the beginning of the glide, after which it uniformly increases to a peak at the end of the glide, as in [ɪʊ] in some pronunciations of *Hugh* [hɪʊ́]. In our examples the more sonorous element of complex nuclei is marked with principal stress, as in [báɪ] and [hɪʊ́], but the less sonorous element of complex nuclei is not marked.

According to whether the stressed element is first or last, complex nuclei are called either falling or rising complex nuclei. In a falling complex nucleus the stressed element is first, as in *boy* [bɔ́ɪ]. In a rising complex nucleus the stressed element is last, as in *Hugh* [hɪʊ́].

R-less Off-glides

Sometimes [ə] is a syllabic peak, but sometimes not. Sometimes it is a non-syllabic off-glide that shares the distribution of syllabic margins such as [r], [t], etc. To indicate this, we write [˘] under [ə] as in [ə̯]. [ə̯] is heard in Eastern New England, metropolitan New York, and parts of the South, as in *r*-less *fear* [fíə̯] and *feared* [fíə̯d].

The articulation of non-syllabic [ə̯], as in *r*-less [fíə̯], is the same as that of syllabic [ə] in some two-syllable pronunciations of *fear*, as [fí-ə̂].[2] The two phone-types differ, however, in distribution. [ə] is a syllabic nucleus under stress, but [ə̯] is not; it is a syllabic margin.

R-full Off-glides

Sometimes non-syllabic [ə̯] has an *r*-quality. To indicate this, some analysts affix the hook of *r* to the right side of [ə̯], as in *r*-full *fear* [fíɚ̯] and *feared* [fíɚ̯ d], but we shall not. In this text

37

we shall use the more convenient symbol [r] as in *r*-full *fear* [fír] and *feared* [fírd].

R-full Nuclei

Syllabic nuclei may also have an *r*-quality. Some analysts indicate this by affixing the hook of *r* to nuclei symbols such as [ɜ] and [ə], as in *r*-full *her* [hɝ] and *bitter* [bítɚ]. We shall simply use [r], as in *r*-full *her* [hɜr] and *bitter* [bítər].

Lengthened Nuclei

Sometimes a nucleus is short, and sometimes it is long. A long nucleus is held longer than a short nucleus. To indicate all degrees of long nuclei, we shall write [ː] after such nuclei, as in some *r*-less pronunciations of *fear* as [fíː].

In *r*-less [fíː] there is no non-syllabic off-glide [ə], as occurs in other *r*-less pronunciations of *fear* as [fíə]. Instead, the nucleus is lengthened or prolonged in duration of time. Thus, [ɪ] in [fíə] is short, and [ɪː] in [fíː] is long.

SUMMARY

Simple Nuclei
Front (U): [i ɪ e ɛ æ a]
    (R): [ü ü]
Central (U): [ɜ ə ʌ ɑ]
Back (R): [u ʊ o ɔ ɒ]
    (U): [ɤ]
Complex Nuclei
Falling: [ɔɪ áɪ áʊ]
Rising: [ɪú]
Lengthened nucleus: [ɪː]
R-less off-glide: [ə]
R-full nucleus: [ɪr]

This concludes our introductory discussion of language, speech production, phonetic symbols, and phone-types. In the next chapter we turn to an examination of the ancestry of English.

NOTES

¹ The glide action of "full" complex nuclei like [ɑɪ] in *buy* [bɑ́ɪ] is distinct from that of "partial" complex nuclei like [eᴵ] sometimes in *bay* [béᴵ]. In the latter, the slight glide movement does not begin until the distinct nucleus [e] is heard. On the other hand, in "true" or "full" complex nuclei the articulation is in continuous drift and is not sufficiently stationary for a distinct nucleus like either [ɑ] or [ɪ] in *buy* [bɑ́ɪ] to be heard. In this book we shall therefore mark nucleus varieties with and without a slight off-glide by single nucleus symbols, such as [i], [e], [o], and [u]. Thus we do not write *bay* as [béᴵ] or [béɪ], but as [bé].

² [^] symbolizes secondary stress in contrast with principal or primary stress [']. In our example we have marked [-ə] with secondary stress for the purpose of illustration, but in actual pronunciation the stress of [-ə] may be weaker.

Ancestry of English

Number of Languages

There are about 2,500 languages spoken around the world.[1] As this figure is only an estimate, there may be about two hundred more or less. If we add 250 "dead" or extinct languages, some of which are only partly known, we reach a total of about 2,750 known languages.

We do not have the accurate figure because we lack many linguistic facts. For example, we know little about the speech habits of several cultures in different parts of the world, like New Guinea and South America. In such cases we do not know whether any two sets of relatively unexplored speech habits constitute two different languages or two dialects of the same language. Until we gain this knowledge, we can only estimate the total number of languages.

Another reason involves the classification of known languages. There is continual controversy whether languages should be classified entirely on linguistic features or on cultural factors as well. Czech and Slovak, because of almost mutual intelligibility, may be called Czechoslovakian, but because their speakers have different cultural characteristics and literatures, they may be regarded as separate languages. Thus, we may find Czechoslovakian in one classification of languages, but Czech and Slovak in another.

Language Classifications

Languages are generally classified on the basis of common linguistic features or descent from a common linguistic ancestor. Many languages belong to language families of which, according to a recent estimate, there are perhaps one hundred.[2] Group classifications, which include several language families, are also used.

Here are the names of some language groups and families:

1. African-Khoin: the languages of the peoples south of the Sahara and west of the Nile.

2. Amerindian: the numerous Indian languages of North, Central, and South America.

3. Basque: the language of the Basques along the northern coast of Spain and the nearby western coast of France.

4. Dravidian: the languages of the peoples of southern India and northern Ceylon.

5. Japanese: the language of the people of Japan.

6. Malayo-Polynesian: the languages of the peoples of Borneo, Hawaii, Indonesia, the Malay Peninsula, Melanesia, Micronesia, Polynesia, and the Philippines.

7. Papuan-Australian: the languages of the peoples of New Guinea and the aborigines of Australia.

8. Semito-Hamitic: the languages of the peoples of southwestern Asia and northern and northeastern Africa, including Amharic, Arabic, Aramaic-Syriac, Hausa, Hebrew, Phoenician, and Somali.

9. Sino-Tibetan: the languages of the peoples of Burma, China, Laos, Thailand, and Tibet.

10. Uralic-Altaic: the languages of the peoples of a vast area stretching from northeastern Asia through Russia to eastern Europe, including Estonian, Finnish, Hungarian, Lapp (north of Arctic Circle), Mongol, Samoyed (northwestern Siberia), and Turkish.

11. Indo-European: the languages of the peoples who once occupied an area stretching from India to Europe, but who later spread to other parts of the world (Australia, North and South America, Africa), including English, French, Spanish, German, Russian, and a number of others.

Proto-Indo-European

The common linguistic ancestor of the Indo-European languages, Proto-Indo-European (PIE), may have been spoken as early as 4000 B.C. The homeland of the people who spoke PIE is not known, but some deductions have been made from comparative studies of the vocabulary of the earliest periods of the Indo-European languages. For example, the occurrence of words for 'snow' and 'winter,' but not for 'camel,' 'tiger,' 'palm,' or 'olive,' suggests a temperate rather than a tropical climate. Three Indo-European words in particular — 'beech,' 'salmon,' and 'turtle' — further suggest that the homeland of these people was an area in northern Europe, an area with rivers flowing into the Baltic and North Seas, and an area not north of Germany.[3]

These clues point toward an original environment in northern Europe, perhaps northern Poland or Lithuania. The last may be the most likely, because Lithuanian preserves several features of PIE phonology and morphology since lost in other Indo-European languages. Furthermore, the Lithuanians have remained for centuries in what may be their original home area.

The so-called migration hypothesis provides a reasonable explanation of the Europe-to-India spread of the Indo-European languages. This hypothesis states that between approximately 3000 and 2000 B.C. the speakers of PIE began a series of migrations from their original habitat, so that different groups of them traveled at various times north, west, and south across Europe, and east to India. Eventually the various dialects of those different PIE groups developed into separate languages.

Historical and archaeological evidence supports the migration hypothesis. For example, we know that northern India was invaded by Indo-European speakers from the northwest sometime before 1500 B.C. We know that Greece was invaded by Indo-European speakers from the north sometime after 2000 B.C. We also know that the Germans spread west across Europe during several migrations.

The best evidence of the linguistic kinship of the Indo-European languages and their development from a common linguistic ancestor, however, is found in linguistically similar words in the daughter languages. Such words are called cognate words because they are derived from a single source. For example, some cognate words for *brother* in the Indo-European languages are Old English *brōðor*, Old Icelandic *brōðir*, Gothic *brōðar*, Old Irish *brāthir*, Lithuanian *broter-*, Old Slavic *bratru*, Latin *frāter*, Greek *phrātēr*, and Sanskrit *bhrātār*, all from PIE **bhrātēr*. Such correspondences clearly indicate kinship and evolution from a common linguistic parent.

Because PIE antedated the extension of writing to Europe, there are no records of PIE. All we know of PIE is based on historical reconstruction from linguistic evidence in the daughter languages. To denote a hypothetical or reconstructed form based on deductions drawn from comparative linguistic evidence, we use an asterisk as in PIE **bhrātēr*. The macron (‾) above the graphemes *a* and *e* in PIE **bhrātēr* indicates that those graphemes represent lengthened or long vowels.

Indo-Hittite

In 1907 several thousand clay tablets were discovered, most of which were written in a language now called Hittite. The language of the Hittites, an ancient people in Asia Minor and northern Syria, is a member of the Anatolian family of languages (Hittite, Luwian, Palaic, Lydian, Lycian). Hittite is known chiefly from wedge shaped or cuneiform inscriptions (Cuneiform Hittite) which date from about 1400 B.C. It is also known from hieroglyphic or mainly pictorial inscriptions (Hieroglyphic Hittite) from about 700 B.C.

Hittite has some affinity with PIE, but there is disagreement about the degree of affinity between them. Some scholars believe that Hittite was an offspring of PIE, while others believe that Indo-Hittite was the hypothetical parent group of both the Indo-European and Anatolian families of languages.

Indo-European Branches

There are many linguistic branches of the Indo-European family of languages. They are Tocharian, Italic, Baltic, Slavic, Albanian, Armenian, Greek, Iranian, Indic, Celtic, and Germanic.

1. Tocharian consists of the language of the Tocharians, an

43

ancient people who lived in Central Asia until about A.D. 1000. Their documents, from the seventh century A.D., are in an eastern and a western dialect.

2. The Italic branch includes French, Italian, Portuguese, Rumanian, Sardinian, and Spanish, all of which are derived from Latin, their common ancestor.

3. The Baltic branch includes Lithuanian, Latvian (also called Lettish), and the now extinct Old Prussian.

4. The Slavic branch includes Russian, Ukrainian, Polish, Czech, Slovak, Slovenian, Bulgarian, Macedonian, and Church Slavic, the liturgical language of the Eastern Orthodox Slavs.

5. The Albanian branch consists of the language of the Albanians.

6. The Armenian branch consists of the language of the Armenians.

7. The Greek branch includes Ancient Greek (the principal dialects of which were the Aeolic, Attic, Doric, and Ionic dialects), Medieval Greek, and Modern Greek.

8. The Iranian branch includes Persian, Kurdish, and Pashto, and such ancient languages as Old Persian and Avestan. The last is the language in which the *Avesta*, the sacred writings of Zoroastrianism, was written.

9. The Indic branch includes many of the ancient and modern languages of India, such as Bengali, Hindi, Gujarati, Marathi, Punjabi, and Sanskrit, the ancient and classical language of the Hindus of India, described in the *Sutras* of the Hindu grammarian Panini (late fourth century, B.C.). Sanskrit includes Vedic Sanskrit, the language of the *Vedas* (one of the collections of Indian sacred writings from the second millennium B.C.), and also Classical Sanskrit, which is still used for sacred or learned writings. Romany, the language of the gypsies, is probably derived from an Indic dialect of northwestern India.

10. The Celtic branch, whose languages once were spoken throughout most of central and southern Europe, has several subgroups including Gaulish, the language of ancient Gaul or France. The northern or Goidelic subgroup of Celtic consists of Gaelic (Ireland), Scottish Gaelic (Scottish Highlands), and Manx (the Isle of Man in the Irish Sea), which is nearly extinct. The southern or Brythonic sub-group of Celtic consists of Welsh

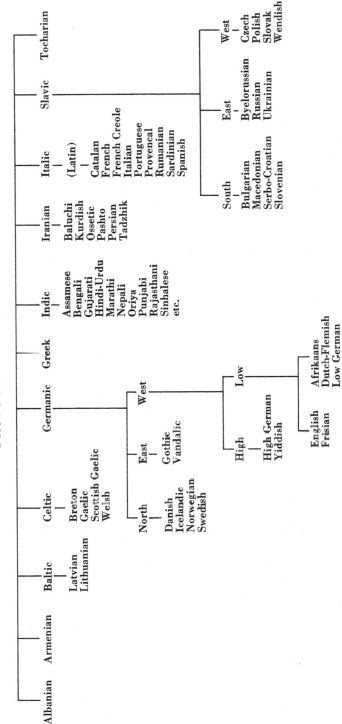

Plate 8. Principal branches of the Indo-European family of languages.

(Wales), Cornish (Cornwall, in southwestern Britain), extinct since the late eighteenth century, and Breton, carried to Brittany (northwestern France) in the fifth and sixth centuries by British Celts fleeing from the invading Anglo-Saxons.

11. The Germanic branch consists of three subgroups: North Germanic — Danish, Icelandic, Norwegian, and Swedish; East Germanic — principally Gothic (extinct); and West Germanic, which is divided into High and Low West Germanic. High West Germanic includes High German and Yiddish. Low West Germanic includes Low German (Plattdeutsch of northern Germany), Dutch, and Anglo-Frisian. The last consists of Frisian, which is spoken in the Frisian Islands off the coast of the Netherlands, and English.

Centum-Satem

The Indo-European branches and Cuneiform Hittite may be classified into the distinct *centum* and *satem* groups according to the development in each of PIE (or Indo-Hittite) velar stop *[k]. In the prehistoric periods of the *centum* languages — Hittite, Celtic, Germanic, Italic, Hellenic, and Tocharian — *[k] was retained in certain words, as initially in Latin *centum* 'hundred.' In the prehistoric periods of the *satem* languages — Albanian, Armenian, Baltic, Slavic, Indic, and Iranian — *[k] became a sibilant (palatal or alveolar), as initially in Avestan *satem* 'hundred.'

A line of cleavage extending roughly from Scandinavia to Greece separates the *satem* or eastern group from the *centum* or western group, with the exception of Tocharian, which is a *centum* language in *satem* territory. (It is possible that the Tocharians carried their *centum* language into the *satem* area as a result of migration.)

Germanic Characteristics

We have called English a member of the Low West Germanic branch of the Indo-European family of languages. English in its oldest period shared four chief characteristics of the Germanic

languages that differentiate them from the other Indo-European languages. These characteristics are:
1. a fixed stress accent
2. verbs with weak inflections
3. adjectives with weak inflections
4. changes resulting from the First Germanic Consonant Shift.

Fixed Stress Accent

PIE accent was free or variable. Sometimes it fell on the stem syllable of a word, as in Latin *páter* 'father,' and sometimes on other syllables, as in Greek *patér* 'father' and Greek *métēr* 'mother.' In the Germanic languages the principal stress accent generally became fixed on the first syllable of a word, as in Old English *fæder* 'father.'

Weak Verbs

The Germanic languages and the other Indo-European languages both had strong or vocalic verbs, that formed the past tense by an internal syllabic change, as in Late Modern English *swim, swam* and Latin *cāp-* 'seize,' *cēp-* 'seized.' Unlike the other Indo-European languages, the Germanic languages also had weak or consonantal verbs, that formed the past tense by the addition of a dental suffix [–d] or [–t], as in Late Modern English *paint, painted* and *walk, walked*.

Weak Adjectives

The Germanic languages and other Indo-European languages both had strong or vocalic adjective inflectional suffixes. In Germanic these suffixes were generally added to an adjective when it was *not* preceded by a demonstrative pronoun, as in Old English *gōd-e menn* 'good men.' But the Germanic languages differed from the other Indo-European languages in also having weak or *n* adjective suffixes, that were generally added to an adjective when it *was* preceded by a demonstrative pronoun, as in Old English *ðā gōd-an menn* 'the good men.'

47

First Consonant Shift

As Proto-Germanic (PGmc), the linguistic ancestor of the Germanic languages, evolved from PIE, certain PGmc consonants (syllable margins) became different from those of other Indo-European languages. These changes are reflected in a systematic series of correspondences between certain Germanic consonants, derived from PIE stops, and consonants in cognate or kindred words in other Indo-European languages.

These collective developments are called the First Germanic Consonant Shift. First stated in 1818 by Rasmus Rask, a Dane, they were treated systematically in 1822 by Jacob Grimm, a German. Grimm's Law describes the development of certain syllabic margins from PIE into PGmc. Here is the major portion of Grimm's Law that relates to English, in phonetic notation:

1. PIE voiceless stops *[p t k] > PGmc voiceless fricatives *[f θ h]. (For the symbol > read "became.")

*[p] > *[f] Latin *p*iscis, Late Modern English *f*ish

*[t] > *[θ] Latin *t*res, Late Modern English *th*ree

*[k] > *[h] Greek *k*ardia, Late Modern English *h*eart

2. PIE voiced stops *[b d g] > PGmc voiceless stops *[p t k].

*[b] > *[p] Latin la*b*ium, Late Modern English li*p*

*[d] > *[t] Latin *d*uo, Late Modern English *t*wo

*[g] > *[k] Latin *g*enus, Late Modern English *k*in

3. PIE voiced aspirated stops *[bh dh gh] > PGmc voiced stops *[b d g]. (Aspirated means "with a strong puff of breath.")

*[bh] > *[b] Sanskrit *bh*rātār, Late Modern English *b*rother

*[dh] > *[d] Sanskrit ma*dh*u, Late Modern English mea*d*

*[gh] > *[g] PIE *[ghostɪs], Late Modern English *g*uest

Grimm's Law may be stated concisely:

$$\underset{\text{*[bh dh gh]}}{3} > \underset{\text{*[b d g]}}{2} > \underset{\text{*[p t k]}}{1} > \text{*[f } \theta \text{ h]}$$

Verner's Law

The First Germanic Consonant Shift also includes certain consonant changes in the Germanic languages not explained by Grimm's Law. Those exceptions were noted in 1876 by Karl Verner, a Dane.

Here is one of the exceptions to Grimm's Law: according to Grimm, PIE *[t] became PGmc *[θ], as in PIE *[tú:] > PGmc *[θú:] 'thou.' Verner noted that specific change was not reflected in all Germanic words. Sometimes, in middle and final position in words, PIE *[t] became PGmc *[θ] and later *[ð], as in PIE *[pəté:r] > PGmc *[faθέr] > *[faðέr] 'father.' As Grimm said, PIE *[t] became PGmc *[θ], but it did not always remain so; sometimes it became PGmc *[ð].

Verner attributed this development and others to the position in PGmc of the principal stress accent in words. He said that the free or variable stress accent of PIE continued to exist in Early PGmc. As a result, the principal stress accent was on the stem syllable in some words. When it was *not*, according to Verner's Law, then PIE *[p t k] and [s] in voiced environments (as between nuclei) became Early PGmc *[f θ h s], respectively, and then *[v ð γ z], as in PIE *[pəté:r] > Early PGmc *[faθέr] > *[faðέr]. Subsequently, Early PGmc *[faðέr] became Late PGmc *[fáðεr], with shift of stress accent to the first syllable.[4]

These examples illustrate Verner's Law in Old English:

PIE *[p] > PGmc *[v] > OE [v] as in *yfel* [úvel] 'evil'

PIE *[t] > PGmc *[ð] > OE [d] as in past plural *snidon* [snídɔn] 'cut'

PIE *[k] > PGmc *[γ] > OE [γ] as in past plural *tugon* [túγn] 'drew,' but OE [y] as in past participle *–tigen* [tíyεn] 'drawn'

PIE *[s] > PGmc *[z] > OE [r̄] as in past plural *curon* [kúr̄ɔn] 'chose'

Both Grimm's Law and Verner's Law are reflected in many forms of Old English strong verbs. In the examples below, Grimm's Law is seen in the present and past indicative singular forms, which in Early PGmc had the principal stress accent on the first syllable. Verner's Law is reflected in the past plural and past participle forms, which in Early PGmc did not have the principal stress accent on the first syllable. The forms cited of the Old English strong verbs *cēosan* 'to choose' and *snīðan* 'to cut' are those of the present tense indicative third singular, the past tense indicative third singular, the past common plural, and the past participle.

Present Indic. 3rd sg.	Past Indic. 3rd sg.	Past Com. pl.	Past pple.
cyst	*cēas*	*curon*	*coren*
[s]	[s]	[r̈]	[r̈]
snīð	*snāð*	*snidon*	*sniden*
[θ]	[θ]	[d]	[d]

SUMMARY

Number of languages, some language classifications, Proto-Indo-European (PIE), Indo-Hittite, Indo-European branches, Centum-Satum groups, Germanic fixed stress accent, weak verbs, weak adjectives, First Germanic Consonant Shift (PGmc), Grimm's Law, and Verner's Law.

NOTES

[1] Siegfried Muller, *The World's Living Languages* (New York, 1964), p. 2.

[2] Muller, p. 3.

[3] Paul Thieme, "The Indo-European Languages," *Scientific American*, CXCIX (October, 1958), 63–74.

[4] At a later date (c. 500 A.D. — c. 700 A.D.) the Second Germanic Consonant Shift differentiated the consonants of High German from those of the Low German languages, as in German *Apfel*, English *apple*; German *tief*, English *deep*; German *zu*, English *to*; German *zwei*, English *two*, and so on.

Periods of English

In this chapter we shall briefly examine the periods of English, their approximate dates, the principal regional dialects of the periods, and background material about the history of Britain and North America.

Prehistoric Britain

In prehistoric times Britain was inhabited by Stone-Age, Bronze-Age, and Iron-Age peoples. Some of them may have arrived there by way of a European land bridge which ceased to exist before 6000 B.C., when the North Sea separated Britain from the European mainland. The last people who migrated there before the beginning of recorded history were Celts and mixed Celtic-Germanic groups from Europe.

Roman Britain

In 54 B.C. Roman troops under Julius Caesar invaded south-eastern Britain (in Latin *Britannia*). The British tribes they overcame were largely Celts, whom the Romans called Britons. The Romans withdrew, in exchange for a money tribute, and did not return for almost a century thereafter. In 43 A.D. Roman troops again invaded Britain. During the next four decades Roman control extended as far north as the Scottish border. Most of Celtic Britain became Roman Britain for almost four hundred years.

Picts and Scots

The Romans did not conquer Scotland, which they called *Caledonia*. It was inhabited by northern tribes called the Picts, an ancient people of uncertain origin. The Scots belonged to a Celtic people who migrated in the fifth century A.D. from Ireland (in Latin *Hibernia*) to northwestern Britain. They conquered the Picts in 846, and subsequently the new territory of the Scots was called *Scot-land*.

Decline of Roman Britain

From about 360 A.D. portions of Roman Britain were periodically ravaged by Picts from the north, Scots from the west, and Saxon sea raiders from northwestern Europe, who attacked the southern shores.

In the late fourth and early fifth centuries, Britain lost the main shield of its military protection when Roman legions rebelled and crossed over to the European continent. The desperate Britons appealed in 410 A.D. to Rome for troops to stave off the assaults of their enemies, but the remote islanders were told to defend themselves. Rome was too busy holding the European borders of its empire against Germanic invaders, who sacked the eternal city in 410 under Alaric, the Visigoth king.

Arrival of Anglo-Saxons

An account of the coming of the Germanic Anglo-Saxons from Europe to Britain is given by the English historian the Venerable Bede (?673–735) in his *History of the English Church and People*. Here is a paraphrase of the main portions of Bede's history:

> To repel the savage attacks of their northern enemies, the Picts, Vortigern, king of the Britons, asked the Saxon peoples across the North Sea for aid. In the year 449 the Angles and the Saxons arrived in Britain in three large ships and were granted land in the eastern part of the island on condition that they protect the country. At first they fought the enemies from the north and defeated them. Then the Anglo-Saxons sent messengers to their European homeland with news of their success, of the fertility of Britain, and of the cowardice of the Britons.
>
> A larger fleet arrived with a great host of warriors, who, on condition

that they fight the enemy, also received land and money from the Britons. The warriors were from the three most formidable races of Germany: the Saxons, Angles, and Jutes. So many of these foreign peoples crowded into the island that the Britons, who had invited them, became fearful.

Then the Germanic warriors made an alliance with the Picts and threatened to turn against the Britons. Provoking a quarrel over supplies, the heathen Germans devastated nearly all of Britain. Buildings were destroyed, priests were slain at the altar, and many people were killed. None remained to bury the dead. Survivors caught in the hills were butchered wholesale, and others, made desperate by hunger, surrendered. These were either slaughtered at once, or enslaved. Some Britons fled to Brittany, in France, but others lived on wretchedly and fearfully in the mountains and forests.

So ends the account of St. Bede, who collated his report from various church records several centuries after the actual events. We are not sure how much truth is in his account, for as a devout Christian cleric he would have been prejudiced against the heathen invaders. However, the outline of his story is probably true.

Anglo-Saxon Conquest

The Germanic warriors from the fringe of northwestern Europe having gained control of the major portion of Britain, seven Anglo-Saxon kingdoms (the Anglo-Saxon heptarchy) eventually emerged. They were Mercia, East Anglia, Essex, Sussex, Wessex, Northumbria, and Kent. In 597 the Roman monk later known as St. Augustine landed in Kent to spread Christianity among the heathen Germanic peoples of southeastern England.

The Anglo-Saxons did not control all of Britain. Britons driven westward to the remote regions along the western coast occupied Wales, Cornwall, Devon, and southwestern Scotland. Occasionally raiders from Ireland attacked the Britons and carried off captives, as St. Patrick, himself a victim, tells in his *Confessions*.

Anglo-Saxons

The English historian Bede referred to the Germanic conquerors of Britain as the *Angli Saxones* 'English Saxons.' He distinguished them from the *Antiqui Saxones* 'Old Saxons' on

the Continent who had not migrated to Britain.[1] Eventually
Old English *Engle* 'the Angles' and later 'the English' came to
be applied to all the Germanic peoples of Old English *Engla-
land* > Middle English *Englelond* > Modern English *England*.
Why the Old English term *Engle* spread is not known, for the
Angles were neither more numerous nor more prominent than
the other Germanic invaders, including the Saxons and so-called
Jutes. At any rate, in the late ninth century King Alfred of
England called his language *Englisc*, from which developed
Middle English *Englysch* and Modern English *English*.

Old English

At first the Germanic dialects spoken by the conquerors of
Britain were identical to those spoken by their Germanic kins-
men in Europe. Between the sixth and ninth centuries, however,
major linguistic changes occurred in the insular dialects, and they
began to differ more and more from those spoken on the Continent. These changes marked the emergence of Old English,
the name given to the language of the Germanic conquerors of
Britain and their descendants.

Periods and Dates

Historians of the English language recognize four periods of
English, which they call Old English (OE), Middle English
(ME), Early Modern English (EModE), and Late Modern
English (LModE). The probable linguistic dates of these periods
and the intervals of transition (T) between them are these:

OE	c. 600 to c. 1000[2]	
	T	c. 1000 to c. 1100
ME	c. 1100 to c. 1400	
	T	c. 1400 to c. 1500
EModE	c. 1500 to c. 1725	
	T	c. 1725 to c. 1825[3]
LModE	c. 1825 to present	

The dates of these periods are essentially arbitrary. The
abbreviation *c.* (*circa* 'approximately') is used before the dates

of these periods, because the emergence of linguistic features that differentiate one period from another was gradual, not sudden. Moreover, they did not emerge at the same rate in all regional dialect areas of England. For example, the linguistic features that came to distinguish ME from OE emerged earlier in the northern region of England than in the southern region of England. In the latter area many older linguistic features were retained for a longer period of time, but in the northern area those features were lost earlier. Therefore, to say the ME period began c. 1100 is a convenient generalization and approximation in time, as it is to say the ME period ended c. 1400 or that the EModE period ended c. 1725.

OE Dialects

Historians of the language speak of four main regional dialects of OE. They are OE Northern (or Northumbrian), OE Midland (or Mercian), OE Southeastern (or Kentish), and OE Southwestern (or West Saxon), the dialect described in chapter Nine of this book.

The area of OE Northern was north of the Humber River (see Plate 9), that of OE Midland between the Humber and Thames Rivers, and that of OE Southeastern the southeastern corner of England. The area of OE Southwestern included the remaining territory south of the Thames and Severn Rivers. These are their approximate boundaries, for their exact limits are not known.

The Danes

In the periods 787–794 and 834–878 England was invaded by Danish and Norwegian warriors from Scandinavia. Collectively called the Danes, these Scandinavian warriors eventually conquered most of eastern and northern England. Because the laws of the Danes prevailed in those sections, the area came to be known as the Danelaw (OE *Denalagu*). King Alfred of Wessex (849–899), called King Alfred the Great, won back the captured territory and became overlord of England.

A second Scandinavian invasion of England took place in 980. In a series of battles that followed, the Danes subdued the Anglo-Saxons, and from 1016 to 1042 Danish kings (Cnut, Harold Harefoot, Harthacnut) ruled England. With the death of the last Danish monarch in 1042, an English king (Edward the Confessor) was restored to the throne.

Anglo-Scandinavian

At the time of the first Norse invasion, the Danes and the Norwegians spoke a common Scandinavian language. About 1000, shortly after the second Norse invasion, a dialectal cleavage separated East Scandinavian (Swedish, Danish) from West Scandinavian (Norwegian, Icelandic).[4] The name given to the language of the Scandinavian invaders and settlers in England is Anglo-Scandinavian, or Anglo-Norse.

Although both were descended from a common Germanic parent, OE and Anglo-Scandinavian differed somewhat in pronunciation and inflection. These linguistic changes arose during the several centuries that followed their Continental separation. Nevertheless, the English and the Scandinavians presumably communicated with each other without too much difficulty. For one thing, both languages shared a common Germanic vocabulary. For another, both were relatively alike in phonology, morphology, and syntax. Anglo-Scandinavian continued to be spoken in parts of England until the twelfth century.

William the Conqueror

When King Edward of England died childless in 1066, the English nobles gave the crown to Earl Harold of Wessex. Across the English Channel in France, Duke William of Normandy, a distant relative of the deceased Edward, challenged Harold's right to the throne and invaded southern England with an army of Normans in 1066. On October 14 at Senlac near Hastings, in southeastern England, the Normans defeated the English. William the Conqueror was crowned King of England that year, and by 1070 he controlled all of England, but not Wales or Scotland.

Plate 9. OE dialect areas.

The political and social changes that resulted from the Conquest were enormous. Many of the highest civil and ecclesiastical offices were given to William's followers, as were the estates of Englishmen who had militarily and politically opposed the new king. There was also a wholesale influx of French artisans, monks, priests, soldiers, traders, and workmen. Thus there were Frenchmen at every social level in England.

Anglo-French

The primary linguistic significance of the Conquest was that French, more accurately that variety of French spoken in England named Anglo-French (AngFr), displaced English as the language of the new royal court, the government, the law courts, the schools, and parliament.[5] AngFr was also spoken by the upper classes in England.[6]

The principal linguistic contributor to AngFr was the Northwestern or Norman dialect of Old French, as spoken by William and most of his retinue.[7] AngFr is often called Anglo-Norman, although that designation obscures the linguistic contributions of emigrants from other areas of France, such as northeastern Walloon and Picardy and western Anjou.[8]

At first, AngFr was a living dialect of Old French. In the immediate generations after the Conquest it underwent the same linguistic changes that were taking place on the Continent, particularly to Northwestern Old French. This happened partly because trade promoted a linguistic interchange between the two countries. Some French nobles in England also sent their children to the Continent to study. In addition, some noblemen held estates in both England and France and frequently traveled back and forth between them.

About a century after the Conquest, AngFr was being spoken not by native speakers of French, as in the beginning, but by those of mixed English-French parentage and of English parentage. The result was that AngFr became increasingly modified by English speech habits. As early as c. 1150 AngFr showed linguistic tendencies that differed from those of Continental Old French.

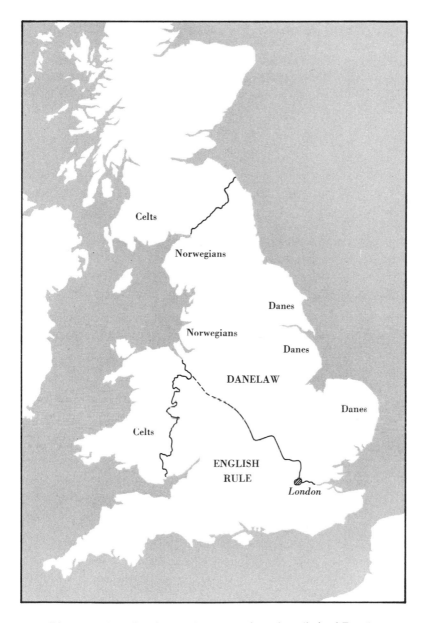

Plate 10. Scandinavian settlements and southern limit of Danelaw.

Decline of Anglo-French

Various political factors contributed to the decline of AngFr in England. They include the loss of direct English control over Normandy (1204–1265), the growth of English nationalism (1272–1400), the attendant reaction against foreigners, and the Hundred Years' War (1337–1453) with France.[9] As AngFr became progressively isolated from Continental French, it no longer shared in the linguistic changes taking place on the Continent, and differed more and more from Continental French.[10]

After about two centuries (1066–c. 1250), the use of AngFr by the upper classes in England slowly began to decrease. AngFr lost its force as a popular and widely spoken language. Eventually it was reduced in status to an artificial social and administrative language used in parliament and records of lawsuits.

Revival of English

The resurgence of English as a language accompanied the growing disuse of AngFr. In the late fourteenth century English again became the national language of England. In 1356–62 English was re-established in law courts, in 1385 in schools, and in 1388 in guild reports submitted to parliament.[11] Beginning about 1423 and noticeably after 1450, a standardized form of written English became common for documentary purposes, such as records, ordinances, and statutes.

ME Dialects

Despite the upper-class use of AngFr in England in the early ME period, English remained the primary language of most of the lower and middle classes of England. English, therefore, was spoken and written throughout the ME period, including the early portion of the Norman Conquest.

Five main dialects of ME are recognized. They are ME Northern, ME West Midland, ME East Midland, ME Southwestern (or Southern), and ME Southeastern (or Kentish). As can be seen on the map of the ME dialect areas (Plate 11), the

Plate 11. ME dialect areas. From Map II "Boundaries of Middle English Dialect Regions," based on "Middle English Dialect Characteristics and Dialect Boundaries" by Samuel Moore, Sanford B. Meech, and Harold Whitehall in *Essays and Studies in English and Comparative Literature*, University of Michigan Publications in Language and Literature, XIII (Ann Arbor, Michigan Press, 1935), 1–60, by permission of The University of Michigan Press. Copyright 1935 by The University of Michigan.

primary territorial difference between the OE and ME dialect areas occurs in the Midland area, by the split of OE Midland into ME West Midland and East Midland.

Southeast Midland

In the late ME period, Southeast Midland (SEMid) emerged as the most influential of the ME dialects.[12] It is the dialect of ME described in this book.

The prominence of SEMid may be attributed to the fact that the SEMid dialect area included the university towns of Cambridge and Oxford, the port city of London, and nearby Westminster, seat of the royal government. Thus, SEMid was the dialect spoken by socially prominent people. It was also geographically in a more or less middle position between the ME northern and southern dialects.

Early Modern English

In the EModE period, as in the ME period, SEMid, the dialect of London, maintained its social prestige as the standard dialect of the royal court and administration. Speakers of other dialects who traveled to or settled in the sixty-mile Greater London area tended to imitate and adopt the more socially fashionable speech habits of Londoners, just as people today adopt certain fashions in clothing and manners to attain social success.[13]

It is from the Greater London dialect of EModE, which was essentially SEMid with some Southwestern and Southeastern features, that the standard varieties of LModE have evolved. It is the dialect of EModE described in Chapter 10 of this book.

Colonial America

Following the voyages of Columbus to the New World, English merchants and the Crown sought a share in the riches of the Americas. With the French in possession of Nova Scotia (1604) and the Spanish in settlements from Florida to New Mexico, the only remaining area open to the British on the North

American Continent was the middle region along the Atlantic Coast.

The first permanent English settlement in North America was made at the mouth of the James River in Virginia in 1607. Subsequently the British established additional settlements,[14] as did the Swedish and Dutch.[15]

Eventually there was a series of wars among the European powers occupying the North American continent, principally Britain, France, and Spain. The British were the victors, and by the Treaty of Paris (1763) Britain gained Canada and virtually all the land east of the Mississippi River, including Florida.[16]

American Dialects

British immigrants to the North American colonies came from all areas of Britain, and at first there was a diversity and mingling of EModE dialects in Colonial America. In New England, however, the majority of early settlers were from eastern and southeastern England. Those in the Virginia Tidewater were largely from central and southern England. The larger portion of those in Pennsylvania and the midland area were from northern and western Britain. Thus, at a relatively early date in American history there were three main geographical bands of settlement — New England, Pennsylvania-midland, and the South. These settlements differed linguistically in regional blends of EModE dialects, but they also were influenced by the standard dialect of Greater-London EModE.

These regional differences were amplified and promoted by the relative isolation of the three bands of settlements for about a century in the early period of Colonial America. The considerable distance separating them made travel difficult, as did the presence of hostile Indians, the lack of roads, and such physical barriers as mountains and forests.

As a result of this relative isolation, the principal port cities of Boston, New York, Philadelphia, Richmond, and Charleston served as centers of trade, culture, and fashion for the new settlements that developed around them. They also set the linguistic fashions for the new settlements. The three main bands of Atlantic Coast dialects of AmE — Northern, Midland,

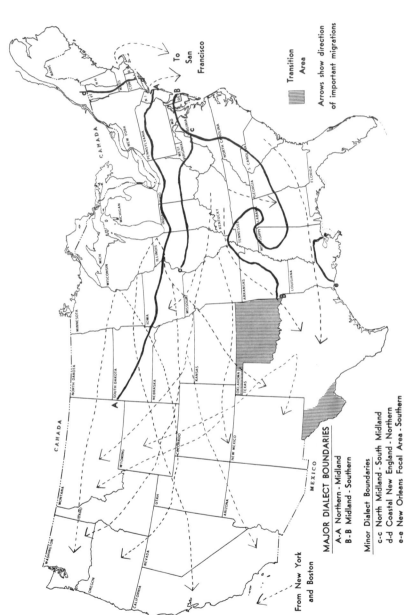

Plate 12. AmE dialect areas. Reprinted from *Dialects-U.S.A.* (National Council of Teachers of English, Champaign, Ill., 1963) by Jean Malmstrom and Annabel Ashley. By permission of Jean Malmstrom and The National Council of Teachers of English. Copyright 1963 by The National Council of Teachers of English.

and Southern — developed from these regional linguistic differences (see Plate 12).

Westward Extension

The increasing numbers of new immigrants to the British colonies in Colonial America in the eighteenth century eventually reached areas far beyond the port cities. Beginning in 1717–1718 the Scotch and Ulster Scotch-Irish, whose speech resembled that of northern Britain, spread to western Pennsylvania, down the Ohio River, as well as into the southern Piedmont and the Southern-Mountain region. Other settlers entered additional areas of Maine, the Mohawk River Valley, southern Georgia, the Blue-Grass region of Kentucky, and the Tennessee Valley.[17] But the primary westward thrust of immigrants occurred after the Revolutionary War (1775–1783) in three geographical waves:

1. From western New England across New York, northern Pennsylvania, northern Ohio, and eventually into Michigan and the Great Plains area.[18]

2. From western Pennsylvania through the Ohio Valley and eventually to the Mississippi River.

3. From the southern Appalachian Mountains, and in part from the southern Atlantic coastal area, across the Gulf States and subsequently to eastern Texas.

Neither eastern New Englanders, engaged in sea-going trade, nor the North Midlanders of Pennsylvania, nor the plantation Southerners along the Atlantic coast contributed much to the westward expansion.

By the time of the first Federal Census in 1790, American settlements stretched from the middle coast of Maine to the middle coast of Georgia, and west to Kentucky, the Tennessee Valley, and the Northwest Territory. The white population of the United States at that time numbered about 3.2 million, of whom approximately seventy-four percent were British (English, Scotch, or Ulster Irish in origin).[19]

Continental United States

Following the Louisiana Purchase from France (1803) and the explorations of Lewis and Clark to the Northwest (1804–

1806), fur traders, missionaries, prospectors, and farmers pushed westward. By 1820 there were settlements along the central and southern Mississippi, and slightly beyond. After the Texan Revolution for independence from Mexico, and the Mexican War (1846–1848), all the land north of the Rio Grande River to the disputed Oregon Territory belonged to the United States. The California Gold Rush (1848), the Mormon trek from Illinois to Utah (1846–1847), the penetration of cattlemen, the migrations after the War Between the States, and the extension of railroads carried a flood of immigrants, settlers, adventurers, and farmers, with a variety of American dialects, to the West.

New streams of immigrants continued to arrive in the nineteenth century. Many Irish came after the Irish potato famine. The Germans, after the revolution of 1848, immigrated to Cincinnati, Milwaukee, St. Louis, and Texas. Chinese and Japanese settled along the Pacific Coast. In the last quarter of the nineteenth century, Swedes and Norwegians immigrated to the Upper Mississippi Valley, and then beyond. After 1890, Italians, Russians, Czechs, Poles, Croatians, Greeks, and other groups came to the cities of the East and Middle West.

From such diverse ethnic groups have come numerous loanwords that reveal the multiple national origins of the speakers of AmE. Examples of such loanwords are given in Chapter 25 of this book.

SUMMARY

Prehistoric Britain, Roman Britain, the Anglo-Saxons, dates and periods of English, OE dialects, the Danes, Anglo-Scandinavian, Norman Conquest, AngFr, revival of English, ME dialects, ME SEMid, Greater-London dialect of EModE, Colonial America, AmE dialects, westward expansion.

NOTES

[1] The earliest accounts of the Germans are found in the *Commentaries on the Gallic War* by the Roman general Julius Caesar, probably written in the winter of 52–51 B.C., and in the treatise *Germania*, probably written in 98 A.D. by the Roman historian Tacitus.

The early German gods included Tiu (OE *Tīw*), god of war and the sky; Woden or Odin (OE *Wōden*), chief god in Germanic mythology; Thor (OE *ður ~ ðor ~ ðunor*), god of thunder; and Freya (Old Icelandic *Freyja*), goddess of love and beauty.

The names of these Germanic gods are reflected in names for the days of the week. For example, OE *Tīwesdæġ* > Modern English Tuesday, OE *Wōdnesdæġ* > Wednesday, OE *ðunresdæġ* > Thursday, and OE *Frīġedæġ* > Friday. On the other hand, OE *Sætern(es)dæġ* > Modern English Saturday, OE *Sunnandæġ* > Sunday, and OE *Monandæġ* > Monday. The first elements in these three Old English words are OE *sæturn* 'Saturn,' borrowed from Latin *Saturnus* 'Roman god of agriculture,' OE *sunne* 'sun,' and OE *mōna* 'moon.'

[2] The linguistic date for the beginning of the OE period is based on David DeCamp, "The Genesis of the Old English Dialects: A New Hypothesis," *Language*, 34 (1958), 323–344.

[3] The linguistic dates for the end of the EModE period and the beginning of the LModE period are taken from Robert A. Peters, "Linguistic Differences Between Early and Late Modern English," *Studia Neophilologica*, XXXVII (1965), 134–138.

[4] The East Scandinavians (Danes) settled in the East Midlands and Yorkshire. The West Scandinavians (Norwegians) settled in northwestern England, part of Wales, Ireland, and the western islands.

[5] From John Trevisa's (1385–87) translation (B. M. Cotton Tiberius D. VII. 50 v) of Ranulph Higden's Latin *Polychronicon*:

> chyldern in scole, agens þe vsage and manere of al oþer nacions buþ compelled for to leue here oune longage and for to construe here lessons and here þinges a freynsch and habbeþ suþthe þe normans come furst into engelond. also gentil men children buþ ytaught for to speke freynsch fram tyme þat a buþ yrokked in here cradel and conneþ speke and playe wiþ a child hys brouch. and oplondysch men wol lykne hamsylf to gentil men and fondeþ wiþ gret bysynes for to speke freynsch for to be more ytold of.

[6] Translated from the *Chronicle* (c. 1300) of Robert of Gloucester (11. 7537–43) quoted in A. C. Baugh, *A History of the English Language*, 2nd ed. (New York, 1957), pp. 135–136.

> 'Thus was in Normans' hands that land brought . . . of the Normans are highmen that are of England and the lowmen of Saxons . . . And the Normans could not speak then but their own speech, and spoke French as they did at home, and their children did also teach, so that high men of this land that of their blood come hold all that speech that they from them took. Except that a man know French some count of him little. But low men hold to English, and to their own speech yet.'

[7] The word *Norman* (< OE *norðmann* 'dweller in the north, Scandinavian') refers to the Northmen from Scandinavia who, in the tenth century, occupied that district on the northern coast of France afterward called

Normandy. The invaders subsequently intermarried with the French and adopted the French language.

⁸ The principal dialects of OFr were Northeastern (Picardy-Walloon), Northwestern (Normandy), Western (Poitou, Saintonge, Anjou), Eastern (Lorraine, Champagne), Southeastern (Burgundy, Franche-Comté), and Central (Ile de France).

⁹ The height of English holdings in France occurred in the twelfth century following the accession of the Angevin dynasty and the marriage of Henry II to Eleanor of Aquitaine. The English then held about two thirds of France. Thereafter, political conflicts resulted in the loss of Normandy. After the Hundred Years' War, English power diminished until only the port of Calais remained in English hands by 1453.

¹⁰ In the prologue (11. 124–26) to "The Canterbury Tales", *The Works of Geoffrey Chaucer*, ed. F. N. Robinson, 2nd ed. (Boston, 1957), p. 18, Chaucer says of the Prioresse: "And Frenssh she spak ful faire and fetishly, after the scole of Stratford atte Bowe, for Frenssh of Parys was to hire unknowe."

¹¹ From Trevisa's translation (*op. cit.*, 59v–51) of Higden's *Polychronicon*:

ffor john cornwall a mayster of gramere, chayngede þe lore in gramer scole and construccion of freynsch in to englysch and richard pencrych lurnede þat manere techyng of hym and oþer men of pencrych. so þat now þe yer of oure lord a þousond þre hondred foure score and fyue of þe secunde kyng richard after þe conquest nyne in al þe gramer scoles of englelond children leueþ frensch and construeþ and lurneþ an englysch and habbeþ þer by avauntage in one syde and desavauntage yn anoþer. Here avauntage ys þat a lurneþ here gramer yn lasse tyme þan childern wer ywoned to do. disavauntage ys þat now childern of gramer scole conneþ no more frensch þan can here lift heele and þat ys harm for ham ... also gentil men habbeþ now moche yleft for to teche here children frensch.

¹² SEMid is reflected in the literary standard (c. 1375–c. 1474) of such ME writers as Geoffrey Chaucer, John Lydgate, and John Gower.

¹³ George Puttenham, *The Arte of English Poesie* (1589), ed. Gladys D. Willcox and Alice Walker (Cambridge, 1936), p. 144, advised:

Ye shall ... take the vsuall speach of the Court, and that of London and the shires lying about London within lx. myles, and not much aboue.

In contrast, he warned against:

neither ... the termes of Northern-men ... nor ... any speach vsed beyond the riuer of Trent ... it is not so Courtly nor so currant as our Southerne English is, no more is the far Westerne mans speach.

¹⁴ British settlements included Plymouth, Mass. (1620); Boston, Mass. (1630); Providence, R. I. (1636); Albemarle County, N. C. (1653); Charleston, S. C. (1670); Philadelphia, Pa. (1682); and Augusta, Ga. (1735).

¹⁵ Dutch Settlements included a colony on Manhattan Island (1613),

Fort Nassau near Albany, N. Y. (1614), New Amsterdam (New York City, 1624), and settlements in Connecticut, Delaware, New Jersey, and Pennsylvania. The Swedish settlement at Wilmington, Del. (1638) was occupied by the Dutch in 1655.

[16] By the Treaty of Versailles (1783) Spain regained Florida, but later sold it to the U. S. in 1819–1821.

[17] Protestant Germans (Pennsylvania Dutch) from the Rhine Palatinate settled north and west of Philadelphia in the Lehigh and Susquehanna Valleys, as well as in the western Carolinas and the Mohawk Valley in New York.

[18] It will be helpful to recall the following surface features of the Atlantic area: from northern New England to central Alabama and Georgia stretch the Appalachian Mountains, the southern half (W. Va.-Md. to Ga.) of which is called the Blue Ridge. The northeastern Appalachian chain, called the Adirondack Mountains, is divided by the Hudson and Mohawk Rivers and the waters flowing north from Lake Champlain. The western Appalachian area consists of parallel mountain ranges, of which the Allegheny Mountains (central Pennsylvania, Maryland, Virginia, West Virginia) and the Cumberland Mountains (Kentucky, Tennessee, Virginia) are the most important. Between the Allegheny Mountains and the Blue Ridge is the Shenandoah Valley.

Along the eastern base of the Appalachian chain is the Piedmont Plateau. That elevated tableland, about 150 miles wide in its middle section, traverses Alabama, Georgia, South Carolina, North Carolina, and Virginia. Its eastern limit is marked by a line of waterfalls and rapids called the fall line. In New England the fall line is near the coast, but southward the fall line traverses inward until it reaches some two hundred miles inland in Georgia.

To the east of the Piedmont Plateau is the Tidewater Belt, a sand-and-clay plain stretching to the Atlantic Ocean. The Tidewater Belt is so near sea level that the tide travels up river to the fall line. The label *the Tidewater* refers specifically to eastern Virginia.

[19] The estimated figures include 3,226,944 whites and approximately 700,000 Negro slaves in Maine, New Hampshire, Vermont, Massachusetts, Rhode Island, Connecticut, New York, New Jersey, Pennsylvania, Delaware, Maryland, Virginia, North Carolina, South Carolina, Georgia, Kentucky, Tennessee, the Northwest Territory, Spanish and French United States. Of the estimated, 3,226,944 whites in the Continental United States in 1790, 1,939,396 were English (60.1%); 261,138 Scotch (8.1%); 190,662 Ulster Irish (5.9%); 116,248 Free-State Irish (3.6%); 279,220 German (8.6%); 100,000 Dutch (3.1%); 73,750 French (2.3%); 21,100 Swedish (0.7%); 25,625 Spanish (0.8%); and 219,805 unassigned (6.8%). See Report of Committee on Linguistic and National Stocks in the Population of the United States, American Council of Learned Societies, in *Report of the American Historical Association for 1931* (Washington, D. C., 1921), I, 124–125.

The Phoneme

In describing the historical consonants, vowels, and diphthongs of English in Chapter 9 and thereafter, we shall use the phoneme as the unit of description. In this chapter we shall briefly explain the concept of the phoneme.

Class of Sounds

A phoneme is a class or family of sounds whose members are called allophones. An allophone is a positional variant of a phoneme. Literally, *allophone* means "a variant phone-type of." By means of distributional analysis, a phone-type in a particular language or period of a language is assigned as an allophone to a specific phoneme.

Allophones, like phone-types, are written between square brackets, as [b]. Phonemes, in contrast, are written between slanted lines, as /b/. To indicate that [b] is an allophone of the phoneme /b/ in a particular language or period of a language, we write /b/ = [b].

Gathering

The customary first step in determining the phonemes of a language is to make an inventory of the phone-types that occur in that language or period of that language. For example, let us assume that in language X one utterance is [ksɛp]. We note, therefore, that the phone-types [k] and [s] and [ɛ] and [p] occur, and that [k] is a voiceless dorso-velar stop, [s] is a voiceless apico-alveolar sibilant, [ε] is a voiced lower mid-front simple syllabic nucleus, and [p] is a voiceless bilabial stop. In this way, we would list and label all the other phone-types that occur in language X.

Environment

The customary second step in phonemic analysis is to describe the environments in which the phone-types of language X occur. For example, the utterance [ksép] may be regarded as consisting of only four linear segments. Excluding stress, we label those four linear segments 1 2 3 4 as follows:

1 2 3 4

[k s ε p]

We note that [k] occurs in position 1, or utterance-initial position, and is followed by [s]. [s], in turn, occurs in position 2, after [k] and before [ε]. [ε] occurs in position 3, after [s] and before [p]. Finally, [p] occurs in position 4, or utterance-final position, and after [ε]. We would similarly list and describe all the other environments in which the phone-types of language X occur.

Contrastive Distribution

We now proceed to an explanation of the principle of contrastive distribution: two phone-types that occur in an identical environment, and that indicate a difference in meaning between utterances, are in contrastive distribution.

Two phone-types that are in contrastive distribution cannot be allophones of the same phoneme; two phone-types in contrastive distribution belong to different phonemes. For example, in AmE two phone-types are [b] as in *bat* [bǽt] and [m] as in *mat* [mǽt]. Both phone-types occupy an identical environment, namely, utterance-initial position and before [æ]. Assuming for the sake of illustration that there are no other observable linguistic features which differentiate the two utterances, our conclusion is that the difference in meaning between *bat* and *mat* is signaled by [b] and [m], more accurately by the phonetic differences between [b] and [m]. Thus, because [b] and [m] are in contrastive distribution, they belong to different phonemes. We assign [b] as an allophone of /b/ and [m] as an allophone of /m/. We write this:

$$/b/ = [b]$$
$$/m/ = [m]$$

Minimal Pair

Two utterances that differ by one phoneme constitute a minimal pair. For example, [bǽt] and [mǽt] in AmE differ by one phoneme; therefore, *bat* [bǽt] and *mat* [mǽt] are a minimal pair, as are *pat* [pǽt] and *pit* [pít], and *sin* [sín] and *sing* [síŋ].

Phonetic Similarity

The allophones of a phoneme must be phonetically similar; they must share a phonetic resemblance. For example, the allophones of OE /f/ were [f] and [v]. Although [f] was voiceless and [v] was voiced, both were phonetically similar as labio-dental fricatives. So too the allophones [g] and [γ] of OE /g/ were phonetically similar. Although [g] was a stop and [γ] was a fricative, both were voiced and dorso-velar. However, it is unlikely that [ŋ], a voiced dorso-velar nasal, and [p], a voiceless bilabial stop, would be allophones of the same phoneme in some language or period of a language because they lack a phonetic resemblance.

Complementary Distribution

The allophones of a phoneme must be in noncontrastive distribution. One kind of noncontrastive distribution is complementary distribution. Two phonetically similar phone-types are in complementary distribution if they occur in mutually exclusive environments. By mutually exclusive we mean that one phone-type normally does not occur in environments in which the other phone-type does. This means A normally does not occur where B does, and vice versa.

For example, [f] and [v] in Old English, as previously stated, were allophones of the phoneme /f/. Both allophones were phonetically similar as labio-dental fricatives, [f] being voiceless and [v] voiced. In Old English [f] normally occurred in utterance-initial position and utterance-final position, as in OE *full* [fúl] and OE *wulf* [wúlf]. On the other hand, [v] normally occurred in Old English between voiced sounds, as in OE *wulfas* [wúlvas]. Hence, [v] normally occurred where [f] did not. In Old English, [f] and [v] occurred in mutually exclusive environments and were in complementary distribution because each occurred where the other normally did not.

Free Variation

Another kind of noncontrastive distribution is free variation. Two phonetically similar phone-types that occupy the same environment without indicating a change in meaning are in free variation. Because such phone-types are not in contrastive distribution, the distinction between them is sub-phonemic, that is, they are in noncontrastive distribution.

For example, let us assume that in language X two phone-types are unaspirated [p] and aspirated [p']. Let us also assume that [p] and [p'] in language X both occur in the same environment, namely utterance-final position after [ɪ], as in [kɪp] 'dog' and [kɪp'] 'dog.' Finally, let us assume that to a native speaker of language X it makes no difference whether [p] or [p'] is used because neither causes a change in meaning. Both utterances mean the same thing — 'dog.' In that event, [p] and [p'] are in free variation.

Phoneme Defined

Having briefly explained some major phonemic principles, we now may define the phoneme: a phoneme is a class of phonetically similar phone-types that are in complementary distribution or free variation in a language or a period of a language. The phone-types that constitute a phoneme are its allophones. They are positional variants of a phoneme.

Phonemic Symbols

As a family or class of closely related speech sounds (phone-types), a phoneme is a single unit and may be written with a single symbol as /f/.

In a phonemic transcription a phonemic symbol, such as /f/ in language X, is used to represent all the allophones of that phoneme. For example, let us assume that in language X both [f] and [v] are allophones of /f/. Because [f] occurs more frequently than [v], we arbitrarily select the symbol *f* to represent the phoneme, namely /f/. Thus, in phonemically transcribing language X, we write /f/ for any occurrence of the allophones [f] or [v], as in these examples:

Phonetic	Phonemic
[fĩ]	/fĩ/
[ĩvɪ]	/ĩfɪ/
[fĩvɪ]	/fĩfɪ/

On the basis of present knowledge about the various periods of English, the majority of the historical phonemes of English are regarded as having had only one principal allophone, as in the case of OE /p/ = [p]. In such an instance, to avoid a needless clutter of symbols, we shall omit listing the principal allophone and simply write OE /p/. Undoubtedly there were other allo-phones of such historical phonemes, but we do not know them because of our incomplete knowledge of Old English.

We shall, however, indicate historical phonemes of English with more than one known principal allophone, as in the case of OE /f/ = [f] [v]. This means that in OE the phoneme /f/ had two principal allophones: [f] and [v]. OE /p/, in contrast, had only one: [p].

No Universal Phonemes

There is no such thing as a universal phoneme, such as /p/ or /t/. There are only phonemes of a language or a period of a language, and they are determined from the distribution of phone-types in that language or period of that language. Thus, because phonemes are distributionally determined classes, a phoneme of a language or a period of a language is relevant only to the language or period of a language being described.

For example, [f] and [v] in OE were allophones of /f/, but in ME they split into the phonemes /f/ and /v/. ME /f/ and OE /f/, therefore, were not the same because their allophones were different: OE /f/ = [f] and [v], but ME /f/ = [f].

As another example, in AmE both [p] and [p'] are allophones of /p/. However, if in some other language it occurs that [p] and [p'] are in contrastive distribution, both would be assigned to different phonemes, perhaps /p/ and /p'/.

In summary, there is no universal phoneme, such as /p/, /z/, /g/, or any other, that is valid for all languages.

Phoneme Classes

In our discussions of phone-types in earlier chapters, we avoided use of the terms vowel and consonant as much as possible in order to reserve those labels for classes of segmental phonemes.

As we previously stated, phonemes are distributionally determined classes. Thus, whether a phone-type in a language or a period of a language is given vowel status or consonant status is essentially a matter of the distribution of that phone-type in the language or period of the language.

For example, segmental phone-types in English that pattern as syllable margins are consonants, such as [s] and [t] in *sit* [sít], and those that pattern as simple nuclei are vowels, such as [ɪ] in [sít]. Thus, on the basis of their distribution, some phone-types in English normally pattern as consonants and others as vowels. In some other language [s] may pattern as a vowel and [ɪ] as a consonant; a particular phone-type that patterns as a consonant in one language does not necessarily pattern as a consonant in some other language. It may be assigned vowel status on the basis of its distribution in that other language, or it may be assigned the phonemic status of some other phoneme class. Much depends upon what types of phoneme classes an analyst wishes to use to describe a language and also meet the criteria of economy and simplicity of description. At any rate, he must first analyze the language to determine the distribution of the phone-types in that language. Only then can he proceed to a determination of the phoneme classes of that language.

In a language such as English the phonemic interpretation of complex nuclei and lengthened simple nuclei depends in large measure on the type of analysis adopted. Although various analyses of such nuclei exist, we do not intend in this elementary text to discuss the technical difficulties or the relative merits of those analyses. In our view, more problems than solutions are presented by interpretations of the overall phonemic systems of the various periods of English which involve such additional segmental phoneme classes as semivowels, covowels, semiconsonants, and omnipotents.

In order to describe the historical phonemes of English we must choose between two methods of analyzing certain nuclei, binary analysis or unitary analysis. For example, in AmE the nucleus [e], the lengthened variety [e:], slightly dipthongal [e^I], and diphthongal [eɪ] all occur in a word such as *eight*. According to one binary analysis of the overall pattern of AmE, [e ~ e: ~ e^I ~ eɪ] are all phonemically interpreted as /ey/, that is, as vowel /e/ plus /y/. On the other hand, according to one unitary analysis of AmE, [e ~ e: ~ e^I ~ eɪ] are all phonemically interpreted as the vowel /e/. Thus, in the binary analysis *eight* is /eyt/, but in the unitary analysis *eight* is /et/. Similarly, in the case of complex nuclei, such as [aʊ] in *out*, the binary analyst interprets it as /aw/, that is, vowel /a/ plus /w/, and the unitary analyst interprets it as /aʊ/, a single vowel unit which he writes with two vowel symbols.

We have chosen to base our phonemic descriptions on unitary analysis in this book. In our view, this method presents fewer difficulties in overall phonemic descriptions of the various historical periods of English.

In this book we maintain that syllabic length is not phonemic in the overall patterns of EModE and AmE. In the case of OE and ME simple nuclei, where phonemic contrasts appear between presumably short nuclei and long nuclei, we interpret these systems of simple nuclei as consisting of contrasts between short vowels and long vowels.

In all the historical periods of English we interpret complex nuclei, marked by a drift in quality during articulation, as complex vowels, called diphthongs. In OE and ME, diphthongs are divided into contrasting subsets of short diphthongs and long diphthongs depending on whether the syllabic peaks of those nuclei are short or long.

Since we have adopted a unitary analysis in this book, the segmental phoneme classes employed herein are consonants, vowels, and diphthongs. Our descriptions do not include other phoneme classes such as semivowels, semiconsonants, and so on.

SUMMARY

Phoneme, allophone, contrastive distribution, complementary distribution, minimal pair, free variation, phonetic similarity consonant, vowel, diphthong.

Old English Phonemes

We begin our examination of the historical sound system of English with a description of the phonemes of the Southwestern dialect of OE. In subsequent chapters we shall examine the phonemes of ME, EModE, and LModE (AmE).

How Do We Know?

Students frequently ask, "How do we know what OE sounded like?" After all, we have no acoustic records of OE. The truth is that we cannot be sure what OE sounded like because our knowledge of it is derived primarily from the analysis of OE manuscripts. Yet we do know that Anglo-Saxon scribes wrote the sounds of the Latin of the period and the sounds of OE with the same Irish-Roman graphemes, and we assume that in many instances the sound values associated with these graphemes were approximately the same in both cases. Thus, knowledge of the pronunciation of Latin in that period has helped scholars to infer the sounds of OE. Supporting evidence includes deductions drawn from linguistic evidence in cognate words in other Germanic languages, as well as historical inferences drawn from ME.

OE Alphabet

The shapes of the graphemes of OE Insular script were different from those we use today. Without special instruction and practice, modern readers would not be able to read *f*, *r*, or *s* in OE Insular script or OE ꝥ, called wynn or OE ȝ, called yogh. For that reason, in this book we shall follow the current practice of using modern Roman type for all the graphemes of the OE alphabet except three. They are OE *æ* or ash, *ð* or eth, and *þ* or thorn. Ash and eth were modifications of Latin graphemes. Thorn was adopted from the runic alphabet.

On the basis of the qualifications stated above, the graphemes of the OE alphabet were *a, æ, b, c, d, e, f, g, h, i, l, m, n, o, p, r, s, t, þ ~ ð, u, w, x, y*, and rarely, *k* and *z*. Anglo-Saxon scribes did not use *j, q,* or *v*.

In OE the graphemes *a, æ, e, i, o, u, y* represented both short and long vowels. As an aid to the reader, we shall place a macron ‾ above these graphemes when they represent long vowels as in *gōd* 'good,' but not when they represent short vowels as in *god* 'God.' The grapheme clusters *ea, eo,* and *ie* represented both short and long diphthongs. We shall mark long diphthongs with a macron as in *hīera* 'higher,' but not short diphthongs as in *hiera* 'their.'

The grapheme *x* represented the consonant cluster /ks/ as in *oxa* /ɔksɑ/. The remaining graphemes of the OE alphabet represented consonants. Some of those graphemes represented more than one consonant or more than one consonant allophone, as in the case of the OE graphemes *c* and *g*. For example, *c* = dorso-velar allophone [k] of OE /k/ and also fronto-palatal allophone [č] of OE /č/. On the other hand, *g* — the dorso-velar allophones [g] and [ɣ] of OE /g/, as well as fronto-palatal allophone [y] of OE /y/. As a further aid to the reader, we shall place a dot above *c* and *g* when they represent palatals, as in *ċidan* /čí:dɑn/ 'to chide' and *ġēar* /yǽ:ɑr̈/ 'year.'

We now turn to an examination of the consonant, vowel, and diphthong phonemes of OE Southwestern (c. 900).

OE Consonants

The stops of OE Southwestern were /p t k b d g/. /p t b d/ were as in *pund* 'pound,' *tō* 'too,' *bān* 'bone,' and *dēad* 'dead.' /k/ was as *c* in *cū* 'cow,' rarely *k* as in *folc ~ folk* 'folk, people.'

/g/ had two allophones: [g] as in *gold* 'gold,' but [γ] between back vowels as in *boga* [bɔ́γɑ] 'bow.'

The fricatives were: /f θ h/. Each had two allophones. Those of /f/ were [f] as in *full* 'full,' *wulf* 'wolf,' but [v] generally between between voiced sounds as in *wulfas* [wúlvɑs] 'wolves.'[1] The allophones of /θ/ were [θ] as in *þīn ~ ðīn* 'thine,' but [ð] generally between voiced sounds as in *ōþer ~ ōðer* [ó:ðɛr̈] 'other, second.' The two allophones of /h/ were [h] initially as in *hūs* 'house,' but [x] elsewhere as in *niht* [níxt] 'night' and *scōh* [šó:x] 'shoe.'

The sibilants were: /s š/. /š/ was as *sc* in *fisc* 'fish.' /s/ had two allophones: [s] as in *sunu* 'son,' but [z] generally between voiced sounds as in *nosu* [nɔ́zʊ] 'nose.' A rare grapheme for [z] was *z*, as in Biblical names such as OE *Zebedes* for Latin *Zebedaei*.

The affricates were: /č ǰ/ as, respectively, *ċ* in *ċidan* 'to chide' and *cg* in *ecg* 'edge.'

The nasals were: /m n/. /m/ was as in *mid* 'with.' /n/ had two allophones: [n] as in *ne* 'not, nor,' but [ŋ] before [g] and [k] as in *singan* [síŋgɑn] 'to sing' and *drincan* [dr̈íŋkɑn] 'to drink.'

The lateral was: /l/ as in *līf* 'life.'

The trill was: /r̈/ as in *rēad* 'red.'

The glides were: /w y/ as, respectively, *w* in *wind* 'wind' and *ġ* in *ġēar* 'year.'[2]

Consonant Clusters

Initial consonant clusters that occurred in OE Southwestern include the following:

/gn/ as in *gnorian* 'murmur.'
/hl/ as in *hlāf* 'loaf, bread.'
/hn/ as in *hnoll* 'top, crown of head.'
/hr̈/ as in *hrōf* 'roof.'
/kn/ as in *cneht* 'boy, youth.'
/wl/ as in *–wlispian* 'to lisp.'
/wr̈/ as in *wrecan* 'to avenge.'

OE Vowels

There were two contrasting sets of vowels in OE. They are usually labeled short and long because of these traditional opinions:

1) the allophones of some of the long vowels differed phonetically in length from those of the short vowels, as in short [æ] and long [æ:]; and 2) that other allophones of the long vowels differed phonetically from those of the short vowels both in length and quality, as in short [ɪ] and long [i:].

The truth is that we do not know exactly how the two sets of vowels differed phonetically. At present we have no better or more probable conjectures than these, which we shall therefore adopt in this text for the purpose of illustration.

To distinguish phonemically OE long vowels from OE short vowels, we shall mark the long vowels with two dots : as in long /æ:/. Short vowels will not be so marked as in short /æ/.

In addition to quantitative and qualitative phonetic differences between the allophones of OE short vowels and long vowels, the phonemic system of OE Southwestern vowels also shows: 1) distinctions of three tongue-heights (high, mid, low); 2) a contrast between front and back vowels; and 3) a contrast between unrounded (U) and rounded (R) vowels,

Short Vowels

	Front		Back
	U	R	U
High	/ɪ/	/ü/	/u/
Mid	/ɛ/		/ɔ/
Low	/æ/		/ɑ/

Examples

/ɪ/ as *i* in *bit* 'he asks.'
/ü/ as *ȳ* in *bȳt* 'bottle.'
/ɛ/ as *e* in *fet* 'he obtains.'
/æ/ as *æ* in *æt* 'at.'
/u/ as *u* in *full* 'full.'
/ɔ/ as *o* in *god* 'god.'
/ɑ/ as *a* in *ham(m)* 'pasture.'

Long Vowels

	Front		Back
	U	R	U
High	/i:/	/ü:/	/u:/
Mid	/e:/		/o:/
Low	/æ:/		/ɑ:/

Examples

/i:/ as *ī* in *bīt* 'he bites.'
/ü:/ as *ȳ* in *bȳt* 'he commands.'
/e:/ as *ē* in *fēt* 'feet.'
/æ:/ as *ǣ* in *ǣt* 'food.'
/u:/ as *ū* in *fūl* 'foul.'
/o:/ as *ō* in *gōd* 'good.'
/ɑ:/ as *ā* in *hām* 'village.'

OE Diphthongs

There probably were three short and three long diphthongs in OE Southwestern. Generally they were falling diphthongs.

Short

/íɛ/ as *ie* in *hiera* 'their.'
/ɛ́ɔ/ as *eo* in *ġeoc* 'yoke.'
/ǽɑ/ as *ea* in *ġear* 'he grunted.'

Long

/í:ɛ/ as *īe* in *hīera* 'higher.'
/é:ɔ/ as *ēo* in *ġeoc* 'support.'
/ǽ:ɑ/ as *ēa* in *ġēar* 'year.'

OE Stress

In keeping with the stress pattern established in Late PGmc, principal stress generally fell on the first syllable of an OE word, as in *súnu* 'son' and *héofon* 'heaven.'

When the first syllable of a noun was a prefix, it was generally stressed as in *únlīf* 'death,' but in verbs it was not stressed, as in *tōbérstan* 'to burst.'

Exceptions included the prefixes *ġe-*, *be-*, and *for-*. The first was never stressed, as in *gebúnden* 'bound,' the other two generally not, as in *bebód* 'command' and *forlórenes* 'forlorn.'

Stress phonemes, and pitch, transition, and terminal phonemes are collectively called suprasegmental phonemes. In general, they are phonemes that occur simultaneously with sequences of one or more linear phonemes and distinguish otherwise identical phoneme sequences. When we study the suprasegmental phonemes of AmE, we shall talk about stress, pitch, transition, and terminal phonemes in more detail. We mention them here only to point out that apart from the OE phoneme of principal stress, which we arbitrarily symbolize /'/, nothing is known about the additional suprasegmental phonemes of OE Southwestern or any other OE dialect, because we have no acoustic records of OE to analyze.

OE Southwestern undoubtedly had other stresses, such as secondary stress, as well as pitch, transition, and terminal phonemes, but we do not know which ones. Some conjectures about the additional stresses of OE have been made on the basis of studies of OE metrics, but there is disagreement about these conjectures. Even if there were agreement, any findings based on studies of OE metrics would not apply to stresses in OE prose because poetry and prose are not the same, and we know very little about stress in OE prose. For that reason, we have confined our discussion of the suprasegmental phonemes of OE Southwestern to principal stress.

SUMMARY

The phonemes of OE Southwestern probably were:

Consonants

6 stops: /p t k b d g/. /g/ = [g] [γ].
3 fricatives: /f θ h/. /f/ = [f] [v].
   /θ/ = [θ] [ð]. /h/ = [h] [x].
2 sibilants: /s š/. /s/ = [s] [z].
2 affricates: /č ǰ/.
2 nasals: /m n/. /n/ = [n] [ŋ].
1 lateral: /l/.
1 trill: /ř/.
2 glides: /w y/.

Vowels

7 short: /ɪ ü ɛ æ ʊ ɔ ɑ/.
7 long: /iː üː eː æː uː oː ɑː/.

Diphthongs

3 short: /íɛ éɔ ǽɑ/.
3 long: /íːɛ éːɔ ǽːɑ/.

Stress

1: principal stress / ' /.

This version of Matthew vi.9–13 is offered as an illustration of OE.

Fæder ūre þū þe eart on heofonum Sīe þīn nama ġehālgod
tō becume þīn rīċe
ġeweorðe þīn willa on eorðan swā swā on heofonum
ūrne ġedæġhwāmlīcan hlāf sele ūs tō dæġ
and forġief ūs ūre gyltas swā swā wē forġiefað ūrum gyltendum
and ne ġelǣd þū ūs on costnunge ac ālīes ūs of yfele[3]

Translation

'Father our, you who are in heavens, be your name hallowed.
Come your kingdom.
Be your will on earth just as in heavens.
Our daily loaf give us today.
And forgive us our sins, just as we forgive our sinners.
And not lead you us into temptation, but release us from evil.'

Phonemic Transcription

/fǽdeɹ úːɹe θuː θe ǽaɹt ɔn héɔfɔnʊm síːɛ θiːn námɑ yeháːlgɔd/
/toːbɛkúme θiːn ɹíːčɛ/
/yɛwéɔɹθe θiːn wíla ɔn éɔɹθan swaːswaː ɔn héɔfɔnʊm/
/úːɹne yedǽyhwɑːmliːkɑn hlɑːf sélɛ uːs toː dǽy/
/and fɔɹyíɛf uːs úːɹe gúltas swaːswaː weː fɔɹyíɛfaθ
    úːɹʊm gúltendʊm/
/and nɛ yelǽːd θuː uːs ɔn kɔ́stnʊnge ak ɑːlíːɛs uːs ɔf úfelɛ/

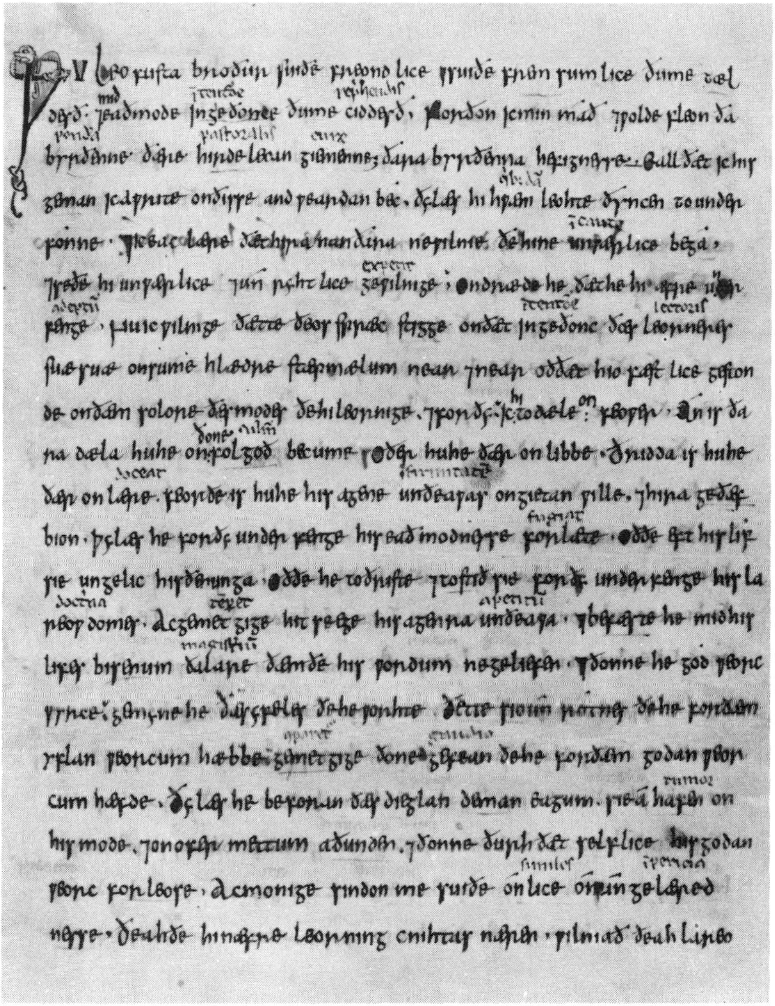

Plate 13. From the *Cura Pastoralis of St. Gregory the Great*, translated into OE by King Alfred (Bod. Lib. MS. Hatton 20, fol. 6r). Copyright of Bodleian Library; reproduced by permission.

NOTES

[1] They were [f], [θ], and [s] when initial and final, but [v], [ð], [z], respectively, when between voiced sounds. Sometimes, however, [f], [θ], and [s] occurred between voiced sounds as in *oflinnan* 'stop,' *geþencan* 'think,' and *āsittan* 'dwell together.'

[2] Some analysts speak of long consonants in OE, but we do not. For evidence against the theory of long consonants, see R. A. Peters, "Phonic and Phonemic Long Consonants in Old English," *Studies in Linguistics*, 19 (1967), 1–6. For an opposite view, see Hans Kurath, "The Loss of Long Consonants and the Rise of Voiced Fricatives in Middle English," *Language*, 32 (1956), 435–445, and William G. Moulton, "The Stops and Spirants of Early Germanic," *Language*, 30 (1954), 1–42.

[3] The OE Southwestern version (Cambridge, Corpus Christi College MS. 140, written c. 1000) is taken from James W. Bright, *The Gospel of Saint Matthew in West Saxon* (Boston, 1910), p. 22. Normalized spellings have been substituted for the MS. entries J 'and,' *sī*, *gewurþe*, *syle*, *forgyf*, *forgyfað*, *ālȳs*.

Middle English Phonemes

In the last chapter we used the Southwestern dialect of OE to describe that period of English, because most surviving OE records are written in that dialect. In describing ME we select instead the Southeast Midland dialect (c. 1300), as the Greater London dialect of EModE is mainly descended from that dialect.

Because in our descriptions of OE and ME we use two different dialects, we must show the correspondences between the two dialects in listing ME developments. For example, OE South-western [ü] remained in ME Southwestern, but the corresponding development in ME SEMid was [ɪ]. Thus, when we say that OE [ü] > ME [ɪ], we mean that the development in ME SEMid corresponding to the development of OE Southwestern [ü] was [ɪ].

Having qualified the descriptions we shall offer in this chapter, we now proceed to the principal phonological and orthographic changes that differentiated ME from OE. We begin with the orthographic changes.

ME Orthographic Changes

Many changes occurred in English spelling in the ME period. Some were English innovations, but the majority resulted from the influence of the French scribes who frequently copied and produced ME manuscripts.

The principal French changes were:

1. *ch* for OE *ċ* = [č] as in OE *ċild* > ME *child* 'child.'
2. *dg* for OE *cg* = [ǰ] as in OE *ecg* > ME *edge* 'edge,' but

$j \sim i \sim g$ initially in French loanwords as *joye ~ ioye* 'joy' and *gentil* 'gentle, noble.'

3. *qu* for OE *cw* = [kw] as in OE *cwēn* > ME *quēēn* 'queen.'[1]

4. *v ~ u* for OE *f* = [v] as in OE *heofon* > ME *hevyn ~ heuene* 'heaven.'

5. *sh* for OE *sċ* = [š] as in OE *sċeal* > ME *shal* 'shall.'

6. *ōū* often for OE *ū* = [u:] as in OE *hūs* > ME *hōūse* 'house.'

7. Near *n, m, v, w,* to prevent confusion in reading a series of downstrokes, *o* often for OE *u* = [ʊ] as in OE *sunu* > ME *sune > sone* 'son.' We shall mark *o* = [ʊ] as *ȯ: sȯne* 'son.'

8. The use in French loanwords of *c* = [s] as in *certayne* 'certain.'

9. The use in Late ME French loanwords of *gu* = [g] as in *guard* 'guard.' Occasionally *gu* was used in native words before a front vowel as in *guest* 'guest' to prevent confusion with *g ~ j* = [ǰ] as in *geste ~ jeste* 'tale.'

10. In the 15th century *īē* from Central French for OE *ē* = [e:] as in OE *spēden* > ME *spēden* > *spīēde(n)* 'to succeed.'

Some of the probable English innovations were:

1. *k* sometimes for OE *c* = [k] as in OE *cyning* > ME *kyng* 'king.'

2. *gh* for OE *h* = [x] as in OE *niht* > ME *nyght* 'night.'

3. *y* for OE *ġ* = [y] as in OE *ġear* > ME *yēre* 'year.'

4. *wh* for OE *hw* = [hw] as in OE *hwæt* > ME *what* 'what.'

5. Gradual disuse of *ð* in favor of *þ* for [θ] and [ð], and then the gradual disuse of *þ* in favor of *th* as in OE *wið ~ wiþ* > ME *wiþ ~ with* > Late ME *with* 'with.'[2]

In short, many French and English changes in the ME period altered English spelling.[3]

ME Consonants

These principal developments occurred in the consonant system of English in the ME period and in the allophones of those consonants:

1. The allophones [f] and [v] of OE /f/ and the allophones [s] and [z] of OE /s/ split in the ME period to become the separate phonemes ME /f/ and /v/, and ME /s/ and /z/. This split resulted from the introduction in the ME period of initial [v] and [z] from French and Latin loanwords. Phonemic contrasts

then arose between [f] and [v] as in ME *fīle* 'to defile' and *vīle* (pl.) 'vile,' and between [s] and [z] as in ME *sēle* 'bliss' and *zēle* 'zeal.'

2. Allophone [γ] of OE /g/ was lost. It merged with various nuclei to form new diphthongs in the ME period, as illustrated in the section in this chapter dealing with ME diphthongs.

The loss of OE [γ] was subphonemic; it did not alter the consonant system of English. OE and ME both had a stop consonant /g/. OE /g/ and ME /g/ differed only in their allophones: OE /g/ = [g] and [γ], but ME /g/ = [g].

Here is the resulting consonant system of ME:

Stops: /p t k b d g/. Respectively, they were as in *pōre* 'poor,' *tōūn* 'town,' *kyng* 'king' and *calf* 'calf,' *bān* 'bone,' *dēp* 'deep,' *gōd* 'good.'

Fricatives: /f v θ h/.[4] /f/ was as in *fōte* 'foot' and /v/ as in *devel ~ deuel* 'devil.'[5] /θ/ had two allophones. They were [θ] as in *þe ~ the* 'the,' but [ð] normally between voiced sounds as in *ōþer ~ ōther* 'other.' /h/ also had two allophones: [h] as in *herte* 'heart' and [x] as *h ~ gh* in *nyht ~ night* 'night.'[6]

Sibilants: /s z š/. /s/ was as *s ~ c* as in *sitē ~ citē* 'city,' /z/ as *z* and *s* in *zēle* 'zeal' and *rēson* 'reason,' and /š/ as *sh* in *shāme* 'shame.'[7]

Affricates: /č ǰ/. /č/ was as *ch* in *chirche* 'church.' /ǰ/ was as *g* in *gentile* 'noble, gentle,' *j* in *joye* 'joy,' and *dg* in *edge* 'edge.'

Nasals: /m n/. /m/ was as in *milde* 'mild.' /n/ had two allophones: [n] as in *nōn* 'noon,' but [ŋ] before [g] and |k| as in *synge(n)* [síŋgən] 'to sing' and *drynke(n)* [dríŋkən] 'to drink.'

Lateral: /l/ as in *lȳf(e)* 'life.'

Trill: /r̈/ as in *rōte* 'root.'

Glides: /w y/. /w/ was as in *wal* 'wall,' and /y/ as *y ~ ġ* in *yēr ~ ġēr* 'year.'

Consonant Clusters

Several reductions occurred in the OE initial consonant clusters that we cited in the last chapter:

1. Loss of [h] in OE initial [hl hn hr̈] as in OE *hlāf* > ME *lōf* 'loaf,'[8] OE *hnecca* > ME *nekke* 'neck,' and OE *hring* > ME *ring* 'ring.'

2. Loss of [l] in OE initial [wl] as in OE *-wlispian* > ME *wlispen* > *lispen* 'to lisp.'

ME Vowels

A number of qualitative and quantitative developments took place in the syllabic system of English in the ME period. The chief *qualitative* changes were:

1. OE [ü] [ü:] through unrounding in Late OE > ME [ɪ] [i:], respectively, as in OE *fyllan* > ME *fillen* 'to fill' and OE *mȳs* > ME *mīs* 'mice.'

2. OE [ɑ] and [æ] > ME [a] as in OE *catte* > ME *cat* 'cat' and OE *fæder* > ME *fader* 'father.'⁹ OE [ɑ], however, remained in ME before [l] as in *all* 'all.'

3. OE [æ:] > ME [ɛ:~e:] as in OE *dǣd* > ME *dę̄d ~ dēd* 'deed.'

4. OE [ɑ:] > ME [ɔ:] as in OE *stān* > ME *stǭn* 'stone.'

5. OE [ɑ ɛ ɔ ʊ] in unstressed syllables > ME [ə] as finally in OE *heofon* [hɛɔfɔn] > ME *heven* [hɛvən] 'heaven.' We shall say more about the leveling of OE nuclei to ME [ə] later in this chapter and in the chapter dealing with English nouns.

Two kinds of *quantitative* developments took place in the syllabic system of English:

A: those that occurred before certain consonant clusters, and

B: those that occurred in open syllables.

A. In Late OE, short nuclei were lengthened before certain consonant clusters. Some of these nuclei were later shortened again, but the following ones remained lengthened in Late ME:

1. All nuclei before /ld/ as in OE *ċild* > ME *chīld* 'child,' but not if a third consonant followed as in OE *ċildru* > ME *childre* > *children* 'children.'

2. [ɪ] and [ɔ] before /mb/ as in OE *climban* > ME *clīmbe* 'to climb' and OE *comb* > ME *cǭmb* 'comb.'

3. [ɪ] and [ʊ] before /nd/ as in OE *bindan* > ME *bȳnde* 'to bind' and OE *grund* > ME *grūnd* 'ground.'

B. In ME a second type of lengthening took place. Nuclei under principal stress were lengthened when they occurred in an open syllable — one that did not end in a consonant.¹⁰

1. After c. 1250, ME [a ɛ ɔ] frequently were lengthened in

open syllables to [a: ɛ: ɔ:], respectively, as in ME *fader* > *fāder ~ fādir* 'father,' OE *etan* > ME *ẹ̄te(n)* 'to eat,' OE *col* > ME *cǭle* 'coal.'

2. In addition, by c. 1400 ME [ɪ] and [ʊ] sometimes underwent both a quantative and qualitative change to [e:] and [o:], respectively, as in OE *wicu* > ME *wēke* 'week' and OE *wudu* > ME *wōde* 'wood.'

As a result of such lengthenings in open syllables in disyllable words but not in closed syllables — those that ended in a consonant — some ME words had long vowels as *fādir* 'father,' but others had short vowels as plural-genitive *fadris*.

The process of analogy also produced such doublets as *fādir ~ fadir*, but later one form became generalized (*fadir*) and the other form (*fādir*) disappeared.[11]

Because of the qualitative and quantitative developments described above, the resultant vowel system of ME was this:

Short Vowels

	Front	Central	Back
High	/ɪ/		/ʊ/
Mid	/ɛ/	/ə/	/ɔ/
Low		/a/	

ME /a/ had two allophones, both written *a*. They were [a] as in ME *ban* 'curse' and [ɑ] before [l] as in ME *all* 'all.'

ME /ɔ/ apparently occurred only in unstressed syllables. Some examples of /ə/ are *e* in ME *wȳse* 'wise,' *a* in ME *aloft* 'aloft,' *u* in ME *undēp* 'shallow,' and *o* in ME *of* 'of,' when the word did not bear principal stress.[12]

The remaining short vowels /ɪ ɛ ʊ ɔ/ were written *i, e, u, o,* respectively, as in ME *hire* 'her,' *wel* 'spring,' *ful* 'full,' and *hol* 'hollow.' /ʊ/ also was written *o*, which we mark *ȯ*, as in *tȯnge* /tʊ́ngə/ 'tongue.'

Long Vowels

	Front	Central	Back
High	/i:/		/u:/
Mid	/e:/ /ɛ:/		/o:/ /ɔ:/
Low		/a:/	

The principal graphemes and grapheme clusters used to represent ME long vowels are illustrated in the following table:

/i:/ $\bar{\imath} \sim \bar{y}$ /u:/ $\bar{u} \sim \bar{o}\bar{u} \sim \bar{o}\bar{w}$
/e:/ $\bar{e} \sim \bar{e}\bar{e} \sim \bar{\imath}\bar{e}$ /o:/ $\bar{o} \sim \bar{o}\bar{o}$
/ɛ:/ $\bar{e} \sim \bar{e}\bar{e} \sim \bar{e}\bar{a}$ /ɔ:/ $\bar{o} \sim \bar{o}\bar{o} \sim \bar{o}\bar{u}$
/a:/ $\bar{a}$

Some Examples:

/i:/ *hīre* 'wages.'
/e:/ *sē* 'see.'
/ɛ:/ *sę̄* 'sea,' *węl* 'wealth.'
/a:/ *bān* 'bone.'
/u:/ *fūl* 'foul.'
/o:/ *nōn* 'noon.'
/ɔ:/ *nǭn* 'none,' *hǭl* 'whole.'

ME Diphthongs

All OE complex nuclei were reduced to simple nuclei by the ME period, generally as follows:

OE			ME		
[ɪɛ]	*hiera*	>	[ɪ ~ ɛ]	*hire ~ here* 'their.'
[i:ɛ]	*hīera*	>	[e:]	*hīēre* 'higher.'[13]
[ɛɔ]	*heorte*	>	[ɛ]	*herte* 'heart.'
[e:ɔ]	*dēop*	>	[e:]	*dēp* 'deep.'
[æɑ]	*hearpe*	>	[a]	*harpe* 'harp.'
[æ:ɑ]	*dēad*	>	[ɛ:]	*dęd ~ dę̄ąd* 'dead.'

New complex nuclei developed in ME from the blending of OE front nuclei with [w y ɣ] and OE back nuclei with [w ɣ]. In ME new complex nuclei also developed from a qualitative change of certain OE nuclei before [x]. The following examples illustrate three of these developments:

1. OE [æ]+[y] > ME [ái] as in OE *dæġ* [dǽy] > ME *day* [dáɪ] 'day.'

2. OE [ɔ]+[ɣ] > ME [ɔ́ʊ] as in OE *boga* [bɔ́ɣɑ] > ME *bowe* [bɔ́ʊə] 'bow.'

3. OE [ɔ]+[xt] > ME [ɔ́ʊxt] as in OE *dohtur* [dɔ́xtʊř] > ME *doughter* [dɔ́ʊxtəř] 'daughter.'

Four principal falling diphthongs arose in ME SEMid from these developments:

/ái/ as *ay* in *day* 'day' and *ey* in *wey* 'way.'
/áu/ as *au* in *cause* 'cause' and *aw* in *drawen* 'to draw.'
/íu/ as *iw* in *niwe* 'new' and *ew* in *dew* 'dew.'
/ɔ́u/ as *ou* in *soule* 'soul' and *ow* in *knowe* 'to know.'

There was, in addition, a fifth principal diphthong /ɔ́i/, written *oi*. It entered ME from French loanwords such as *chois* 'choice.'

ME Suprasegmentals

Principal or primary stress / ' / was as in ME *ful* /fúl/ 'full.' We do not know what the other stresses and suprasegmental phonemes of ME were. Probably, the reduction of OE [ɑ ɛ ɔ ʊ] to ME [ə] in unstressed syllables was conditioned by a change from secondary stress / ^ / or tertiary stress / ` / in those syllables in OE to weak stress / ˘ / in ME. We shall conjecture, therefore, that there were at least two stresses in ME: principal or primary stress / ' / and weak stress / ˘ / as in ME *oxe* /ɔ́ksə̆/ 'ox.'

SUMMARY

The phonemes of ME SEMid probably were:

Consonants

6 stops: /p t k b d g/.
4 fricatives: /f v θ h/. /θ/ = [θ] [ð]. /h/ = [h] [x].
3 sibilants: /s z š/.
2 affricates: /č ǰ/.
2 nasals: /m n/. /n/ = [n] [ŋ].
1 lateral: /l/.
1 trill: /ř/.
2 glides: /w y/.

Vowels

6 short: /ɪ ɛ ə a ʊ ɔ/.
7 long: /iː eː ɛː aː uː oː ɔː/.

93

Diphthongs

5 short: /ái áu íu ɔ́ɪ ɔ́u/.

Stresses

2: primary / ' /, weak / ˘ /.

SPECIMEN OF ME

ME version of Matthew vi.9–13.

Ōure fādir that art in heuenes, halwid bē thī nāme;
Thī kyngdōm cumme tō; bē thī wille dōn as in heuen and in ērthe;
Ġif tō ūs this day ōūre brēēd ǫuer ōther substaunce;
And forġēue tō ūs ōūre dettis, as wē forġēue tō ōūre dettōūrs;
And lēēde ūs nat in tō temptaciōūn, būt delyuere ūs frǫ ȳuel.[14]

Translation

'Our father that art in heavens, hallowed be thy name;
Thy kingdom come to; be thy will done as in heaven and in earth;
Give to us this day our bread over other substance;
And forgive to us our debts, as we forgive to our debtors;
And lead us not into temptation, but deliver us from evil.'

Phonemic Transcription

/úːɹ̈ə fáːdɪɹ̈ θat aɹ̈t ɪn hévənəs hálwɪd beː θi: náːmə/
/θi: kíngdoːm kúmə toː/ /beː θi: wílə doːn as ɪn hévən and ɪn éːɹ̈θə/
/yɪf toː uːs θɪs dáɪ úːɹ̈ə bɹ̈eːd ɔ́ːvəɹ̈ óːθəɹ̈ sʊbstáʊnsə/
/and fɔɹ̈yéːvə toː uːs úːɹ̈ə détɪs as weː fɔɹ̈yéːvə toː úːɹ̈ə dɛtúːɹ̈s/
/and lɛːd uːs nat ɪn toː tɛmptasɪúːn buːt dɛlívəɹ̈ uːs fɹ̈ɔ́ íːvəl/

NOTES

[1] Throughout this chapter macrons have been added to ME graphemes and grapheme clusters that represent a long vowel.

[2] In the handwriting of the Late ME period the grapheme þ came to be written with an open top as Ⲩ. For that grapheme printers in the EModE period substituted *y* because it most resembled Ⲩ. Thus, they printed *y*ᵉ 'the' and *y*ᵗ 'that.' In the LModE period those unacquainted with the practice of early printers have translated *y*ᵉ 'the' as 'ye.' As a result, we encounter today pseudo-archaic misnomers like *Ye Olde Tea Shoppe.*

[3] In ME the spelling *sk* is found primarily in loanwords or derivatives of earlier loanwords, as (Scandinavian) *skyll ~ skil* 'skill,' (French) *skārsli* 'scarcely,' (Latin) *skōle* 'school,' and (Dutch) *skipper* 'master of a ship.'

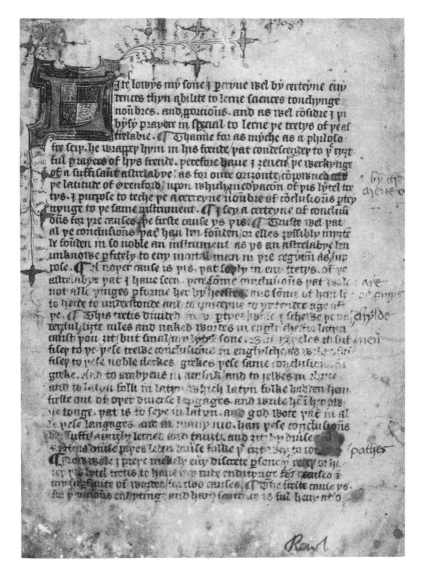

Plate 14. From Geoffrey Chaucer's *A Treatise on the Astrolabe* (Bod. Lib. MS. Rawl. D. 913, fol. 23r). Copyright of Bodleian Library; reproduced by permission.

[4] As in OE, [f], [s], [θ] sometimes occurred in ME between vowels instead of [v], [z], [ð], respectively, as in ME *bifōren* 'before,' *asonder* 'asunder,' and *lengthe* 'length.' Intervocalic [s] frequently occurred in French loanwords, such as *spāce* /spá:sə/ 'space' and *condicioun* /kɔndɪsɪú:n/ 'condition.'

[5] In ME the graphemes *v* and *u* represented /v/ as in *haven ~ hauen* and /ʊ/ as in *vnder ~ under.*

[6] Initial *h* was silent in many French loanwords, such as /ɔnú:r̈/ *honour* 'honor,' /úmblə/ *humble* 'humble,' and /ú:r̈ə/ *houre ~ oure* 'hour.'

[7] Initial voiceless [s] and [f] frequently became voiced [z] and [v] respectively in ME Southeastern, as in SE *zuych(e)* 'such' and *vox* 'fox,' but not in ME Midland, as in Mid *such(e)* and *fox.*

[8] As an aid to the reader, we have placed small hooks under *ǫ* (and later also the graphemic variants *ǫǫ ǫ̆*) =[ɔ:] and under *ę̄* (*ę̄ę̄ ę̄ą̄*) =[e:] to distinguish them, respectively, from *ō* (*ōō*) =[o:] and *ē* (*ēē īē*) =[e:].

[9] Scholarly opinion varies about the phonetic quality of ME /a/. Some analysts have suggested [æ], but [æ] probably represents a later value.

[10] Lengthening occurred only in disyllabic words. In such two-syllable words a single consonant after a vowel belongs to the next syllable, as in *fā-dir.* Lengthening did not occur in three-syllable (trisyllabic) words.

[11] Analogy is that linguistic process by which words become imitative of more familiar words and patterns without themselves having undergone the same linguistic development that those more familiar words and patterns underwent. For example, in LModE the new plural *curriculums* exists besides the older plural *curricula* through analogy with other noun plurals ending in *-s.*

[12] Some prefix changes include: OE [bɛ-] as in *beginnan* > ME [bɪ-] as in *bigynne(n)*; OE [ɔf-] as in *ofdune* > ME [ə-] as in *adōūn*; OE [ɔn-] as in *onbutan* > ME [ə-] as in *abōūten*; OE [ɑnd-] as in *andlang* > ME [ə-] as in *along.*

[13] ME *hīēre* [hé:r̈ə] 'higher' > Late ME [hí:ər̈].

[14] ME *ȳvel ~ ēvel* 'evil.' The ME SEMid Wycliffe version (1389) is taken from *The Gothic and Anglo-Saxon Gospels*, ed. Joseph Bosworth, 3rd ed. (London, 1888), p. 25.

11

Early Modern English Phonemes

In this chapter we shall examine the phonemic system of the Greater-London dialect (c. 1650) of EModE. We also shall examine the various phonological and orthographic developments that differentiated EModE from ME.

Orthographic Changes

The orthographic or graphemic changes in the writing system of EModE were few. The grapheme ʃ was used as a variant of s as in ʃeene ~ seene 'seen,' but in the period of transition (c. 1725–c 1825) to LModE the grapheme ʃ gradually fell into disuse and eventually disappeared. The only other graphemic development of note was the gradual restriction in use at the end of the EModE period of the graphemes *j* and *v* to represent consonants, and of *i* and *u* to represent vowels.

EModE Consonants

These principal developments occurred in the EModE period in the consonant system of English and in the allophones of those consonants:

1. The allophones [θ] and [ð] of ME /θ/ split in the EModE period to become the separate phonemes EModE /θ/ and /ð/. This split resulted from the voicing of ME [θ] when it occurred in initial position in some words. ME [θ] thus became EModE [ð] as in ME *þi* [θiː] > EModE *thy* [ðʌɪ].[1] A phonemic contrast

then arose between [ð] and [θ] as initially in EModE *thy* [ðʌ́ɪ] and EModE *thigh* [θʌ́ɪ].[2]

2. The allophones [n] and [ŋ] of ME /n/ split in the EModE period to become the separate EModE phonemes /n/ and /ŋ/. This split resulted from the development ME [ŋg] > EModE [ŋ] as in ME *singe* [síŋgə] > *[síŋg] > EModE *sing* [síŋ]. EModE [ŋ] and [n] then contrasted phonemically, as finally in EModE *sing* [síŋ] and EModE *sin* [sín].

3. Emergence of EModE /ž/. The phoneme /ž/ did not occur in ME. It developed in EModE from the assimilation of the medial sequence [zy] to [ž], as in EModE *leasure* [lɛ́zyuɹ] > [lɛ́žəɹ] 'leisure.'[3] A phonemic contrast then developed between EModE [ž] and, for example, [s] as medially in EModE *leasure* [lɛ́žəɹ] 'leisure' and EModE *lesser* [lɛ́səɹ]. Two additional examples of the EModE development [zy] > [ž] are EModE *vision* [vízyun] > [vížən] and EModE *plesshur* [plɛ́zyuɹ] > [plɛ́žəɹ] 'pleasure.'[4] The EModE medial sequence [zy], from which [ž] developed, occurred only in words that in ME were borrowed from French and Latin.

4. Allophone [x] of ME /h/ was lost. In ME [x] occurred in medial and final positions, but not in initial position. In EModE, [x] was lost medially, as in ME *nyght* [níxt] > EModE *night* [nʌ́ɪt] and ME *taughte* [táuxtə] > EModE *taught* [tɔ́t]. [x] also was lost in final position in EModE, as in ME *saugh* [sáux] > EModE *saw* [sɔ́], but sometimes it became EModE [f] as in ME *laughe* [láuxə] > EModE *laugh ~ loffe* [lǽf ~ láf].

The loss of ME [x] was subphonemic. ME /h/ and EModE /h/ differed only in their allophones: ME /h/ = [h] and [x], but following the loss of [x], EModE /h/ = [h].

5. Subphonemic changes in the quality of EModE /r/. In ME, /r̄/ = trill [r̄] in all positions. ME trill [r̄] in EModE, in initial position, as in *ring* and *red*, was either a weak trill [r̄] or was so weakened that [r] occurred. We are uncertain about this. Between nuclei, as in *direct*, EModE /r/ probably was [r]. Before consonants and in final position, as in *farm* and *far*, respectively, fricative [ɹ] probably occurred.

Because of unsubstantial knowledge at present about the qualitative values of the allophones of EModE /r/, for convenience we shall write allophone [r] initially and between vowels, but allophone [ɹ] in all other positions. Thus, our conjecture is that ME trill /r̈/ − [r̈], but EModE /r/ = non-trill [r] and fricative [ɹ].

As a result of the changes described above, the consonants of the London dialect of EModE probably were:

Stops: /p t k b d g/ as in *pallace* 'palace,' *tel* 'to tell,' *cut* and *king, best, doe* 'to do,' and *giue* 'to give.'[5]

Fricatives: /f v θ ð h/ as in *fair* and *Philip, voice* and *liues* 'lives,' *oath, that,* and *he.*

Sibilants: /s z š ž/ as in *sin* and *city, zeale* 'zeal,' *should* and *chiualry* 'chivalry,' *vision* and *measure.*

Affricates: /č ǰ/ as in *childe* 'child' and *iudge* 'judge.'

Nasals: /m n ŋ/ as in *man, name, sing.*

Lateral: /l/ as in *loue* 'love.'

Glides: /w y r/. /w y/ as in *will* and *yeer* 'year'. /r/, according to our conjecture, had two principal allophones: [r] as in *red* and *direct,* but [ɹ] as in *farm* and *far.*[6]

Consonant Clusters

In the chapter dealing with OE, we cited the initial consonant clusters /hn hl hr̈ wl gn wr̈ kn/. In the last chapter we said the first four of those consonant clusters became ME /n l r̈ l/, respectively. In ME the clusters /gn wr̈ kn/ remained, but in EModE they were reduced as follows:

1. Loss of [g] in ME initial [gn] as in ME *gnawen* [gnáuən] > EModE *gnaw* [nɔ́].

2. Loss of [w] in ME initial [wr̈] as in ME *wrōng* [wr̈ɔ́ːŋg] > EModE [rɔ́ŋ].

3. Loss of [k] in ME initial [kn] as in ME *knyght* [kníxt] > EModE *knight* [náɪt]. The reduction ME [kn] > EModE [n] occurred c. 1680–1700.

In addition, [w] sometimes was lost in initial [hw] as in ME *what* [hwát] > EModE *what* [hwát ~ wát] and ME *whō* [hwóː] > EModE *who* [hú].

Great Vowel Shift

In the period from c. 1400 to c. 1650–1700, the syllabic system of English underwent an extensive series of changes, the Great Vowel Shift, sometimes called the Great Syllabic Shift.

As a term the Great Vowel Shift generally refers only to those changes that affected ME long nuclei. The label should properly refer to all the "shifts" or changes that ME nuclei underwent.

We can only approximately describe London English nuclei, for the phonetic evidence we must use is frequently difficult to interpret. The principal reason is that London English was not so much a dialect as a mixture of several regional and class dialects that existed side by side in the London area. Furthermore, the changes collectively labeled the Great Vowel Shift did not uniformly affect the speech of all dialect speakers in the London area at the same time. Consequently, the linguistic state of Greater London English c. 1650 was quite fluid; double and triple pronunciations of words occurred. For example newer [æ] probably alternated with older [a] in *man*, and the variations [a ~ ɒ ~ ɔ] probably occurred as in *war*. Many of the finer details of the Greater-London dialect of EModE, spoken in an area of about sixty miles around London, are beyond the scope of this book. We shall only examine the principal effects that resulted from the Great Vowel Shift.

A major change in the vowel system of English caused by the Great Vowel Shift was the loss of length as a feature of differentiation among vowels. In the OE and ME periods, you will recall, there were two sets of vowels which we phonemically differentiated as short and long. In the EModE period, however, that phonemic distinction was lost. Although many of the EModE vowels had both short and long allophonic variants, as in *seen* [sín ~ sí:n] and *both* [bóθ ~ bó:θ], the phonemic contrast between nuclei was one of quality, as in *sin* [sín] and *seen* [sín], not quantity. Thus, in the descriptions that follow, length is not indicated in EModE vowels or their allophones because it was a non-distinctive or subphonemic feature of the syllabic system of EModE.

Here are two lists to illustrate the principal changes resulting from the Great Vowel Shift: the first shows the phonetic developments affecting the allophones of ME long vowels; and the second shows the phonetic developments affecting the allophones of ME short vowels.

Long Vowels

1. ME [a:] > EModE [e] as in ME *nāme* [ná:mə] > EModE *name* [ném].

2. ME [ɛ:] > EModE [e ~ i] as in ME *drẹm* [dřɛ́:m] > EModE *dream* [dɹém ~ dɹím].

3. ME [e:] > EModE [i] as in ME *grēte* [gřé:tə] > EModE *greet* [gɹít].

4. ME [i:] > EModE [ʌɪ] as in ME *chīld* [čí:ld] > EModE *childe* [čʌ́ɪld].

5. ME [ɔ:] > EModE [o] as in ME *stǫn* [stɔ́:n] > EModE *stone* [stón].

6. ME [o:] > EModE [u] as in ME *mōne* [mó:nə] > EModE *moone* [mún].

7. ME [u:] > EModE [ʌu] as in ME *hūs* [hú:s] > EModE *house* [hʌ́us].

Although other developments than these occurred in specific environments,[7] for pedagogical purposes the general phonetic drift of the changes affecting the ME long nuclei may be diagrammed as follows, minus length marks:

Front	Back
[ʌɪ] ← [i]	[u] → [ʌu]
↑	↑
[e]	[o]
↑	↑
[a] [ɛ]	[ɔ]

Short Vowels

1. ME [ʊ] > EModE [ʌ] as in ME *sǒne* [súnə] > EModE *sonne* [sʌ́n].

2. ME [ɔ] > EModE [ɒ ~ ɑ] as in ME *God* [gɔ́d] > EModE *God* [gɒ́d ~ gɑ́d].

3. ME [a] > EModE [æ] as in ME *man* [mán] > EModE *man* [mǽn].

In addition to these developments, many other changes affected short nuclei in specific environments. For example, ME [ɛ] before [ř] > EModE [a ~ ɜ] as in ME *person* [pɛ́řsən] > EModE *parson ~ person* [pɑ́ɹsən ~ pɜ́ɹsən]. Examples of other changes of this sort are beyond the scope of our study.

EModE Vowels

The EModE vowel system of Greater-London English after the Great Vowel Shift probably consisted of eleven vowels:

	Front	Central	Back
High	/i/ /ɪ/		/u/ /ʊ/
Mid	/e/ /ɛ/	/ə/	/o/ /ɔ/
Low	/æ/		/ɑ/

/æ/ had two principal allophones: [æ] and [a] as in *ask* [ǽsk ~ ásk]. Both allophones were free variants. One or the other could occur in the same environment without a change in the meaning of the word in which they occurred.

/ə/ had three allophones: [ʌ] as in *sonne* [sʌn] 'son,' [ɜ] as in *word* [wɜɹd], and [ə] as in *among* [əmʌŋ].

The allophones of /ɑ/ were the free variants [ɑ] and [ɒ] as in *want* [wɑ́nt ~ wɒ́nt].[8] /ɑ/ varied with /æ/ in many words such as *ask* /ǽsk ~ ásk/, *path* /pǽθ ~ páθ/, *half* /hǽf ~ háf/.

These examples illustrate EModE /i ɪ e ɛ æ ə u ʊ o ɔ ɑ/:

/i/ *beet, bier.*
/ɪ/ *bit.*
/e/ *bait.*
/ɛ/ *bet, bear, beer.*
/æ/ *bat, cat, hat.*
/ə/ *but, beard, bird, heard, herd.*
/u/ *boot, fool.*
/ʊ/ *full.*
/o/ *boat, foal.*
/ɔ/ *bought, caught.*
/ɑ/ *−bote* 'compensation,' *cote* 'cottage,' *hot.*

EModE Diphthongs

All five ME complex nuclei underwent change in the transition from ME to EModE. Four of these complex nuclei were reduced to simple nuclei, and the fifth was changed in quality but remained a complex nucleus, as illustrated in the following table:

1. ME [aɪ] > EModE [e] as in ME *day* [dáɪ] > EModE *day* [de].

2. ME [aʊ] > EModE [ɔ] as in ME *cause* [káʊzɔ] > EModE *cause* [kɔ́z].

3. ME [ɔʊ] > EModE [o] as in ME *knowe* [knɔ́ʊə] > EModE *know* [nó].

4. ME [ɪʊ] > EModE [u] as in ME *niwe* [níʊə] > EModE *new* [nú], also older [níʊ].

5. ME [ɔɪ] > EModE [ʌɪ] as in ME *ioye* [ǰɔ́ɪə] > EModE *ioy* [ǰʌ́ɪ]. The change of ME [ɔɪ] to EModE [ʌɪ] is attested by such EModE rhymes as Shakespeare's *groin*: *swine*, Pope's *toil*; *pile*, and Dryden's *joins*: *lines*.

As a result of these changes, and others previously described, there were only two diphthongs in the Greater-London dialect of EModE: /ɔ́ɪ/ and /ɔ́ʊ/ as, respectively, in *ioy* /ǰɔ́ɪ/ and *house* /hɔ́ʊs/. EModE /əɪ/ = [ʌɪ], and /əʊ/ = [ʌʊ]. The latter, you will recall, developed from ME [u:] > EModE [ʌʊ], as in ME *hūs* [hú:s] > EModE *house* [hʌ́ʊs].

EModE Suprasegmentals

In EModE, as in ME, there were at least two stresses: primary stress / ′ / and weak stress / ˘ /, as in *heauen* /hέvə̆n/ 'heaven.' Undoubtedly there were other stresses in EModE, but we do not know what they were, nor do we know what the other suprasegmental phonemes of EModE were.

SUMMARY

The phonemes of the Greater-London dialect of EModE probably were:

Consonants

6 stops: /p t k b d g/.
5 fricatives: /f v θ ð h/.
4 sibilants: /s z š ž/.
2 affricates: /č ǰ/.
3 nasals: /m n ŋ/.
1 lateral: /l/.
3 glides: /w y r/. /r/ = [r] [ɹ].

Vowels

11: /i ɪ e ɛ æ ə u ʊ o ɔ ɑ/. /æ/ = [æ] [a]. /ə/ = [ʌ]
[ɜ] [ə]. /ɑ/ = [ɑ] [ɒ].

Diphthongs

2: /ɔ́ɪ ɔ́ʊ/. /ɔ́ɪ/ = [ʌɪ]. /ɔ́ʊ/ = [ʌʊ].

Stresses

2: / ˈ ˇ /.

SPECIMEN OF EMODE

EModE version of Matthew vi.9–13.

Our Father, which art in heauen, hallowed be thy Name.
Thy kingdome come. Thy will be done, in earth as it is in heauen.
Giue us this day our dayly bread.
And forgiue us our debts, as we forgiue our debters.
And leade us not into temptation, but deliuer us from euill.[9]

Phonemic Transcription

/ɔ́ʊr fǽðər hwɪ́č ært ɪn hévən hǽləd bi ðɔ́ɪ nem/
/ðɔ́ɪ kíŋdəm kəm/ /ðɔ́ɪ wɪl bi dən ɪn ərθ æz ɪt ɪz ɪn hévən/
/gɪv əs ðɪs de ɔ́ʊr déli bred/
/æn fɔ́rgɪv əs ɔ́ʊr dɛts əz wi fɔ́rgɪv ɔ́ʊr détərz/
/æn led əs nɑt íntə témtešən bət dəlívər əs frɑm ívɪl/

NOTES

[1] Also initially in *that, the, they, them, these, there, then, than.*

[2] There was also a frequent voicing of ME final [θ], as well as [f s], to EModE [ð v z], respectively, as in ME *with* [wíθ] > EModE *with* [wíð] before voiced sounds as in *with all* [wíðɔl], ME *of* [ɔ́f] > EModE *of* [óv ~ ʌ́v], and ME *his* [hís] > EModE *his* [híz].

[3] Assimilation is that linguistic process by which a sound is partially or totally adapted to the articulation of an adjacent sound, as in [fm] > [m] in OE *wifman* [wì:fmɑn] > *wômman* [wúmən] 'woman.'

[4] Similarly, EModE [sy] > [š] c. 1650 as in EModE *special* [spésyal] > [spɛ́šəl]; EModE [ty] > [č] c. 1670–1700 as in EModE *fortune* [fɔ́rtyʊn] > [fɔ́ɹčən]; and EModE [dy] > [ǰ] c. 1670–1700 as in EModE *soldier* [sóldyəɹ] > [sóljə̆ɹ ~ sójə̆ɹ].

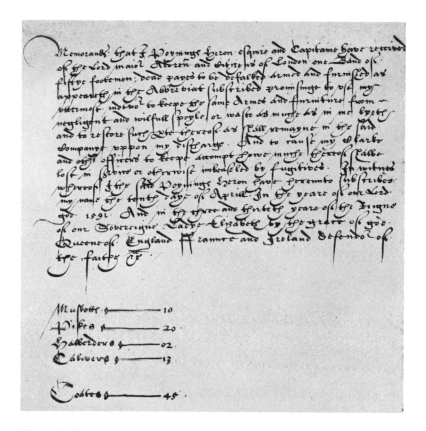

Plate 15. Secretary hand (1591). From Public Record Office, State Papers Domestic, Elizabeth, Vol. 238, fol. 221. British Crown copyright; reproduced by permission of the Controller of H. M. Stationery Office.

⁵ Sometimes ME [d] between nuclei > EModE [ð] as in ME *fādir* [fá:dɪrʲ] > [fádɪrʲ] > EModE *father* [fáðəɹ ~ fǽðəɹ].

⁶ Because we are uncertain about the values of EModE /r/, for convenience we have classified EModE /r/ as a glide. This tentative classification is subject to revision if more definite evidence concerning EModE /r/ becomes available. Such evidence may point to the ultimate classification of EModE /r/ as a fricative or possibly even a trill.

⁷ For example, ME [o:]+[d] or [t] or [k] > EModE [ʊ], [ʌ], [u] as in ME *bōk(e)* [bó:kə] > EModE *book* [bʊ́k], ME *blōd(e)* [bló:də] > EModE *blood* [blʌ́d], ME *fōde* [fó:də] > EModE *food* [fúd]. In addition, sometimes ME long nuclei were shortened as in ME *bōte* [bó:tə] > EModE –*bote* [bát ~ bʊ́t] 'compensation.'

⁸ No phonemic contrast between EModE [æ] and [a], between [a] and [ɑ], or between [ɑ] and [ɒ], appears probable c. 1650.

⁹ The EModE King James or Authorized version from *The Holy Bible* (London, 1611), p. 14. The following EModE variant version is that of William Tyndale (1526), taken from *The Gothic and Anglo-Saxon Gospels*, ed. Joseph Bosworth, 3rd ed. (London, 1888), p. 25:

> *O oure father which arte in heven, halowed be thy name; Let thy kingdom come; thy wyll be fulfilled, as well in erth, as hit is in heven; Geve vs this daye oure dayly breade; And forgeve vs oure treaspases, even as we forgeve them which treaspas vs; Leede vs not into temptacion, but delyvre vs ffrom (sic) yvell.*

American English Phonemes

In this chapter we shall examine the phonemes of LModE, the last of the four periods of English. We shall also examine the principal sound developments that came to differentiate LModE from EModE.

World Varieties

Because of various British military conquests, migrations, and settlements dating from the seventeenth century, the English language spread around the world to the West Indies, North America, India, Africa, Burma, the Malay Peninsula and Archipelago, Australia, and New Zealand. From that linguistic extension several varieties of English other than British English (BrE) have developed. They include American English (AmE), Australian English, Canadian English, Caribbean or West Indian English, and South African English. We have selected AmE from these world varieties of English as the basis of our description of LModE.

AmE Dialects

Data about AmE dialects published in *The Linguistic Atlas of the United States and Canada* has been mostly limited to the eastern half of the United States.[1] The collection of material about many areas west of the Mississippi River is not complete. Therefore we cannot offer a thorough analysis of the phonemic system of AmE but will restrict our discussion to the three main dialect areas of the eastern United States: Northern, Midland, and Southern (see map in Chapter seven).

Northern (N) includes that area of the United States north of a line extending westward from northern New Jersey across northern Pennsylvania, Ohio, Indiana, and Illinois to the Upper Mississippi Valley. Two principal sub-areas of Northern are Eastern New England (ENE) and Metropolitan New York (MNY).

Midland is divided into North Midland (NMid) and South Midland (SMid). The area of North Midland includes most of New Jersey, Pennsylvania, northern Delaware, northern Maryland, northern West Virginia, central Ohio, central Indiana, and central Illinois. A principal sub-area of NMid is western Pennsylvania (WPa). South Midland includes southern West Virginia, southern Ohio, southern Indiana, southern Illinois, most of Kentucky, eastern Tennessee, western Virginia, North Carolina, South Carolina, northern Georgia, and most of northern Alabama and northern Mississippi.

Southern (S) includes the remaining area in the South, excluding the Southern-Mountain region of South Midland.

In summary, the principal dialect areas of the eastern United States are:

1. Northern (N), including the two sub-areas: Eastern New England (ENE) and Metropolitan New York (MNY).

2. Midland, consisting of North Midland (NMid), including the sub-area of western Pennsylvania (WPa), and South Midland (SMid).

3. Southern (S).

AmE Consonants

In the evolution from EModE to AmE, the principal development in the consonant system involved qualitative changes in the allophones of EModE /r/ and their split into the separate AmE consonant phonemes /r/ and /ɹ/. Those dialects of AmE in which /ɹ/ occurs instead of /r/ are called *r*-less dialects, and those dialects in which /r/ occurs instead of /ɹ/ are called *r*-full dialects.

It is possible that the allophone of EModE /r/ in initial position, as in EModE *red*, was weak trill [r̃] or apico-alveolar [r]. In AmE, however, the phone-type that commonly occurs in initial position, as in *red*, is [r].

After initial /t/ or /d/, EModE fricative [ɹ] remains in AmE, usually as the voiceless variety after /t/ and the voiced variety after /d/, as in *tread* and *dread*. [r], however, occurs after /b/ or /g/ as in *bray* and *grey*.

In pre-consonant and post-vowel positions, EModE fricative [ɹ] generally is [r] in *r*-full dialects of AmE as in EModE *beard* [bɔ́ɹd] > AmE [bírd ~ bírd] and EModE *fear* [fíɹ] > AmE [fír ~ fír].

In *r*-less dialects (ENE, MNY, and some S), EModE fricative [ɹ] after high and mid nuclei generally is non-syllabic [ə̯] as in *beard* [bíə̯d ~ bíə̯d] and *fear* [fíə̯ ~ fíə̯]. In these dialects [ə̯] is generally lost after low nuclei as in *cart* [kát ~ kát], but not after mid nuclei as in *war* [wɔ́ə̯] and *ward* [wɔ́ə̯d].

To summarize, in initial position (*red*) and post-consonant position (*tread*), all dialects of AmE have /r/ = [r] and [ɹ]. In *r*-full dialects the consonant /r/ = [r] occurs in pre-consonant position (*beard*) and post-vowel position (*fear*), and in *r*-less dialects the consonant /ə̯/ = [ə̯] occurs. In short, EModE /r/ = [r] [ɹ] > AmE /r/ = [r] [ɹ], and also, in *r*-less dialects, AmE /ə̯/.

The distribution of *r*-less /ə̯/ in post-vowel position, as in *fear* [fíə̯], is restricted by the occurrence of linking *r*. In place of final [ə̯], as in *fear* [fíə̯], a number of *r*-less speakers in ENE, MNY, and parts of S have linking [r] before a word beginning with a vowel, as in *fear it* [fír ɪt]. They pronounce final post-vowel *r* not as [ə̯] but as [r] when the following word begins with a vowel. Compare, for example, the distribution of /r/ and /ə̯/ in *r*-less *fear is fear* /fɪr ɪz fɪə̯/.

Intrusive *r* also occurs in the speech of some *r*-less speakers in ENE and MNY. Intrusive *r* is an unhistorical or added [r], as in *ma and pa* [mar ən pa] and *law and order* [lɔr ən ɔdə].

Here, then, is the consonant system of AmE:

Stops: /p t k b d g/ as in *pill, till, kill, bill, dill*, and *gill*.[2]
Fricatives: /f θ v ð h/ as in *fin, thin, vat, that, hat*.
Sibilants: /s š z ž/ as in *sip, ship, ruse* 'stratagem,' *rouge*.
Affricates: /č ǰ/ as in *choice* and *Joyce*.

Nasals: /m n ŋ/ as in *ram, ran, rang.*
Lateral: /l/ as in *lamb.*
Glides: /w y r ɹ̠/. /w y/ as in *wet* and *yet*. /r/ as in *red* and *direct*, r-full *far, farm.* /r/ = [r] [ɹ]. /ɹ̠/ as in r-less *fear, feared.*

Grease/Greasy-Line

Imagine a line that runs approximately from southwestern Connecticut westward above the top of New Jersey, drops southward to Philadelphia, then rises to the northern corner of Pennsylvania, cuts through central Ohio, turns northward to include most of Indiana, and then cuts south through central Illinois and southern Iowa. This is a significant line. North of it speakers normally use /s/ in *grease* and *greasy*, as in /grís/ and /grísi/.

In an area of transition along the line, /s/ and /z/ alternate as in /grís ~ gríz/ and /grísi ~ grízi/. The area of transition is relatively narrow to the west of Philadelphia, but to the northeast of that city it widens to include most of northern New Jersey, New York City, and eastern Long Island.

South of the area of transition, speakers normally use /z/, as in /griz/ and /grizi/.

We may summarize these statements in the following generalizations:

N = /s/ as in /grís/ and /grísi/.
NMid = /s ~ z/ as in /grís ~ gríz/ and /grísi ~ grízi/.
SMid and S = /z/ as in /gríz/ and /grízi/.

AmE

These changes presumably occurred in the syllabic system of English in the evolution from EModE to AmE:

1. It became fashionable to use certain EModE syllabic nuclei, and the variant EModE nuclei fell into disuse, as in EModE *dream* [dɹém ~ dɹím] > AmE [dɹím].

2. EModE [a ~ ɑ] > frequently AmE r-less [ɑ] as in EModE *far* [fáɹ ~ fɑɹ] > *[fɑ̯ɹ] > AmE MNY, S [fɑ]. It is, however, possible that [ɑ] occurred in EModE *far* [fɑɹ].

We are equally uncertain about other qualitative distinctions between AmE and EModE simple nuclei, such as whether or not AmE [ɨ] also occurred in EModE.

In the description of AmE vowels presented below, it will be seen that the vowels of AmE in the eastern half of the United States vary phonemically from dialect to dialect not only in number but also in quality.

The nuclei of AmE also vary phonetically in length according to tension and environment, but syllabic length in our opinion is not phonemic in AmE. This, however, is still a controversial matter. Indeed, there is general disagreement among analysts concerning the phonemic interpretation of AmE nuclei. Some have offered a binary analysis and others a unitary analysis, as we have, but our unitary analysis does not entirely agree with other unitary analyses that have been presented. This neither means that our description is correct nor that all other interpretations are wrong; it means that there are several ways of phonemically symbolizing the phonetic data of AmE nuclei in the eastern United States, and that one's choice is primarily a matter of interpretation and preference. Perhaps we will eventually reach an agreement about the vowel phonemes of AmE, although this seems unlikely for the present, or at least until the *Linguistic Atlas* is completed.

High and Mid Vowels

The high and mid vowels of Northern, Midland, and Southern are front /i ɪ e ɛ/, central /ɨ ə/, and back /u ʊ o ɔ/.

Examples

/i/ as in *beet, bee, seat.*
/ɪ/ as in *bit, beer, bid, gist (the gist of it).*
/e/ as in *bait, bay, gate, mate.*
/ɛ/ as in *bet, bear, neck, jest.*

/ɨ/ has two principal allophones: [ɨ] and [ɜ]. The latter occurs in *r*-less pronunciations in ENE, S, frequently in MNY in such words as *bird, word, work, turn, heard, herd, hurt, stir.* [ɨ] may be heard in such words as *wish* and *sister*, in which other speakers use [ɪ]. [ɨ] and [ɪ] contrast phonemically in the speech of those who use [ɨ] in *just (He just left)* and [ɪ] in *gist (the gist of it).*

Many speakers have [ɨ] in unstressed positions as in *rapid* [rǽpɨd], *houses* [háuzɨz], *haunted* [hɔ́ntɨd], in which other speakers may have [ɪ] or [ə].

/ə/ has two principal allophones: [ʌ] and [ə]. The former is frequent in *bud, cut,* and *but.* [ə] occurs in unstressed syllables, as initially in *again* and finally as in *sofa.*

/u/ as in *pool, do, moon, boot.*

/ʊ/ as in *pull, could, full, put.* Regionally, /u/, /ʊ/, and /ə/ alternate in such words as *root, room,* and *soot.*

/o/ as in *pole, open, home,* and *gonna* (*He's gonna win*).[3]

/ɔ/ has two principal allophones: [ɒ] and [ɔ]. The latter is common in most dialect areas in the eastern United States, whereas [ɒ] predominates in WPa, ENE, and parts of the Great Lakes area. /ɔ/ as generally in *law.* /ɔ/ also as in *dog,* but S /ɔ ~ ɑ ~ ʒo/.

Summary of High and Mid Vowels

	Front	Central	Back[4]
High	/i/ /ɪ/	/ɨ/	/u/ /ʊ/
Mid	/e/ /ɛ/	/ə/	/o/ /ɔ/

Low Vowels

Analysts disagree about how to interpret the low nuclei of AmE. Our analysis represents a compromise drawn from various phonemic interpretations of the low-nuclei range.

/æ/ occurs in all eastern dialects in such words as *hat, fat,* and *bag.* It also regularly occurs in such words as *aunt, glass,* and *half,* which in ENE have /a/. In the eastern dialects, however, there is a rather wide variation of /a ɑ ɚ/ and their range of allophones:[5]

> I: *R*-full areas
> N, Mid /ɑ/ = [ɑ] [a]
> WPa /ɑ/ = [ɑ]

> II: *R*-less areas
> ENE /a/ = [a] [ɑ]
> S, MNY /ɑ/ = generally [ɑ]
> S, MNY /ɚ/ = generally [ɚ]

Some Examples

	far	*barn*	*father*	*John*
N, Mid	/ɑ	ɑ	ɑ	ɑ
WPa	ɔ	ɑ	ɔ	ɔ
ENE	a	a	a	ɔ ~ a
MNY, S	ɚ	ɚ	ɚ	ɑ ~ ɔ ~ ɚ/

A few additional examples of low-vowel variations among the eastern dialects are these:

water: /ɔ/, SMid /ɑ ~ ɔ/
cot: /ɑ/, ENE, WPa /ɔ/
caught: /ɔ/
ask: /æ/, ENE /a ~ æ/
aunt: /æ/, ENE /a/, S /æ ~ ɑ/
orange: /ɔ/, ENE, MNY, Eastern Pa, S /ɑ/
half: /æ/, ENE /a/, Western NE /æ ~ a/, S /æ ~ ɑ/
log: N /ɔ ~ ɑ/, ENE /ɔ ~ a/, MNY /ɑ/, WPa, SMid /ɔ/, S /ɑ ~ ɚ ~ ɔ/

Summary of High, Mid, and Low Vowels

	Front	Central	Back
High	/i/ /ɪ/	/ɨ/	/u/ /ʊ/
Mid	/e/ /ɛ/	/ə/	/o/ /ɔ/
Low	/æ/ /a/	/ɑ/	/ɚ/

Diphthongs

The EModE complex nuclei [ʌɪ] and [ʌʊ] survive to some extent in AmE, as in some Southern pronunciations of *out* as [ʌʊt] and of *twice* as [twʌɪs], but more often these EModE nuclei have other qualitative values in AmE dialects. For example, EModE [ʌʊ] in *house* > AmE [áʊ ~ ɑʊ ~ ə́ʊ], alongside older [ʌʊ]. Similarly, EModE [ʌɪ] in *wife* > frequently AmE [aɪ ~ áɪ]; and EModE [ʌɪ] in *joy* > frequently AmE [ɔ́ɪ].

The many varieties of complex nuclei in the AmE dialects east of the Mississippi River are given various phonemic interpretations by different analysts. In our opinion, the principal diphthongs of AmE in the eastern states are /áɪ ɑ́ɪ ə́ɪ ɔ́ɪ ɔ́ɪ ǽʊ áʊ ɑ́ʊ ə́ʊ/.[6]

Examples

twice /twáɪs ~ twɑ́ɪs ~ twɔ́ɪs/.
poison /pɔ́ɪzən ~ páɪzən ~ póɪzən/.
house /háʊs ~ hǽʊs ~ hɔ́ʊs ~ hɑ́ʊs/.

Stress

Stress is the relative loudness or prominence of speech. In AmE there are at least four contrasting degrees of stress. They are heavy or primary stress / ′ /, medium or secondary stress / ˆ /, light or tertiary stress / ` /, and weak or zero stress / ˘ /.

Examples

Rústy̆
Ădieú
Whât dŏ yóu wànt?
Thĕ whîte gréenhòuse

Pitch

Pitch is the relative highness or lowness of speech. There are four contrasting degrees of pitch in AmE. They are low pitch /1/, normal pitch /2/, high pitch /3/, and very high pitch /4/.

Examples

3 3 1
Yes.

2 2   3
Really?

4 4 1
Help!

2   3   1
Close the door.

Open Transition

The open transition phoneme / + / occurs between words or between the syllables of a word, as in *I scream* /áɪ+skrìm/ versus *ice cream* /áɪs+krìm/ and *that stuff* /ðǽt+stɔ́f/ versus *that's tough* /ðǽts+tɔ́f/.

Often / + / symbolizes a time phenomenon, one that involves audible lengthening of a preceding segment.[7] / + / also symbolizes other phonetic effects on preceding and following segments, such as variations in voice and aspiration, but we shall not enter into those details.[8]

Absence of the various phonetic effects phonemically symbolized by /+/ is called close transition. Segments with close transition are written together without intervening blank space, as in *nitrate* /náɪtrèt/ in contrast to *night-rate* /náɪt+rèt/.

Analysts disagree about the validity of the /+/ phoneme in AmE. Many analysts give phonemic status to the phonetic effects symbolized by /+/, but others do not. This question is among the many that await future solution.

Terminals

In AmE there are three terminals that mark the ends of syntactic divisions in utterances.[9]

/ ↗ /, or rising terminal, phonemically symbolizes what may be described as an upturn. Phonetically, at the very end of a sequence of pitches, there is a rise in pitch above the last pitch.

Examples

^{2 2 3}
Tea / ↗ /?

^{2   3   3}
Is she here / ↗ /?

^{2   3   3   3 4   4}
What's that / ↗ /? *A hat* / ↗ /?

^{2 2 2   2 2 2   2   2 2   3 3 1}
One / ↗ /, *two* / ↗ /, *three* / ↗ /, *four* / ↘ /.

/ ↘ /, or falling terminal, phonemically symbolizes what may be described as a downturn. Phonetically, at the end of a sequence of pitches, there is a fall in pitch which precedes the fading of the voice into silence.

Examples

^{3 3 1}
Yes / ↘ /.

^{2   3   1}
John loves Marsha / ↘ /.

^{2   3   1}
What is she doing / ↘ /?

^{3 3 1   3 3 1   3   3 1   3 3   1}
One / ↘ /, *two* / ↘ /, *three* / ↘ /, *four* / ↘ /.

/ → /, or level terminal, phonemically symbolizes a pitch that stays on the same level. Phonetically, the last segment of the word is prolonged about twice as long as the time phenomenon symbolized by /+/. The same pitch level is maintained until the beginning of the next pitch pattern, but the first pitch of that new pattern may be lower or higher.

Examples

$\overset{2}{I}$ waited an $\overset{3}{h}$our $\overset{2}{/} → /,$ but he $\overset{2}{d}$idn't $\overset{3}{a}$rrive $\overset{1}{/} \searrow /.$

$\overset{2}{Y}$ou don't think it'll $\overset{3}{r}$ain $\overset{2}{/} → /,$ do $\overset{2}{y}$o$\overset{2}{u}$ $\overset{3}{/} \nearrow /?$

$\overset{2}{I}$ $\overset{3}{ca}$n$\overset{1}{'}$t $/ → /,$ he $\overset{1}{s}$a$\overset{1}{i}$d $\overset{1}{/} \searrow /.$

$\overset{3}{O}$n$\overset{3}{e}$ $\overset{3}{/} → /,$ t$\overset{3}{w}$o$\overset{3}{}$ $\overset{3}{/} → /,$ $\overset{3}{t}$hre$\overset{3}{e}$ $\overset{3}{/} → /,$ $\overset{3}{f}$ou$\overset{3}{r}$ $\overset{1}{/} \searrow /.$

Occasionally / → / occurs at the end of a sentence. When it does, the utterance is regarded by the hearer as incomplete or broken off, as in $\overset{2}{J}$ohn said $\overset{2}{h}$e / → / . . . .

SUMMARY

Consonants

6 stops: /p t k b d g/.
5 fricatives: /f v θ ð h/.
4 sibilants: /s z š ž/.
2 affricates: /č ǰ/.
3 nasals: /m n ŋ/.
1 lateral: /l/.
4 glides: /w y r ʒ/. /r/ = [r] [ɹ].

Vowels

14: /i ɪ e ɛ æ a ɨ ə ɑ u ʊ o ɔ ɵ/. /ɨ/ = [ɨ] [ɜ]. /ə/ = [ʌ] [ə]. /ɔ/ = [ɒ] [ɔ]. N, Mid /ɑ/ = [ɑ] [a]. WPa /a/ = [ɑ]. ENE /a/ = [a] [ɑ]. S, MNY /ɑ/ = [ɑ], /ɵ/ = [ɵ].

Diphthongs

9: /áɪ áɪ ɔ́ɪ óɪ ɔ́ɪ ǽʊ áʊ áʊ ɔ́ʊ/.

Suprasegmentals

4 stresses: / ′ ^ ` ˇ /.
4 pitches: /1 2 3 4/.
1 open transition: /+/.
3 terminals: / ↗ ↘ → /.

Specimen of LMode

Matthew 6.9–13 from *The New English Bible: New Testament.* Copyright © The Delegates of the Oxford University Press and The Syndics of The Cambridge University Press, 1961. Reprinted by permission.

Our Father in heaven, Thy name be hallowed:
Thy kingdom come, Thy will be done, On earth as in heaven.
Give us today our daily bread.[10]
Forgive us the wrong we have done, As we have forgiven those who have
    wronged us.
And do not bring us to the test, But save us from the evil one.

Phonemic Transcription I

/àwər fɑ ðər ɪn hɛvɪn ðaɪ nem bi hælowd/
/ðaɪ kɪŋdəm kəm/ /ðaɪ wɪl bi dən ʌn ərθ æzɪn hɛvɪn/
/gɪvəs təde ɑur deh brɛd/
/fərgɪvəs ðə rɔŋ wiəv dən əz wiəv fəɪgɪvən ðoz huəv rɔŋd əs/
/æn du nɑt brɪŋəs tu ðə tɛst bət sevəs frəm ðə ivəl wən/

Phonemic Transcription II

² ³ ² ² ² ³ ² ¹
/ awšr+fɑ̂ðšr+ìn+hévĭn → ðaɪ+nêm+bì+hǽlŏwd ↘ /

² ³ ¹ ² ¹ ² ³
/ ðaɪ+kíŋdšm+kšm ↘ ðaɪ+wíl+bì+dân ↘ ân+ɔ́rθ+ǽzĭn+

¹
    hèvĭn ↘ /

² ³ ¹
/ gîvəs+tšdé+ɑ̂ur+dêlĭ+brɛ̀d ↘ /

² ³ ² ² ³
/ fərgîvǎs+ðš+rɔ́ŋ+wîšv+dšn → šz+wìəv+fərgîvšn+ðóz+

¹
    hùšv+rɔ́ŋd+šs ↘ /

² ³ ² ² ³
/ ǽn+dû+nɑ̀t+bríŋšs+tû+ðš+tɛ̀st → bšt+sêvǎs+frəm+ðš+

³ ¹
    ívšl+wšn ↘ /

NOTES

[1] See Hans Kurath and Raven I. McDavid, Jr., *The Pronunciation of English in the United States* (Ann Arbor, 1961); E. Bagby Atwood, *A Survey of Verb Forms in the Eastern United States* (Ann Arbor, 1953); Kurath, *A Word Geography of the Eastern United States* (Ann Arbor, 1949); Kurath and Bernard Bloch, eds., *Linguistic Atlas of New England*: 3 vols. in 6 parts (Providence, 1939–1943); Kurath et al., eds., *Handbook of the Linguistic Geography of New England* (Washington, D. C., 1939).

[2] For [t] between vowels and in some other medial positions, some speakers of AmE have a tap [ɾ] as in *latter* [lǽɾər]. Tap [ɾ] is a single flap or tap of the apex of the tongue against the upper gums. It is also heard in Southern British English as in *very* [vέɾi]. Tap [ɾ], an allophone of AmE /t/, is also written as a partially voiced [t̬] by some analysts, as in *very* [vέt̬i].

[3] Some speakers have /o/ in *hoarse, mourning* and /ɔ/ in *horse, morning*. Others have /ɔ/ or /o/ in all four words.

[4] Some New England speakers, primarily in ENE, also have a shortened and centralized phoneme /ɵ/ in such words as *stone, whole,* and *road*. For them, /ɵ/, as in *road*, contrasts with /o/, as in *rode*. /ɵ/, however, is recessive; it is receding or tending to recede. For that reason we do not include it among our principal vowels.

[5] See Kurath and McDavid, *Pronunciation of English*, pp. 6–7, and passim; Kurath, *A Phonology and Prosody of Modern English* (Ann Arbor, 1964), pp. 108–112, and passim.

[6] In parts of New England and the State of New York, the diphthong /ɪu/ as in *new* has some currency, but it is recessive. More commonly the vowel /u/ occurs, less often /yu/ as in the variants /nú ~ nɪu ~ nyú/. See Kurath and McDavid, *Pronunciation of English*, pp. 113, 174.

[7] See Martin Joos, "The Definition of Juncture and Terminals," *Second Texas Conference on Problems of Linguistic Analysis in English*, 1957 (Austin, 1962), pp. 4–18.

[8] For convenience, /+/ is generally classified as a suprasegmental, but actually it is not a suprasegmental. Phonetically /+/ shows overlapping with the segmentals.

[9] The open transition phoneme and the terminal phonemes are sometimes collectively called juncture phonemes, but that label is not used in this book.

[10] Variant *our bread for the morrow, New English Bible*, p. 11, footnote a.

The Morpheme

In this chapter we shall talk about the components of words and define the term morpheme as a preliminary to the description that begins in the next chapter of the major classes of historical English words.

A *word* may be defined as a linguistic form that can be spoken meaningfully in isolation. It is more technically defined as a linguistic construction consisting of one or more bases, with or without one or more affixes (prebases and postbases). Let us examine what is meant by base, prebase, and postbase.

Base

A base is a linguistic construction to which prebases and postbases are added. For example, *joy* is a base (B). To that B we may add the prebase (PB) *en-* as in *en-joy*. To the PB-B *en-joy*, we may add the postbase (PoB) *-able* as in *en-joy-able.* Thus, the order of the elements in *en-joy-able* is PB-B-PoB. PBs precede Bs, PoBs follow Bs.

There are free bases and bound bases. A base such as *joy* is called a minimum free form or simply a free base. Other examples of free bases are *dog, boy, man*, and so on. In contrast, a bound base is a bound form, i.e., it cannot occur in isolation as a word. For example, the construction *re-ceive* contains the PB *re-* and the bound base *-ceive*. *Leg-ible* contains the bound base *leg-* and the PoB *-ible*. Note that PBs as *re-* and PoBs as *-ible* also are bound forms, but they are not bound bases. PBs and PoBs are called affixes. They are attached to either free or bound bases.

We have thus far given as examples words consisting of a single base, either free or bound, with either a PB or a PoB. Here are some examples of words containing more than one PB or PoB.

PB-B-PoB-PoB	*un-gain-li-ness*
PB-PB-B-PoB	*un-en-joy-able, in-con-ceive-able*

Some words consist of two or more bases, with or without affixes. The technical name given to a linguistic construction with more than one base is phrase, and words that are phrases are called morphological phrases. Some examples are these:

B-B	*street-car*
B-B-B	*long-shore-man*
B-B-PoB	*flame-throw-er*
PB-B-B	*non-union-shop*

Inflectional Suffix

In addition to PBs and PoBs, there is a third kind of affix, called an inflectional suffix (IS). It is a bound form that conveys a grammatical signal, such as number (boy-*s*), tense (walk-*ed*), or case (you-*r*). A PB such as *en-* in *en-joy* and a PoB such as *-er* in *sing-er* do not convey such grammatical signals.

In English an IS normally comes after a PoB, as in *sing-er-s*. Sometimes, however, an IS comes after another IS as in *ox-en-'s*. Another exception is the plural *mothers-in-law*, in which the order of elements is B-IS-PoB-PoB, but note *mother-in-law's* (B-PoB-PoB-IS).

Form Class

In this book we define a form class as a class of words having certain morphologic features in common. This is a comparatively narrow definition.

We shall talk about three kinds of form classes:

1. Form classes marked by ISs as *boy-boys*, *walk-walked*, and

you-your. The words in such IS classes also may have character-istic PoBs as *-dom* in *kingdoms* and *-ment* in *payments*.

2. Form classes marked by PoBs but not ISs, as *colder-coldest*, and *quickly*. In this book *-er*, *-est*, and *-ly* shall be called PoBs, although in some texts *-er* and *-est*, as in *cold-er* and *cold-est*, are labeled ISs. As we shall see in a later chapter, *-er* and *-est*, as in *cold-er* and *cold-est*, are historically PoBs.

3. Form classes marked neither by ISs nor PoBs as *and, of, from, in, to*, and so on.

In short, we shall talk about form classes marked by ISs, form classes marked by PoBs, and form classes marked by the absence of ISs and PoBs.

Historical Form Classes

In OE there were four form classes marked by ISs: nouns, pronouns, verbs, and adjectives. In LModE there are only three: nouns, pronouns, and verbs. In OE there was only one form class marked by PoBs, the class called adverbs. In LModE, however, there are two PoB form classes: adverbs and adjectives.

In OE, as in LModE, there were many sets of form classes marked neither by ISs nor PoBs. The constructions that con-stitute such form classes we shall call function words (FWs). Prepositions and conjunctions are two FW classes. We shall have more to say about them and other FW classes in the chapters dealing with English syntax.

Paradigm

Two terms we shall use in connection with form classes marked by ISs are paradigm and stem.

A paradigm is a listing of all the forms of a form-class word. For example, in LModE the paradigm of the noun *man* is *man, men, man's, men's*, and the paradigm of the verb *sing* is *sing, sings, sang, sung, singing*.

Stem

A stem is that part of a morphological construction to which an IS is added. For example, *boy* is the stem in the noun paradigm *boy, boy-s, boy-'s, boy-s'*. In the verb paradigm *walk, walk-s, walk-ed, walk-ing,* the stem is *walk*.

Stems may be single bases or morphological phrases, with or without PBs or PoBs. as in these examples:

$$\text{Stem} + \text{IS}$$
$$boy + \text{-}s$$
$$cat\text{-}boat + \text{-}s$$
$$non\text{-}sing\text{-}er + \text{-}s$$
$$en\text{-}fold + \text{-}ed$$
$$black\text{-}en + \text{-}ed$$

Morpheme

PBs, Bs, PoBs, and ISs are morphemes. They are the smallest meaningful units in a language. To indicate this, we write morphemes between curved braces as { }. For example, {'glass'} is one morpheme, but *glasses* contains two morphemes: {'glass'} and {noun pl.}. Neither {'glass'} nor {noun pl.} are divisible into smaller units of meaning.

Although the meaning of a morpheme is frequently clear, as in {'boy'}, {'tree'}, {'girl'}, sometimes the meaning of a morpheme is uncertain or undefinable, as {'cran-'} in *cran-berry* and {'-ceive'} in *de-ceive*.

There are lexical morphemes and grammatical morphemes. In this book lexical morphemes are enclosed within single quotation marks inside braces as in {'boy'}. In contrast, grammatical morphemes are not enclosed within single quotation marks as in {noun pl.}.

Bs, PBs, and PoBs are lexical morphemes that make up stems. They have "vocabulary" meaning(s), that is they have "dictionary" meaning(s). For example, some meanings of the lexical morpheme {'dog'} are: 1. any of a large, varied group of domesticated animals, 2. in metereology, a parhelion, 3. in astronomy, the constellations the Great Dog or the Little Dog, and so on.

ISs, on the other hand, are grammatical morphemes that convey grammatical signals such as number, tense, and case. {noun pl.} and {past tense} are grammatical morphemes.

Allomorph

The variant phonemic "shapes" of a morpheme are its allomorphs. Written as units of one or more phonemes, allomorphs are enclosed between slanted lines as / /.

The allomorphs of a morpheme are identical in meaning, but they differ phonemically. For example, /-s/ in *hats* /hæts/, /-z/ in *bags* /bǽgz/, and /-ɪn/ in *oxen* /áksɪn/ are some allomorphs of the morpheme {noun pl.}. /-s/, /-z/, and /-ɪn/ all have the same meaning, but they differ phonemically.

The allomorphs of a morpheme are in complementary distribution or free variation, that is, in noncontrastive distribution. The allomorphs /-s/ and /-z/ of {noun pl.}, for example, are in complementary distribution. /-s/ occurs after voiceless sounds as in *caps* /kǽps/, and /-z/ occurs after voiced sounds as in *cabs* /kǽbz/.[1] Some allomorphs of {noun pl.} are in free variation as finally in the variant plurals *gladioli ~ gladioluses* /glǽdiólaɪ ~ glǽdiólǝsɪz/.

We may now proceed to give a more complete definition of the morpheme as a group of semantically similar allomorphs in complementary distribution or free variation.

Nonsequential IS

The order of the IS /-z/ in *boy-s* is sequential. It is added directly to the end of the stem *boy*.

A nonsequential IS is not added directly to the end of the stem, but is added internally. For example, *man* /mæn/ and *men* /mɛn/ differ by the vowels /æ/ in /mæn/ and /ɛ/ in /mɛn/. There are several ways of describing the grammatical contrast of number between singular *man* and plural *men*; the method we prefer is to assume that the stem morpheme {'man'} has two allomorphs: /mæn/ and /m-n/. This permits us to describe /mɛn/ as stem allomorph /m-n/+nonsequential IS /-ɛ-/. To indicate that /-ɛ-/ is a nonsequential IS, we put hyphens before and after it as in /-ɛ-/. /-ɛ-/ is another allomorph of {noun pl.}.

Zero Allomorph

To describe the contrast between singular *sheep* and plural *sheep*, we shall make use of the concept of the zero allomorph, written /∅/. Thus, we describe singular *sheep* as /šíp/ and plural sheep as /šíp/+/∅/, in which zero plural IS is written /∅/.

Constituents

Immediate constituents (ICs) are the components into which a linguistic construction is divided in a first analysis. For example, the ICs of *singers* are *singer-s*.[2] The ICs of *unwanted* are *un-wanted*.

Ultimate constituents (UCs) are the components of a linguistic construction on its lowest or final level of analysis. For example, the UCs of *singers* are *sing-er-s*. The UCs of *unwanted* are *un-want-ed*.

Superfix

Lexical (PB, B, PoB) and grammatical (IS) morphemes are segmental morphemes. There also are suprasegmental morphemes called superfixes and intonation contours.

A superfix, also called a stress morpheme, consists of a meaningful pattern of stress phonemes, with or without /+/. Superfixes help distinguish words and phrases consisting of otherwise identical sequences of segmental phonemes.

For example, the "verb" superfix { ˇ ′ }, with allomorphs / ˇ ′ / and / ˇ+′ / as in /sǎspɛ́kt/ and /sǎs+pɛ́kt/, differs from the "noun" superfix { ′ ˋ }, with allomorphs / ′ ˋ / and / ′+ˋ / as in /sǽspɛkt/ and /sǽs+pɛ̀kt/. So too, the "morphological phrase" superfix { ′+ˋ }, as in /blǽk+bìrd/, differs from the "modifier-noun" superfix { ^ +′ }, as in /blæ̀k+bírd/.

Intonation Contour

An intonation contour consists of a meaningful pattern of pitches and a terminal. Intonation contours, such as {231 ↘ } in /²jân+ləvz³+máršə¹↘/, as {233 ↗ } in /²ìz+šǐ³+hír³↗/, and others illustrated under "Terminals" in Chapter 12, accompany syntactic structures as phrases and sentences.

SUMMARY

Word, free and bound base (B), prebase (PB), postbase (PoB), sequential and nonsequential inflectional suffix (IS), form class, paradigm, stem, morpheme { }, allomorph / /, zero allomorph /Ø/, immediate constituent (IC), ultimate constituent (UC).

Segmental morphemes — lexical (PB, B, PoB) and grammatical (IS).

Suprasegmental morphemes — superfix { ' ` } and intonation contour {231 ↘ }.

NOTES

[1] /–s/ and /–z/ do not occur after the sibilants /s z š ž/ or the affricates /č ǰ/. /ɪz/ does, as in *places* /plésɪz/ and *peaches* /píčɪz/, alternating dialectally with /ɪz/ and /əz/.

[2] Most analysts use a slanted bar to separate ICs as in *singer/s.*

14

Historical Nouns

The subject matter of this chapter is the historical noun system of English. We shall begin with an examination of OE South-western nouns and then proceed to an examination of ME SEMid nouns, EModE London-area nouns, and finally LModE (AmE) nouns. We will follow this procedure in succeeding chapters to describe historical English pronouns, verbs, adjectives, and adverbs.

OE Nouns

There are two kinds of constructions in OE noun paradigms:

1. Stem+IS as plural genitive *hunda* 'hounds' = *hund*+*a*, and

2. Stem without IS as singular nominative *hund* 'hound.'

The stem of an OE noun was an allomorph of a combined morpheme of grammatical gender (masculine, feminine, or neuter) and lexical meaning. For example, {masc. 'hound'} = /húnd/ as in *hund-a*.

The IS of an OE noun was an allomorph of a combined morpheme of number (singular or plural) and one of four cases (nominative, accusative, dative, genitive). For example, {pl. g.} = /a/ as in *hund-a*. The nominative singular forms of OE nouns, and frequently those of the accusative singular, were without inflection. They consisted only of the noun stem, as sg. n.a. *hund*.

Gender

The gender of an OE noun stem was of the type called grammatical gender. It was an arbitrary "sex" designation. That means the gender of an OE noun stem did not necessarily match the gender that we today might associate with the lexical meaning of the OE noun stem. For example, OE *wīf* 'woman, wife' was neuter, OE *man(n)* 'man' was masculine, OE *stān* 'stone' was masculine, OE *tunge* 'tongue' was feminine, and OE *mæġden* 'girl' was neuter.

OE Noun Classes

One method of classifying English nouns is according to their plural suffixes. For example, the OE nouns we shall study may be classified as follows on the basis of contrasts between their singular and plural nominative-accusative forms:

1. −*s* plural: sg. *catt*, pl. *cattas*
2. −∅ plural: sg. *sċēap*, pl. *sċēap*
3. −*a* plural: sg. *sunu*, pl. *suna*
4. −*n* plural: sg. *oxa*, pl. *oxan*
5. −*e*− plural: sg. *mann*, pl. *menn*
6. −∅ ~ −*u* plural: sg. *ċild*, pl. *ċild* ~ *ċildru*

We shall examine the paradigms of the following OE nouns:

1. Masculine *catt* 'cat'
2. Neuter *sċēap* 'sheep'
3. Masculine *sunu* 'son'
4. Masculine *oxa* 'ox'
5. Masculine *hunta* 'hunter'
6. Masculine *mann* 'man'
7. Neuter *ċild* 'child'

OE Paradigms

The OE noun *catt* had a six-form paradigm. That means there were six different forms in the paradigm of OE *catt*, the uninflected stem *catt* plus five inflected forms — *catt-es, catt-e, catt-as, catt-a, catt-um*, as follows:[1]

1. {masc. 'cat'} = stem allomorph /kát/.

sg. n.a.[2]	*catt*	/kɑt/
sg. d.	*catte*	/kɑt/+/ɛ/
sg. g.	*cattes*	/kɑt/+/ɛs/
pl. n.a.	*cattas*	/kɑt/+/ɑs/
pl. d.	*cattum*	/kɑt/+/ʊm/
pl. g.	*catta*	/kɑt/+/ɑ/

2. {neut. 'sheep'} = /šǽ:ɑp/.
Here is another six-form paradigm:

sg. n.a.	*sċēap*	/šæ:ɑp/
sg. d.	*sċēape*	/šæ:ɑp/+/ɛ/
sg. g.	*sċēapes*	/šæ:ɑp/+/ɛs/
pl. n.a.	*sċēap*	/šæ:ɑp/+/Ø/
pl. d.	*sċēapum*	/šæ:ɑp/+/ʊm/
pl. g.	*sċēapa*	/šæ:ɑp/+/ɑ/

3. {masc. 'son'} = /súnʊ/, /sún-/.
Here is a three-form paradigm:

sg. n.a.	*sunu*	/sʊnʊ/
sg. d.g., pl. n.a.g.	*suna*	/sʊn/+/ɑ/
pl. d.	*sunum*	/sʊn/+/ʊm/

4. {masc. 'ox'} = /ɔ́ksɑ/, /ɔ́ksɛ-/, /ɔ́ks-/.
Here is a four-form paradigm:

sg. n.	*oxa*	/ɔksɑ/
sg. a.d.g., pl. n.a.	*oxan*	/ɔksɑ/+/n/
pl. d.	*oxum*	/ɔks/+/ʊm/
pl. g.	*oxena*	/ɔksɛ/+/nɑ/

5. {masc. 'hunter'} = /húntɑ/, /húntɛ-/, /húnt-/.
Here is another four-form paradigm:

sg. n.	*hunta*	/hʊntɑ/
sg. a.d.g., pl. n.a.	*huntan*	/hʊntɑ/+/n/
pl. d.	*huntum*	/hʊnt/+/ʊm/
pl. g.	*huntena*	/hʊntɛ/+/nɑ/

6. {masc. 'man'} = /mán/, /mǽn/.
Here is a five-form paradigm:

sg. n.a.	*man(n)*	/mɑn/
sg. d., pl. n.a.	*men(n)*	/mɛn/+/-ɛ-/[3]
sg. g.	*mannes*	/mɑn/+/ɛs/
pl. d.	*mannum*	/mɑn/+/ʊm/
pl. g.	*manna*	/mɑn/+/ɑ/

7. {neut. 'child'} = /číld/, /číldǐ-/

Here is a six-form paradigm:

sg. n.a.	čild	/čɪld/
sg. d.	čilde	/čɪld/+/ɛ/
sg. g.	čildes	/čɪld/+/ɛs/
pl. n.a.	čild ~ čildru	/čɪld/+/Ø/ ~ /čɪldǐ/+/ʊ/
pl. d.	čildrum	/čɪldǐ/+/ʊm/
pl. g.	čildra	/čɪldǐ/+/ɑ/

ME Nouns

English nouns underwent a number of changes by the ME period. First, there were those changes that affected all English form classes:

1. OE [ɑ ɛ ɔ ʊ] in unstressed syllables > ME [ə], written *e*, as in the following examples:

OE *cattas* [kátɑs] > ME *cattes* [kátəs].

OE *cattes* [kátɛs] > ME *cattes* [kátəs].

OE *nacod* [nákɔd] > ME *nāked* [ná:kɔd].

OE *sunum* [súnʊm] > ME *sunen* [súnən].

OE [ɪ], however, remained in unstressed syllables as in OE *engliš* [éŋglɪš] > ME *english* [éŋglɪš].

2. OE [m] in unstressed syllables > ME [n] as in OE pl. d. *sunum* [súnʊm] > ME *sunen* [súnən], but subsequently final [n] frequently was lost as in ME *sunen ~ sune*.

Two factors may have contributed to the leveling and looses in final unstressed ISs:

1. Weakening of stress. Primary stress in OE was fixed generally on the first syllable of a word. By the end of the OE period such stress emphasis on the first syllable of a word may have contributed to a further weakening of stress in final unstressed syllables, especially ISs. As a result, former distinctions among nuclei in final unstressed ISs were lost through leveling under weakened stress to [ə].

2. ISs made obscure. Another factor which may have contributed to the leveling of OE [ɑ ɛ ʊ ɔ] to ME [ə] was the linguistic communication in England between English and Scandinavian speakers. In these two languages the form classes were similar but not identical. For one thing, there were differ-

ences in ISs. Perhaps in attempting to communicate with each other more easily, English and Scandinavian speakers tended to eliminate differences in their respective inflectional systems by stressing the lexical stems of inflected words and obscuring final ISs.

English nouns also underwent these additional changes in the ME period:

1. The loss of OE grammatical gender and the parallel rise of so-called natural gender. For example, OE noun-stem morpheme {masc. 'stone'} > ME {neut. 'stone'}, OE {neut. 'wife'} > ME {fem. 'wife'}, and so on. Accordingly, henceforth we shall not cite the gender of English nouns.[4]

In OE the gender of an OE noun stem was indicated primarily by the gender signal of the pronoun or adjective used with the noun, as in (masc.) *se mann, swēte mann* and (fem.) *sēo wīf, swētu wīf*. With the leveling of OE final nuclei in unstressed syllables to ME [ə], the formerly distinct gender signals of adjectives and most pronouns were lost as in *þe man, swēte man* and *þe wīf, swēte wīf*. Thereafter, the gender of a noun was known by the so-called natural gender associated with the lexical meaning of the noun stem and also by the gender of the third person singular personal pronoun that referred to a noun antecedent, as in *þe man . . . hē* and *þe wīf . . . shē*.

2. The merging of OE nominative, accusative, and dative singular forms into a ME singular common-case form, as in OE sg. n.a. *catt* and sg. d. *catte* > ME sg. common *cat*.

3. OE sg. gen. *−es* [−ɛs] > ME *−es* [−əs] and by analogy was extended as the ME singular possessive-case IS to nouns which in OE had sg. gen. ISs other than *−es*, as in OE sg. g. *suna,* > ME sg. possessive *sónes*.

4. OE pl. n.a. *−as* [−ɑs] > ME *−es* [−əs] and by analogy was extended as the ME plural nominative-accusative case IS to many but not all nouns which in OE had pl. n.a. ISs other than *−as* as in OE pl. n.a. *suna* > ME pl. n.a. *sones*.

5. The merging into one ME common-plural IS *−es* [−əs] of OE plural-dative ISs, most plural-genitive ISs, and the ME common n.a. pl. *−es* [−əs], as in OE pl. d. *sunum,* pl. g. *suna* and ME pl. n.a. *sónes* > ME pl. common *sónes*.

As a result of the above changes, English nouns underwent

a reduction in case-number forms from as many as four (n.a.g.d.) in OE to two singular (common, possessive) and usually one plural (common), or sometimes two plural (common, possessive) forms in Late ME.

The following examples illustrate the changes that OE nouns underwent in Early ME and Late ME. A blank, marked —, indicates that no form occurred in ME.

		OE	Early ME			Late ME
sg.	n.a.	*catt*	*catt*	sg.	c.	*cat*
	d.	*catte*	*catte*			
	g.	*cattes*	*cattes*[5]		p.	*cattes*
pl.	n.a.	*cattas*	*cattes*	pl.	c.	*cattes*
	d.	*cattum*	*catte(n)*			
	g.	*catta*	*catte*		p.	—
sg.	n.a.	*sċēap*	*shēp*	sg.	c.	*shēēp*
	d.	*sċēape*	*shēpe*			
	g.	*sċēapes*	*shēpes*		p.	*shēēpes*
pl.	n.a.	*sċēap*	*shēp*	pl.	c.	*shēēp*
	d.	*sċēapum*	*shēpe(n)*			
	g.	*sċēapa*	*shēpe*		p.	—
sg.	n.a.	*sunu*	*sune*	sg.	c.	*sóne*
	d.	*suna*	*sune*			
	g.	*suna*	*sune*		p.	*sónes*
pl.	n.a.	*suna*	*sune*	pl.	c.	*sónes*
	d.	*sunum*	*sune(n)*			
	g.	*suna*	*sune*		p.	—

Note: OE pl. n.a. *suna* became an –*s* plural in Late ME, but OE pl. n.a. *sċēap* > Late ME *shēēp* remained a zero (Ø) plural.

		OE	Early ME			Late ME
sg.	n.	*oxa*	*oxe*	sg.	c.	*oxe*
	a.d.	*oxan*	*oxe(n)*			
	g.	*oxan*	*oxe(n)*		p.	*oxes*
pl.	n.a.	*oxan*	*oxe(n)*	pl.	c.	*oxen*
	d.	*oxum*	*oxe(n)*			
	g.	*oxena*	*oxene, oxe(n)*		p.	—

sg. n.	*hunta*	*hunte*	sg. c.	*hunte*
a.d.	*huntan*	*hunte(n)*		
g.	*huntan*	*hunte(n)*	p.	*huntes*
pl. n.a.	*huntan*	*hunte(n)*	pl. c.	*huntes*
d.	*huntum*	*hunte(n)*		
g.	*huntena*	*huntene, hunte(n)*	p.	—

Note: OE *hunta* became an *−s* plural in Late ME, but OE *oxa* remained an *−n* plural in Late ME.

	OE	Early ME	Late ME	
sg. n.a.	*man(n)*	*man*	sg. c.	*man*
d.	*men(n)*	*manne*		
g.	*mannes*	*mannes*	p.	*mannes*
pl. n.a.	*men(n)*	*men*	pl. c.	*men*
d.	*mannum*	*manne(n)*		
g.	*manna*	*manne*	p.	*mennes*
sg. n.a.	*ċild*	*chīld*	sg. c.	*chīld*
d.	*ċilde*	*chīlde*		
g.	*ċildes*	*chīldes*	p.	*chīldes*
pl. n.a.	*ċild ~ ċildru*	*chīld ~ childre*[6]	pl. c.	*children*
d.	*ċildrum*	*childre(n)*		
g.	*ċildra*	*childre ~ childer*	p.	—

Note: OE pl. n.a. *ċild ~ ċildru* became an *−n* plural in Late ME. Actually, Late ME *children* is a double plural: OE *−u* > Early ME *−e* > Late ME *−e+n=−en*.

ME Paradigms

As a result of these changes, the nouns we have described had these paradigms in ME:

Common Case		Possessive Case
1. {'cat'} = /kát/.		
sg. *cat* /kat/		*cattes* /kat/+/əs/
pl. *cattes* /kat/+/əs/		—
2. {'sheep'} = /šé:p/.		
sg. *shēēp* /še:p/		*shēēpes* /še:p/+/əs/
pl. *shēēp* /še:p/+/∅/		—

3. {'son'} = /súnə/, /sún-/.
   sg. *sóne* /sʊnə/   *sónes* /sʊn/+/əs/
   pl. *sónes* /sʊn/+/əs/   —

4. {'ox'} = /ɔ́ksə/, /ɔ́ks-/.
   sg. *oxe* /ɔksə/   *oxes* /ɔks/+/əs/
   pl. *oxen* /ɔks/+/ən/   —

5. {'hunter'} = /húntə/, /húnt-/.
   sg. *hunte* /hʊntə/   *huntes* /hʊnt/+/əs/
   pl. *huntes* /hʊnt/+/əs/   —

6. {'man'} = /mán/, /m-n/.
   sg. *man* /man/   *mannes* /man/+/əs/
   pl. *men* /m-n/+/-ɛ-/   *mennes* /m-n/+/-ɛ-/+/əs/

7. {'child'} = /čí:ld/, /číldï-/.
   sg. *chīld* /či:ld/   *chīldes* /či:ld/+/əs/
   pl. *children* /čɪldï/+/ən/   —

ME French Loans

Nouns borrowed from French during the ME period were adapted to the pattern of English nouns. In the twelfth century, most OFr feminine nouns were inflected as follows:

	Sg.	Pl.
n.	*flor(s)*	*flors*
non-n.	*flor*	*flors*

In the thirteenth century, the Late OFr tendency toward loss of sg. n. −*s* led to the paradigmatic reduction:

	Sg.	Pl.
	flor	*flors*

Consequently, OFr *flor* and *flors* were adopted into ME as sg. *flōūr* 'flower,' pl. *flōūres*, the last remodeled by analogy to conform with the common ME noun plural IS −*es*.

In similar fashion, most OFr masculine-noun paradigms by the thirteenth century were inflected like this:

	Sg.	Pl.
n.	*ber(s)*	*baron*
non-n.	*baron*	*barons*

Of these, the oblique or non-nominative constructions *baron* and *barons* were adopted into ME as sg. *barōūn* 'baron,' pl. *barōūns*.

New possessive forms were subsequently added to such ME loans as *flōūr*, *flōūres* and *barōūn*, *barōūns*, through analogy with other ME noun paradigms:

	Common	Possessive
sg.	*flōūr*	*flōūres*
pl.	*flōūres*	—
sg.	*barōūn*	*barōūns*
pl.	*barōūns*	—

EModE Nouns

These major developments took place in English nouns by the EModE period:

1. Voicing of final [–s] in [–əs] to [–z], as in ME *cattes* [kátəs] > EModE *cates* [kǽtəz] and ME *sónes* [súnəs] > EModE *sonnes* [sʌ́nəz].

2. Loss of [-ə-] in unstressed final syllables, as in *sonnes* [sʌ́nəz] > [sʌ́nz], but [-ə-] was retained after stem final [s z š ž j], as in EModE *faces* [fésəz].

3. Following the loss of [-ə-], as described above, final [–z] > [–s] after voiceless sounds, as in EModE *cates* [kǽtəz] > [kǽtz] > [kǽts].

4. Loss of final [–ə], as in ME *sóne* [súnə] > EModE *sonne* [sʌ́n].

5. The emergence through analogy of new paradigmatic forms, as pl. common *sheeps*, alongside *sheep*, and pl. possessive *childrens* and *cats*.

EModE Paradigms

The resultant EModE noun paradigms were as follows:

	Common		Possessive
1. {'cat'} = /kǽt/.			
sg. *cat*	/kæt/		*cats* /kæt/+/s/
pl. *cats*[7]	/kæt/+/s/		*cats* /kæt/+/s/+/∅/

NOTE: In EModE nouns, as also in the case of ME and LModE nouns, the number suffix occurs first and is followed by the case suffix in the order: stem+number suffix+case suffix. Thus, in analyzing pl. possessive *cats*, we begin with the pl. common *cats* = /kǽt/+/s/, and then we add /∅/ to indicate a zero allomorph of the possessive case. This gives us pl. possessive *cats* = /kǽt/+/s/+/∅/.

2. {'sheep'} = /šép/.
   sg. *sheep* /šep/[8]   *sheeps* /šep/+/s/
   pl. *sheep ~ sheeps* /šep/+   —
       /∅ ~ s/

3. {'son'} = /sɔ́n/.
   sg. *sonne* /sən/   *sonnes* /sən/+/z/
   pl. *sonnes* /sən/+/z/   *sonnes* /sən/+/z/+/∅/

4. {'ox'} = /áks/.
   sg. *ox* /ɑks/   *oxes* /ɑks/+/əz/
   pl. *oxen* /ɑks/+/ən/   —

5. {'hunter'} = /hɔ́ntər/.
   sg. *hunter* /həntər/   *hunters* /həntər/+/z/
   pl. *hunters* /həntər/+/z/   *hunters* /hənter/+/z/+/∅/

NOTE: -e in ME sg. *hunte* > -er in EModE *hunter* through analogy with other EModE nouns in -er.

6. {'man'} = /mǽn/, /m-n/.
   sg. *man* /mæn/   *mans* /mæn/+/z/
   pl. *men* /m-n/+/-ɛ-/   *mens* /m-n/+/-ɛ-/+/z/[9]

7. {'child'} = /čɔ́ɪld/, /číldr-/.
   sg. *child* /čəɪld/   *childes* /čəɪld/+/z/
   pl. *children* /čɪldr/+/ən/   *children's* /čɪldr/+/ən/+/z/

LModE Nouns

The primary differences between EModE nouns and LModE nouns are these:

1. Phonetic differences in ISs: EModE [-ən] > AmE [-ɪn], as in EModE pl. c. *oxen* [áksən] > AmE *oxen* [áksɪn]; and

EModE[–əz] > AmE [–ɪz], as in EModE sg. poss. *oxes* [áksəz] > AmE *ox's* [áksɪz].

2. The development in LModE of analogical forms such as pl. possessive *sheeps'*.

3. The prevailing practice in LModE of inflecting new nouns as –*s* plurals, as LModE *telephones, automobiles*, etc.

LModE Paradigms

The noun paradigms of AmE are as follows:

Common	Possessive
1. {'cat'} = /kǽt/.	
sg. *cat* /kæt/	*cat's* /kæt/+/s/
pl. *cats* /kæt/+/s/	*cats'* /kæt/+/s/+/Ø/
2. {'sheep'} = /šíp/.	
sg. *sheep* /šip/	*sheep's* /šip/+/s/
pl. *sheep* /šip/+/Ø/	*sheeps'* /šip/+/Ø/+/s/
3. {'son'} = /sə́n/.	
sg. *son* /sən/	*son's* /sən/+/z/
pl. *sons* /sən/+/z/	*sons'* /sən/+/z/+/Ø/
4. {'ox'} = /áks/.	
sg. *ox* /ɑks/	*ox's* /ɑks/+/ɪz/
pl. *oxen* /ɑks/+/ɪn/	*oxen's* /ɑks/+/ɪn/+/z/
5. {'hunter'} = /hə́ntər/.	
sg. *hunter* /həntər/	*hunter's* /həntər/+/z/
pl. *hunters* /həntər/+/z/	*hunters'* /həntər/+/z/+/Ø/
6. {'man'} = /mǽn/, /mɛ́n/.	
sg. *man* /mæn/	*man's* /mæn/+/z/
pl. *men* /m-n/+/-ɛ-/	*men's* /m-n/+/-ɛ-/+/z/
7. {'child'} = /čáɪld/, /číldr-/.	
sg. *child* /čaɪld/	*child's* /čaɪld/+/z/
pl. *children* /čɪldr/+/ɪn/	*children's* /čɪldr/+/ɪn/+/z/

SUMMARY

The major morphological developments in the noun system of English in the evolution from OE to LModE were these:

1. A reduction of cases from four in OE (nominative, accusative, dative, genitive) to two in ME (common, possessive).

2. Some historical changes in noun plural suffixes:

OE	LModE
−*a suna*	> −*s sons*
−*n huntan*	> −*s hunters*
−∅ ~ −*u čild* ~ *čildru*	> −*n children*

3. The creation through analogy of new EModE pl. poss. forms, such as *children's*.

NOTES

[1] In OE, as in all periods of English, some nouns normally had only singular forms, such as *ādam* 'Adam' and *lundenburg* 'London,' and some nouns had only plural forms, such as *engle, englan* 'Angles, English,' *seaxe, seaxan* 'Saxons.' For a more detailed analysis of OE nouns, see R. A. Peters, "Case-Number Morphs of Old English Nouns," *Linguistics*, 14 (1965), 41–51.

[2] n. = nominative case, a. = accusative case, d. = dative case, and g. = genitive case. They designate morphological variants in a paradigm. For the syntactic relationships of those case forms to other words in OE syntactic constructions, see "Case" in Chapter 19 of this book.

[3] Syllabic differences in noun constructions, as between (pl. n.a.) *menn* and (sg. n.a.) *mann*, were the result of mutation in the prehistoric period of OE. Mutation, also called umlaut, is the change of a syllabic nucleus as a result of partial assimilation to a following sound, especially the fronting of a back vowel by a fronted sound as [ɪ] in a following syllable. For example, the prehistoric OE (pl. n.a.) form for 'men' was *[mánɪ]. The influence of *[−ɪ], a high front sound, influenced the change of *[−a−], a low back sound, to *[−ɛ−], a mid front sound, one more like *[−ɪ]. Following the development *[mánɪ] > *[ménɪ], final *[−ɪ] was lost, and the resultant form was OE (pl. n.a.) *menn* [mén]. Mutation in prehistoric OE was also responsible for the syllabic differences in such OE noun contrasts as *fōt* 'foot' and *fēt* 'feet,' *mūs* 'mouse' and *mȳs* 'mice,' *tōþ* 'tooth' and *tēþ* 'teeth,' *gōs* 'goose' and *gēs* 'geese,' such OE adjective stems as *lang-* 'long' and *lengr-* 'longer,' and such OE verb forms as *cēosan* 'to choose' and *cīest* 'he chooses,' to cite a few examples. For additional information about mutation in OE, as well as a brief account of other OE sound changes not described here (such as dipthongization, the influence of nasals, and the influence of [w]), see Randolph Quirk and C. L. Wrenn, *An Old English Grammar* (New York, 1957).

[4] The validity of natural gender in regard to English nouns is questionable. For example, the natural gender of LModE *man* is said to be masculine, *sister* feminine, and *baby, parent, people* neuter. But we may variously substitute *he* (masc.), *she* (fem.), *it* (neut.), *they* (genderless) for these nouns:

man/men: he-they   *sister/sisters*: she-they
baby/babies: he, she, it-they   *parent/parents*: he, she-they
people: they

It is therefore apparent that there is no necessary correlation between gender and the lexical meaning of a LModE noun, except in the case of some singular forms. The same is true of ME and EModE nouns. As a result, some analysts do not speak of gender in connection with ME, EModE, and LModE nouns.

[5] Occasionally genitives with zero suffix also occurred in ME, as in *the forest sȳde* 'the forest's edge' and *gentilmen children* 'gentlemen's children.'

[6] Other ME multiple plurals included *brēthren ~ brōþeres* 'brothers,' *lǫmber ~ lǫmbren ~ lambes* 'lambs,' *calvre ~ calvren ~ calues* 'calves.'

[7] In EModE the apostrophe was not regularly used to mark the possessive singular until c. 1700. At a later date it was extended to the possessive plural. For a discussion of these developments, read the brief account of the evolution of English punctuation in Chapter 27.

[8] ME [-é:-] usually became EModE [-í-], as in ME *grēte* [gŕé:tə] > EModE *greet* [gɹít], although in the case of ME *shēēp* [šé:p] the development to EModE [-í-] apparently took place after the time of Shakespeare. In his plays, for example, *sheep* rhymes with *keepe* and *sleepe*, both with [-é-]. Later, EModE *sheep* [šép] > [šíp].

[9] The same order occurred in ME pl. poss. *mennes*, namely /m-n/ + /-ɛ-/ + /əs/.

Historical Pronouns

English pronouns, like English nouns, may be analyzed as morphological constructions consisting of either a stem or a stem plus IS. The relative complexity of such a description of English pronouns far outweighs its practical benefit to the beginning student of the history of the English language. For that reason, we shall abandon such analysis in the case of English pronouns and simply list the historical forms and their phonemic transcriptions.

OE Pronouns

There were three groups of OE pronouns, traditionally called personal pronouns, interrogative pronouns, and demonstrative pronouns, the last consisting of two subgroups.

We shall first examine the personal pronouns and describe their evolution from OE to LModE. After that, we shall examine the interrogative and then the demonstrative pronouns.

OE Personal Pronouns

In OE the personal pronouns indicated four cases (n.a.d.g.), three persons (first, second, third), three numbers (sg. 'one,' dual 'two only,' pl. 'more than two') in the first- and second-person forms but two numbers (sg. and pl.) in the third-person forms, and three genders (masc., fem., neut.) in the third-person singular forms:

First person

sg. 'I'	dual 'we two'	pl. 'we'
n. *ic* /íč/	*wit* /wít/	*wē* /wé:/
a.d. *mē* /mé:/	*unc* /únk/	*ūs* /ú:s/
g. *mīn* /mí:n/	*uncer* /únkɛř/	*ūre* /ú:řɛ/

Second person

sg. 'thou'	dual 'you two'	pl. 'you'
n. *ðū* /θú:/	*ġit* /yít/	*ġē* /yé:/
a.d. *ðē* /θé:/	*inc* /ínč/	*ēow* /é:ɔw/
g. *ðīn* /θí:n/	*incer* /ínčɛř/	*ēower* /é:ɔwɛř/

Third person

sg. masc. 'he'	fem. 'she'	neuter 'it'
n. *hē* /hé:/	n. *hēo* /hé:ɔ/	n.a. *hit* /hít/
a. *hine* /hínɛ/	a. *hīe* /hí:ɛ/	
d. *him* /hím/	d.g. *hiere* /híɛřɛ/	d. *him* /hím/
g. *his* /hís/		g. *his* /hís/

pl. 'they'
n.a. *hīe* /hí:ɛ/
d.   *him* /hím/
g.   *hiera* /híɛřɑ/

ME Personal Pronouns

The following developments occurred in the ME period:

1. The loss of dual-number forms.

2. The loss of some sg. accusative forms, and the merger of the remaining sg. accusative forms with those of the sg. dative to produce new object-case forms. As a result, the personal pronouns were reduced to three case forms: subject (< n.), object (< d.a.), and possessive (< g.).

3. The progressive use in the fourteenth century of ME North Midland *s(c)hē* as the third-person singular feminine subject form. The origin of *shē ~ schē* is not known, but the pronoun may have developed from OE *hēo* or Old Scandinavian *sjā*.[1]

4. Before the end of the twelfth century in ME Northern and North Midland, the native third-person plural forms (n.a.) *hī*, (d.) *hem*, (g.) *hire ~ here* came to be displaced by *þei, þeim, þeir* from Old Scandinavian *þei-r, þeim, þeir-(a)*, respectively.

The subject form *þei* was subsequently adopted in Southeast Midland, but the use of object *þeim* and possessive *þeir* was rare before the fifteenth century, the native forms *hem, hire ~ here* being used instead.

5. By the thirteenth century the second-person plural pronouns *yē, yōū, yōūr* came to be used as singular forms to denote respect in addressing superiors and adults. The old singular forms *þōū, þē, þy(n)*, in contrast, were used in addressing familiars and inferiors. However, the use of both sets of second-person pronouns was irregular in ME.

6. The use of the object-case variants *hit ~ it* in the third-person singular.

The resultant ME personal pronouns were:

First person

	sg.	pl.
subj.	*I ~ ich* /í: ~ íč/[2]	*wē* /wé:/
obj.	*mē* /mé:/	*ūs ~ us* /ú:s ~ ús/
poss.	*mȳ ~ mȳn* /mí: ~ mí:n/	*ōūr ~ ōūre* /ú:ř ~ ú:řə/

Second person

	sg.	pl.
subj.	*þū* /θú:/	*yē* /yé:/
obj.	*þē* /θé:/	*yōū* /yú:/
poss.	*þī ~ þīn* /θí: ~ θí:n/	*yōur* /yú:ř/

Third person

sg.	sg.	sg.
subj. *hē* /hé:/	subj. *she* /šé:/	subj. *hit ~ it* /hít ~ ít/
obj. *him* /hím/	poss., obj. *hir(e) ~ her(e)* /híř ~ hířə ~ hɛř ~ hɛřə/	obj. *hit ~ it ~ him* /hít ~ ít ~ hím/
poss. *his* /hís/		poss. *his* /hís/

Third person pl.

subj. *þai ~ þei* /θáɪ/
obj. *hem* /hɛm/
poss. *hir(e) ~ her(e)*
/híř ~ hířə ~
hɛř ~ hɛřə/

EModE Personal Pronouns

These changes occurred in the English personal pronouns by the time of EModE:

1. The loss of final −e [−ə], as in ME *her(e)* > EModE *her*.
2. *You* displaced *ye* as the second-person plural subject form.
3. The second-person singular forms *thou, thee, thy ~ thyn* were displaced, respectively, by the plural forms *you, you, your*. Older *thou, thee, thy ~ thyn*, however, subsequently survived in the speech of Quakers and in poetic and religious use.
4. The new analogical pronoun *its* replaced *his*.
5. *Them* and *their* from North Midland replaced the native forms *hem* and *hir(e) ~ her(e)*, respectively, in the fifteenth century.
6. The introduction in the fifteenth century from North Midland of *ours, yours, hers, theirs* from Late ME *ōūres, yōūres, hires ~ heres, þeires*.

Consequently, the EModE personal pronouns were:

First person
    sg.   pl.
  subj. *I* /ə́ɪ/   *we(e)* /wí/
  obj. *me(e)* /mí/   *us* /ə́s/
  poss. *my ~ mine* /mə́ɪ ~ mə́ɪn/ *our ~ ours* /ə́ʊr ~ ə́ʊrz/

Second person
        subj., obj. *you* /yú/
        poss.   *your ~ yours* /yúr ~ yúrz/[3]

Third person
  sg.   sg.   sg.
subj. *he(e)* /hí/   subj. *she* /ší/   subj., obj. *it* /ít/
obj. *him* /hím/   obj. *her* /hə́r/   poss.   *its* /íts/
poss. *his* /híz/   poss. *her ~ hers*
                 /hə́r ~ hə́rz/

Third person pl.
        subj. *they* /ðé/
        obj. *them* /ðɛ́m/
        poss. *their ~ theirs* /ðɛ́r ~ ðɛ́rz/

LModE Personal Pronouns

The personal pronouns of EModE and LModE are morphologically alike; they differ only phonemically. For example, EModE /əi əʊ/ are respectively /aɪ aʊ ~ a/ in AmE as follows:

I, me, my, mine	/aí mí máɪ máɪn
we, us, our, ours	wí ə́s áʊr ~ ár áʊrz ~ árz
you, your, yours	yú yɔ́r yɔ́rz
he, him, his	hí hím híz
she, her, hers	ší hə́r hə́rz
it, its	ít íts
they, them, their, theirs	ðé ðέm ðέr ðέrz/

OE Interrogative Pronouns

The OE interrogative pronouns indicated five cases: n.a.d.g. and instrumental (i.). All OE interrogative pronouns were numberless. Distinctions of gender occurred only in the contrast between neuter n.a. *hwæt* and masculine n. *hwā,* a. *hwone.* The remaining interrogative pronouns were genderless.

Masculine 'who'   Neuter 'what'

n. *hwā* /hwá:/   n.a. *hwæt* /hwǽt/

a. *hwone* /hwɔ́nɛ/

         d. *hwǣm* /hwǣ:m/

         g. *hwæs* /hwǽs/

         i. *hwȳ* /hwǘ:/

ME Interrogative Pronouns

In the ME period the interrogative pronouns underwent a reduction from five cases (n.a.d.g.i.) to three (subj., obj., poss.) with loss of gender:

subj.	*whō*	/hwó:/
obj.	*whōm*	/hwó:m/
poss.	*whōs*	/hwó:s/

OE *hwæt* > ME *what* /hwát/, an uninflected FW. ME *what* was not a pronoun because it lacked possessive and objective forms. *What* remained a FW in EModE and remains so in LModE.

EModE Interrogative Pronouns

Following the change ME [hw] > EModE [h], the EModE forms of the interrogative were:

subj.	*who*	/hú/
obj.	*whom(e)*	/húm/
poss.	*whose*	/húz/

LModE Interrogative Pronouns

The LModE forms of the interrogative pronouns are the same as those of EModE, namely:

subj.	*who*	/hú/
obj.	*whom*	/húm/
poss.	*whose*	/húz/

OE Demonstrative Pronouns

There were two sets of OE demonstrative pronouns: (A) the 'the, that' set, and (B) the 'this' set. We shall call them the Demon A set and the Demon B set.

The Demon A set and the Demon B set both indicated five cases (n.a.d.g.i.), two numbers (sg. and pl.), and three genders (masc., fem., and neut.) in the singular. The plural forms were genderless.

Demon A set

Sg. masc.	neut.	fem.	pl.
n. *sē* /sé:/	n.a. *ðæt* /θǽt/	n. *sēo* /sé:ɔ/	n.a. *ðā* /θá:/
a. *ðone* /θɔ́nε/		a. *ðā* /θá:/	
d. *ðǣm* /θǽ:m/		d.g. *ðǣre* /θǽ:r̈ε/	d. *ðǣm* /θǽ:m/
g. *ðæs* /θǽs/			g. *ðāra* /θá:r̈a/
i. *ðȳ ~ ðon* /θú: ~ θɔ́n/			

Demon B set

Sg. masc.	neut.	fem.	pl.
n. *ðes* /θέs/	n.a. *ðis* /θís/	n. *ðēos* /θé:ɔs/	n.a. *ðās* /θá:s/
a. *ðisne* /θísnε/		a. *ðās* /θá:s/	
d. *ðissum* /θísʊm/		d.g. *ðisse* /θísε/	d. *ðissum* /θísʊm/
g. *ðisses* /θísεs/			g. *ðissa* /θísa/
i. *ðȳs* /θú:s/			

ME Demonstrative Pronouns

In the ME period the OE Demon A pronouns were reduced to the following forms:

þe ~ the /θə́/
þat ~ that /θát/
þǭ ~ thǭ /θɔ́ː/ 'these, those'[4]

The OE Demon B set of pronouns were reduced to these forms:

þis /θís/ 'this'
þise ~ þēse /θízə ~ θéːzə/ 'these'[5]

All these Demon A and Demon B constructions were FWs in ME. They were not pronouns because they lacked possessive and objective forms. Thus, the OE Demon A and Demon B pronouns disappeared in ME.

SUMMARY

In OE there were three sets of pronouns:

1. Personal
2. Interrogative
3. Demonstrative
   A. 'the, that'
   B. 'this'

The personal pronouns were reduced from four cases (n.a.d.g.) and as many as three numbers (sg., dual, pl.) in OE to three cases (subj., obj., poss.) and two numbers (sg., pl.) in ME. In ME *shē* and *þai* and in EModE *their* and *them* were adopted from Northeast Midland. In EModE *thou, thee, thy ~ thyn* were displaced by plural *you, you, your,* and *his* was displaced by the analogical form *its. Ours, yours, hers, theirs* were introduced from North Midland in the fifteenth century.

The interrogative pronouns were reduced from five cases (n.a.d.g.i.) in OE to three in ME: subj. *whō,* obj. *whōm,* poss. *whōs.* OE neuter *hwæt* became the ME FW *what.*

The OE demonstrative A and B pronouns indicated five cases (n.a.d.g.i.), two numbers (sg., pl.), and three genders (masc., fem., neut.). In ME the A set was reduced to the FWs *the, that, thō,* and the B set to the FWs *þis, þise ~ þēse.*

NOTES

¹ The form *sċæ* occurs in the Peterborough Chronicle entry of 1140.

² OE *ich* [ǐč] > ME Ī [íː] probably through loss of final [č].

³ /u/ or /ɔ/ occurred in EModE *your* instead of EModE [ʌʊ] < ME [uː]. ME [uː] > EModE [u] in *you* instead of [ʌʊ].

⁴ North Midland *thǭs* /θǒːs/ displaced ME *thǭ* in EModE, and the resultant EModE forms were *the* /ðə̌/, *that* /ðǽt/, *those* /ðǒːz/. The same forms occur in LModE.

⁵ ME *þise* was lost in EModE, as was final *−e* in the other forms. Thus, the EModE (and LModE) forms are *this* /ðǐs/ and *these* /ðíz/.

16

Historical Verbs

OE verbs consisted of a stem such as *sing* or a stem plus IS, such as *sing-eð*. The stem was a combined morpheme of lexical meaning and tense (present or past). For example, {present 'sing'} = /síng-/ as in *sing-* and {past 'sing'} = /sáng/ as in *sang.*

OE Verb Classes

OE verbs are grouped into three classes, depending on how past tense is indicated in verb stems: strong verbs, weak verbs, and so-called anomalous or irregular verbs.

Strong verbs indicated past tense by a change of the stem nucleus, as in the contrast between /síng-/ and /sáng/. Weak verbs indicated past tense by the addition of the dental suffix /–d/, as in the contrast between /hǽːl / *hāl* and /hǽːld-/ *hǽld-*, or the dental suffix /–t/, as in the contrast between /kús-/ *cyss-* and /kúst-/ *cyst-*. Irregular verbs indicated past tense by means of a different base, as in the contrast between /ɛ́ɔm/ *eom* and /wǽs/ *wæs*.

OE Finite ISs

There were two kinds of verb ISs, finite ISs and non-finite ISs. An OE finite IS was a combined morpheme of nu.aber (singular or plural), mood (indicative, subjunctive, or imperative — see "Mood," Chapter 19 in this book), and sometimes person (first, second, or third), as {3rd sg. indic.} = /–εθ/ *–eð* in *sing-eð*. Some OE finite ISs were personless, however, such as the present and past subjunctive, the indicative plural, and the imperative plural.

OE Non-finite ISs

The ISs of the OE infinitive, present participle, and past participle did not indicate number, mood, or person, as did finite OE ISs. The ISs of the infinitive, present participle, and past participle were non-finite verb morphemes that indicated, respectively, {infin.}, {pres. part.}, and {past part.}.

{infin.} = /–ɑn/ as in *sing-an* 'sing'[1]

{pres. part.} = /–ɛndɛ/ as in *sing-ende* 'singing'

{past part.} of strong verbs = /–ɛn/ as in *sung-en* 'sung,' and {past part.} of weak verbs = usually /–ɛd/ as in *cyss-ed* 'kissed.' Irregular verbs, such as the verb *bēon* 'be,' lacked a past participle in OE.

Some past participles had the PB /yɛ-/ *ǧe-*, as in *ǧe-sungen ~ sungen* 'sung' and *ǧe-cyssed ~ cyssed* 'kissed.'

OE Paradigms

We begin our description of the historical verb system of English with an analysis of the paradigms of the OE strong verb *singan* 'sing,' the OE weak verb *cyssan* 'kiss,' and the combined OE irregular verbs *bēon, wesan* 'be.'

1. Strong verb

{'sing'} = /síng/, /sÍ-ng/.

Present tense

Indicative

Sg. 1	*singe*	/sɪng/+/ɛ/
2	*singest*	/sɪng/+/ɛst/
3	*singeð*	/sɪng/+/ɛθ/
Pl.	*singað*	/sɪng/+/ɑθ/

Subjunctive

Sg.	*singe*	/sɪng/+/ɛ/
Pl.	*singen*	/sɪng/+/ɛn/

Imperative

Sg.	sing	/sɪng/
Pl.	singaðᵈ	/sɪng/+/aθ/

Part.	singende	/sɪng/+/ɛnde/

Past tense
Indicative

Sg. common²	sang	/s–ng/+/–ɑ–/+/∅/
2	sunge	/s–ng/+/–ʊ–/+/ɛ/
Pl.	sungon	/s–ng/+/–ʊ–/+/ɔn/

Subjunctive

Sg.	sunge	/s–ng/+/–ʊ–/+/ɛ/
Pl.	sungen	/s–ng/+/–ʊ–/+/–ɛn/

Part.	ġesungen	/yɛs⁻ng/+/–ʊ–/+/ɛn/

2. Weak verb
  {'kiss'} = /kǘs/.

Present tense
Indicative

Sg. 1	cysse	/küs/+/ɛ/
2	cysest	/küs/+/ɛst/
3	cysoðᵈ	/kʊ̈s/+/ɛθ/
Pl.	cyssaðᵈ	/küs/+/aθ/

Subjunctive

Sg.	cysse	/kūs/+/ɛ/
Pl.	cyssen	/küs/+/ɛn/

Imperative

Sg.	cyss	/küs/
Pl.	cyssaðᵈ	/küs/+/aθ/

Part.	cyssende	/küs/+/ɛndɛ/

Past tense
Indicative

Sg. common	cyste	/küs/+/t/+/ɛ/
2	cystest	/küs/+/t/+/ɛst/
Pl.	cyston	/küs/+/t/+/ɔn/

Subjunctive

Sg.   *cyste*   /küs/+/t/+/ɛ/

Pl.   *cysten*   /küs/+/t/+/ɛn/

Part.   *ġecyssed*   /yɛkū́s/+/ɛd/

3. Irregular verb

The paradigm of the combined OE verbs *bēon, wesan* 'be' contained several different bases, as a consequence of the combination into one paradigm in PGmc of the three separate PIE verb bases *bheu, *es/os, *wes/wos (> OE *bēon, is, wesan*).

Because of the relative complexity of a structural analysis of the OE 'be' bases and their ISs, it will be simpler merely to list the paradigmatic forms of 'be' and their phonemic transcriptions:

Present tense

Indicative

Sg. 1	*eom*	/ɛ́ɔm/	*bēo*	/bé:ɔ/
2	*eart*	/ǽaï̈t/	*bist*	/bíst/
3	*is*	/ís/	*biᵭ*	/bíθ/
Pl.	*sindon*	/síndɔn/	*bēoᵭ*	/bé:ɔθ/

Subjunctive

Sg.	*sīe*	/sí:ɛ/
Pl.	*sīen*	/sí:ɛn/

Imperative

Sg.	*wes*	/wɛ́s/
Pl.	*wesaᵭ*	/wɛ́saθ/

Part.   *wesende*   /wɛ́sɛndɛ/

Past tense

Indicative

Sg. common	*wæs*	/wǽs/
2	*wǣre*	/wǽ:ï̈ɛ/
Pl.	*wǣron*	/wǽ:ï̈ɔn/

Subjunctive

Sg.	*wǣre*	/wǽ:ï̈ɛ/
Pl.	*wǣren*	/wǽ:ï̈ɛn/

ME Verbs

These changes took place in the English verb system in the ME period:

1. Leveling of syllabic nuclei in OE ISs to ME −e [−ə], as in OE singeð ˌsíŋgɛθ] > ME singeð [síŋgəθ].

2. OE present participle IS −ende [−ɛndɛ] was replaced in the Midlands by the new ME IS −inge [−ɪŋgə], as in OE sing−ende [síŋgɛndɛ] > ME sing−inge [síŋg−ɪŋgə]. ME −inge < ME Southwestern and Southeastern noun PoB −ing(e) < OE noun PoB −ung ~ −ing, as in OE bodung 'preaching' and OE rǣding 'reading.'

3. OE past participle PB ǧe− [yɛ−] > ME y− ~ i− [ɪ−], as in OE ǧesungen [yɛsúŋgɛn] > ME (y)sungen ~ (i)sungen [ɪsúŋgən ~ súŋgən]

4. OE present indicative plural IS −að [−aθ] was replaced in the Midlands by ME −en [−ən]. Through the leveling of syllabic nuclei in OE ISs to ME −e [−ə], both OE present indicative sg. singeð [síŋgɛθ] and OE present indicative pl. singað [síŋgaθ], for example, became ME singeð [síŋgəθ]. To provide a new contrast between singular and plural numbers in the indicative present, the former OE subjunctive IS −en [−ɛn] > ME −en [−ən] was used as the new ME indicative plural IS, as in the contrast between ME present indicative sg. singeð [síŋgəθ] and present indicative pl. singen [síŋgən].

5. OE infinitive IS −an [−an] > ME −en [−ən] and later −e [−ə], as in OE singan [síŋgan] > ME singe(n) [síŋgən ~ síŋgə].

6. About one third of the OE strong verbs were lost in the ME period, and other strong verbs became weak verbs. For example, the verb 'help' in ME had the strong past tense forms (sg.) halp and (pl.) holpen, as well as the weak form (sg.) helpede. There was also a strong past participle form (y)holpen as well as the weak form helped. In the EModE period, most of the strong forms of such "mixed" verbs went out of use while the weak forms were retained, as in LModE past tense helped and past participle helped.

7. Extensive remodeling of the paradigm of the irregular verb 'be:' loss of OE present indicative bēo, bist, bið, beoð, sindon; the introduction by analogy of present indicative pl. bēn

and from Northern analogical *are(n)*; loss of OE subjunctive sg. *sīe* and pl. *sīen* and replacement by ME sg. *bē* and pl. *bēn*; loss of OE imperative *wes* and *wesað* and replacement by ME *bē* and *bēð*; replacement of OE present participle *wesende* by analogical ME *bēing*; the addition through analogy of the ME past participle *ybēn* [ɪbé:n].

ME Paradigms

The paradigms of the ME strong verb *singe(n)* 'sing,' the ME weak verb *kisse(n)* 'kiss,' and the ME irregular verb *bē(n)* 'be' were as follows:

1. Strong verb

    {'sing'} = /síng/, /sⁱng/.

Present tense

Indicative

Sg. 1	*singe*	/sɪng/+/ə/
2	*singest*	/sɪng/+/əst/
3	*singeð*	/sɪng/+/əθ/
Pl.	*singen*	/sɪng/+/ən/

Subjunctive

Sg.	*singe*	/sɪng/+/ə/
Pl.	*singen*	/sɪng/+/ən/

Imperative

Sg.	*sing*	/sɪng/
Pl.	*singeð*	/sɪng/+/əθ/

Part.	*singinge*	/sɪng/+/ɪngə/

Past tense

Indicative

Sg. common	*sang*	/sⁱng/+/-a-/+/Ø/
2	*sunge*	/s-ng/+/-ʊ-/+/ə/
Pl.	*sungen*	/s-ng/+/-ʊ-/+/ən/

Subjunctive

Sg.	*sunge*	/s-ng/+/-ʊ-/+/ə/
Pl.	*sungen*	/s-ng/+/-ʊ-/+/ən/

Part.	*isungen*	/ɪs-ng/+/-ʊ-/+/ən/

2. Weak verb

{'kiss'} = /kís/.

Present tense

Indicative

Sg.	1	*kisse*	/kɪs/+/ə/
	2	*kissest*	/kɪs/+/əst/
	3	*kisseð*	/kɪs/+/əθ/
Pl.		*kissen*	/kɪs/+/ən/

Subjunctive

Sg.	*kisse*	/kɪs/+/ə/
Pl.	*kissen*	/kɪs/+/ən/

Imperative

Sg.	*kiss*	/kɪs/
Pl.	*kisseð*	/kɪs/+/əθ/

Part. *kissinge* /kɪs/+/ɪngə/

Past tense

Indicative

Sg. common	*kiste*	/kɪs/+/t/+/ə/
2	*kistest*	/kɪs/+/t/+/əst/
Pl.	*kisten*	/kɪs/+/t/+/ən/

Subjunctive

Sg.	*kiste*	/kɪs/+/t/+/ə/
Pl.	*kisten*	/kɪs/+/t/+/ən/

Part. *ikist* /ɪkís/ | /t/

3. Irregular verb

Present tense

Indicative

Sg.	1	*am*	/ám/
	2	*art*	/árt/
	3	*is*	/ís/
Pl.		*bēn ~ are(n)*	/bé:n ~ árən/

Subjunctive

Sg.	*bē*	/bé:/
Pl.	*bēn*	/bé:n/

		Imperative
Sg.	bē	/bé:/
Pl.	bēð	/bé:θ/

Part.	bēing	/bé:ɪng/

		Past tense
		Indicative
Sg. common	was	/wás/
2	wēre	/wé:r̃ə/
Pl.	wēren	/wé:r̃ən/

		Subjunctive
Sg.	wēre	/wé:r̃ə/
Pl.	wēren	/wé:r̃ən/

Part.	ybēn	/ɪbé:n/

EModE Verbs

In the EModE period the following developments occurred in English verbs:

1. Loss of ME final *–e* [–ə] and *–e(n)* [–ə ~ –ən], as in ME *singe* [síŋgə] > EModE *sing* [síŋ] and ME *singe(n)* [síŋgə ~ síŋgən] > EModE *sing* [síŋ]. Consequently, the following morphological forms were lost in EModE:

2. The infinitive in *–e(n)*: ME *singe(n)* > EModE *sing*.

3. The present indic. sg. 1 in *–e*: ME *singe* > EModE *sing*.

4. The present indic. pl. in *–en*: ME *singen* > EModE *sing*.

5. The subjunctive in *–e* and *–en*: ME sg. *singe* and ME pl. *singen* > both EModE *sing*.

6. The pl. imperative in *–eð*: ME pl. *singeð* > EModE *sing*.

7. As a result of the losses in strong and weak verbs as stated in 1–6 above, the ME infinitive, the present indicative sg. 1 and pl., the subjunctive, and the pl. imperative all had the present-tense base form in EModE, such as *sing* and *kiss*.

8. Adoption of Late ME present indic. sg. 3 ISs *–es ~ –s* from North Midland, as in EModE *kisses* and *sings*, as alternate ISs along with older present indic. sg. 3 IS *–eth*, as in EModE *kisseth* and *singeth*.

9. Development in the paradigm of EModE 'be' of the past indic. sg. 2 forms *wast ~ wert* through analogy with *EModE* sg. 2 forms such as *canst, dost, shalt, wilt.*

10. The analogical leveling in the paradigm of *sing* of ME past tense forms to the common EModE form *sung*, as in ME past sg. common *sang*, sg. 2 *sunge*, and pl. *sungen* > all EModE past common *sung*.

11. EModE strong and weak verbs became moodless. The ME paradigms of these verbs indicated three moods (indicative, subjunctive, imperative), but with the loss of the ME subjunctive and imperative (5–6 above), EModE strong and weak verbs became moodless in the absence of any morphological contrasts for mood. In the paradigm of EModE 'be,' however, the subjunctive remained (see below).

12. Loss in the paradigm of 'be' of ME imper. sg. *bē* and pl. *bēð*.

13. The development through analogy in the paradigm of EModE 'be' of present subj. sg. 2 *beest ~ be'st*, and the loss of ME present subj. sg. *bē*, pl. *bēn*; past subj. sg. *wēre*; pl. *wēren*.

14. Loss of ME past participle PB *y– ~ i–*, as in ME *ysungen ~ iȝungon* > EModE *sung*.

EModE Paradigms

1. Strong verb
   {'sing'} = /sɪ́ŋ/, /s²ŋ/.

	Present tense	
Base	*sing*	/sɪŋ/
Sg. 2	*singest*	/sɪŋ/+/ɔst/
3	*singeth ~ sings*	/sɪŋ/+/əθ ~ z/
Part.	*singing*	/sɪŋ/+/ɪŋ/

	Past tense	
Common	*sung*[3]	/s–ŋ/+/–ə–/
Participle	*sung*	/s–ŋ/+/–ə–/

2. Weak verb
   {'kiss'} = /kɪ́s/.

	Present tense	
Base	*kiss*	/kɪs/
Sg. 2	*kissest*	/kɪs/+/əst/
3	*kisseth ~ kisses*	/kɪs/+/əθ ~ əz/
Part.	*kissing*	/kɪs/+/ɪŋ/
	Past tense	
Common	*kiss'd*	/kɪs/+/t/
Part.	*kiss'd*	/kɪs/+/t/

3. Irregular verb

	Present tense	
	Indicative	
Base	*be*	/bí/
Sg. 1	*am*	/ǽm/
2	*are ~ art*[4]	/ár ~ árt/
3	*is*	/íz/
Pl.	*are*	/ár/
	Subjunctive	
Sg.	*beest ~ be'st*	/bíəst ~ bíst/
	Past tense	
Sg. common	*was*	/wáz/
2	*wast ~ wert*	/wást ~ wέrt/
Pl.	*were*	/wέr/
Part.	*bin ~ been*	/bín ~ bín/

LModE Verbs

English verbs underwent these changes in LModE:

1. Loss of EModE present tense second-person IS –*est*, as in EModE *singest* > LModE *sing*, except for retention of –*est* in poetic and religious use, as in *thou singest*.

2. Loss of EModE present tense third-person IS –*eth*, as in EModE *singeth ~ sings* > LModE *sings*, except for retention of –*eth* in poetic and religious use, as in *he singeth*.

3. In the paradigm of the verb 'sing,' the loss of EModE

past common *sung* and the adoption (c. 1850) of the EModE variant *sang*, as in EModE (c. 1760) *sung ~ sang* > LModE *sang* [sǽŋ].[5]

4. Loss in the paradigm of the irregular verb 'be' of EModE present indic. sg. 2 *art* and past sg. 2 *wast ~ wert*, except for retention of *art* and *wert* in poetic and religious use, as in *thou art* and *thou wert*.

5. Loss in the paradigm of 'be' of EModE present subj. sg. *beest ~ be'st*. As a result, the paradigm of 'be' became moodless by the time of LModE. As you will recall, strong and weak verbs previously became moodless in EModE.

LModE (AmE) Paradigms

1. Strong verb
   {'sing'} = /síŋ/, /s∸ŋ/.

   ### Present tense

Base	*sing*	/sɪŋ/
Sg. 3	*sings*	/sɪŋ/+/z/
Part.	*singing*	/sɪŋ/+/ɪŋ/

   ### Past tense

Common	*sung*	/s ŋ/ ǀ / ᴂ /
Part.	*sung*	/s-ŋ/+/-ə-/

2. Weak verb
   {'kiss'} = /kís/.

   ### Present tense

Base	*kiss*	/kɪs/
Sg. 3	*kisses*	/kɪs/+/ɪz/
Part.	*kissing*	/kɪs/+/ɪŋ/

   ### Past tense

Common	*kissed*	/kɪs/+/t/
Part.	*kissed*	/kɪs/+/t/

157

3. Irregular verb

Present tense

Base	*be*[6]	/bí/
Sg. 1	*am*	/ǽm/
3	*is*	/íz/
Common	*are*	/ár/
Part.	*being*	/bíɪŋ/

Past tense

Sg. common	*was*	/wɔ́z/
Sg. 2 and pl.	*were*	/wɔ́r/
Part.	*been*	/bín/

SUMMARY

Finite OE verb forms indicated two tenses (present, past), three moods (indicative, subjunctive, imperative), and as many as three persons (first, second, third). Strong verbs indicated past tense by a change of syllabic nucleus, and weak verbs by the addition of a dental suffix. The OE infinitive in *–an*, the present participle in *–ende*, and the past participle in *–en* (strong) or *–ed* (weak) were non-finite verb forms. They did not indicate tense, mood, or person.

In the ME period, OE IS nuclei were leveled to ME *–e* [–ə], OE pres. part *–ende* > ME *–inge*, OE past part. PB *ǧe–* > ME *y– ~ i–*, OE infin. *–an* > ME *–en*, OE pres indic. pl. *–að* > ME *–en*. The paradigm of 'be' underwent extensive remodeling. Also, about one third of the OE strong verbs were lost, and other strong verbs became weak verbs.

In the EModE period, ME *–e* and *–e(n)* were lost, as were ME past part. PB *y– ~ i–*. Alternate pres. 3rd sg. *–es ~ –s* were adopted. Following the loss of ME infinitive, imperative, subjunctive, pres. indic. sg. 1 and pl. forms, strong and weak verbs became moodless in EModE. The verb 'be' underwent further extensive remodeling in EModE, but the analogical pres. subj. sg. forms *beest ~ be'st* were retained.

158

In LModE, EModE pres. 2nd *–est* and pres. 3rd *–eth* were lost. EModE past common *sung* was lost, and the alternate form *sang* was adopted in LModE. There were further losses in the paradigm of 'be,' so that following the loss of the pres. subj. sg. forms, the forms of 'be' became moodless.

NOTES

[1] There was also a phrasal infinitive consisting of *tō*+stem+IS /–ɛnɛ/ *–enne*, as in *tō sing-enne* 'to sing.' Later, OE *–enne* [–ɛnɛ] > ME *–en* [–ən], as in ME *tō sing-en*. With the loss of final *–en* [–ən] in EModE, ME *tō sing-en* > EModE *to sing* > LModE *to sing*. OE *–enne*, with later variant *–anne*, was derived from a PGmc noun IS which indicated neuter sg. d.

[2] Common = first and third persons.

[3] The variant *sang* [sǽŋ] also occurred by 1763. See Robert Lowth, *A Short Introduction to English Grammar*, 2nd ed., corrected (London, 1763), p. 83.

[4] *Are* as a singular form was used with the pronoun *you*, whereas *art* was restricted in use to the older pronoun *thou*.

[5] See *OED*, IX, 876.

[6] *Be* is used in constructions such as *I request (that) it be painted*, and after *if*, as in *If he be late....* *Be* also is used after *to*, as in *She wants to be happy*, and in subjectless sentences such as *Be quiet! Are* is used with the pronouns *you, we, they*. Some analysts classify 'be' as a function word (FW) auxiliary or helping verb. They restrict the label *verb* to LModE word sets that pattern as *sing* and *kiss*. See W. F. Twaddell, *The English Verb Auxiliaries* (Providence, 1963), pp. 16–17.

Historical Adjectives

OE adjectives consisted of a stem such as *swēt*, or a stem plus IS, such as *swēt–um*. The stem contained a lexical morpheme as {'sweet'} = /swé:t–/.[1] The IS was a combined morpheme of case and number as {pl. d.} = /–ʊm/ in *swēt–um*. Sometimes the IS morpheme also included gender as {masc. sg. a.} = /–nɛ/ in *swēt–ne*.

OE Stems

Most OE adjectives had three stems, traditionally called the positive degree, comparative degree, and superlative degree. The positive-degree stem consisted of an allomorph of the lexical morpheme as /swe:t–/. The comparative- and superlative-degree stems were formed by adding a comparative-degree PoB or a superlative-degree PoB to an allomorph of the lexical morpheme as /swé:t–/+comparative PoB /–ř/ > /swé:tř–/ 'sweeter' and /swé:t–/+superlative PoB /–ɛst/ > /swé:tɛst/ 'sweetest.'[2]

The following sets illustrate the comparative- and superlative-degree PoBs of many OE adjectives:

1. The /ř/, /ɔst/–set.
    {'hard'} = /hǽařd–/.
    heard–   /hæ̃ařd/
    heardr–   /hæ̃ařd/ + /ř/
    heardost–   /hæ̃ařd/ + /ɔst/

2. The /ř/, /ɛst/–set.
        {'long'} = /láng–/, /léng–/.
        lang–   /lɑng/
        lengr–   /lɛng/ + /ř/
        lengest– /lɛng/ + /ɛst/
3. The /ř/, /st/–set.
        {'good'} = /gó:d–/, /bɛ́t–/.
        gōd–   /go:d/
        betr–   /bɛt/ + /ř/
        betst–   /bɛt/ + /st/
4. The /Ø/, /t/–set.
        {'little'} = /lű:tɛl–/, /lǽ:s–/.
        lȳtel–   /lü:tɛl/
        lǽss–   /læ:s/ + /Ø/
        lǽst–   /læ:s/ + /t/

OE Paradigms

There were two sets of OE adjective ISs, traditionally called the strong-adjective paradigm and the weak- or *n-* adjective paradigm. These ISs were added to OE adjective stems.

1. The strong paradigm.

The strong paradigm indicated five cases (n.a.d.g.i.), two numbers (sg. and pl.), and three genders (masc., fem., neut.). The pl. g. and d. were genderless.

The following two sub-sets of strong adjective ISs are representative of many OE adjectives. For convenience, the two sub-sets are labeled the Strong A set and the Strong B set. The OE adjective stems cited below are *swēt–* 'sweet' and *gōd–* 'good.' The lack of an IS is indicated by —.

Strong A set.

		Masc.		Neut.		Fem.
sg. n.	/swé:t/ +		/ɛ/			/ʊ/
a.	/swé:t/ +	/nɛ/			/ɛ/	
d.	/swé:t/ +		/ʊm/			/řɛ/
g.	/swé:t/ +		/ɛs/			/řɛ/
i.	/swé:t/ +		/ɛ/			—
pl. n.a.	/swé:t/ +	/ɛ/		/ʊ/		/ɑ/

Common

d.	/swé:t/+	/ʊm/
g.	/swé:t/+	/ïɑ/

Strong B set.

		Masc.	Neut.	Fem.
sg. n.	/gó:d/+	—	—	—
a.	/gó:d/+	/nɛ/	—	/ɛ/
d.	/gó:d/+	/ʊm/		/ïɛ/
g.	/gó:d/+	/ɛs/		/ïɛ/
i.	/gó:d/+	/ɛ/		—
pl. n.a.	/gó:d/+	/ɛ/	—	/ɑ/

Common

d.	/gó:d/+	/ʊm/
g.	/gó:d/+	/ïɑ/

2. The weak paradigm.

The weak or *n* paradigm indicated four cases (n.a.d.g.), two numbers (sg. and pl.), and three genders (masc., fem., neut.) in the sg. n.a. only. The remaining inflectional suffixes were genderless.

		Masc.	Neut.	Fem.
sg. n.	/swé:t/ or /gó:d/+	/ɑ/	/ɛ/	
a.	/swé:t/ or /gó:d/+	/ɑn/	/ɛ/	/ɑn/

Common

sg. d.g., pl. n. a.	/swé:t/ or /gó:d/+	/ɑn/
d.	/swé:t/ or /gó:d/+	/ʊm/
g.	/swé:t/ or /gó:d/+	/ïɑ ~ ɛnɑ/

Syntactic Uses

The use of the OE strong- or weak-adjective paradigm depended on the relationship of the OE adjective to neighboring words. Although a description of those relationships is properly the concern of OE syntax, it will be helpful to list some of them here.

A weak paradigm IS was added to an OE adjective stem:

1. When the adjective was preceded by a demonstrative pronoun, as (masc. sg. a.) *ðone* in *ðone gōdan man* 'the good man.'

2. Frequently, but not always, when the adjective was preceded by a genitive case personal pronoun, as in *his mǣran hālgan* 'his glorious saints.' Often the genitive case personal pronouns *mīn, uncer, ūre, ðīn, incer, ēower* became morphological adjectives when (strong) adjective inflections were added to them as *mīn* > (masc. sg. a.) *mīn-ne* in *mīnne stronglican stōl* 'my sturdy throne.'[3]

In contrast, the strong paradigm was used when the adjective was *not* preceded by a demonstrative or personal pronoun as in (masc. pl. n.) *gōd-e menn* 'good men,' and (sg. n.) *is gōd* 'is good,' *is brādost* 'is widest.'[4]

ME Adjectives

The following changes occurred in OE comparative and superlative PoBs in the ME period:

1. OE comparative PoB *-r* [-r̈] as in *betr-* > ME *-er* [-ər̈] as in ME *beter-*.

2. With the leveling of OE nuclei in unstressed syllables to [-ə], usually written *-e*, OE superlative PoBs *-ost* [-ɔst] and *-est* [-ɛst] > ME *-est* [-əst].

The resultant ME sets of adjective stems were as follows:

1. The /ər̈/, /əst/-set.
   {'hard'} = /hár̈d-/.
   hard-   /har̈d/
   harder-   /har̈d/+/ər̈/
   hardest-   /har̈d/+/əst/
   {'long'} = /lɔ́:ng-/, /lɛ́ng-/
   lōng-   /lɔ:ng/
   lenger-   /lɛng/+/ər̈/
   lengest-   /lɛng/+/əst/

2. The /ər̈/, /st/-set.
   {'good'} = /gó:d-/, /bɛ́t-/, /bɛ́-/.
   gōd-   /go:d/
   beter-   /bɛt/+/ər̈/
   best-   /bɛ/+/st/

3. The /Ø/, /t/–set.
{'little'} = /lítəl–/, /lɛ́:s–/, /lɛ́s–/.
litel–   /lɪtəl/
lęss– ~ less– /lɛ:s ~ lɛs/+/Ø/
lęst–   /lɛ:s/+/t/

ME Paradigms

The OE strong- and weak-adjective paradigms had already undergone extensive reduction by the ME period:

1. OE nuclei in unstressed ISs were leveled to ME [–ə], written –*e*.

2. All OE case distinctions were lost in ME, as were all OE gender distinctions. Thus, the OE IS combined morpheme of (gender) -number-case > ME IS morpheme of number only.

As a result, the ME strong- and weak-adjective paradigms of *gōd–* 'good' and *swēt–* 'sweet' were these:

1. The strong paradigm.

	Sg.	Pl.
/gó:d/ +	—	/ə/
/swé:t/+	/ə/	/ə/

2. The weak paradigm.

	Sg.	Pl.
/gó:d/ +	/ə/	
/swé:t/+	/ə/	

As these paradigms show, the only grammatical contrast was for number (sg. and pl.), as between strong sg. *gōd* in *gōd man* 'good man' and strong pl. *gōde* in *gōde men* 'good men.'[5] There was, however, confusion in the use of strong and weak adjective ISs. For example, –*e* was often added to the strong sg. as *gōd* > *gōde* in *gōde man* 'good man,' and sometimes –*e* was omitted from the strong pl. as *gōde* > *gōd* in *gōd men* 'good men.'

EModE Adjectives

After the progressive disappearance of final IS –*e* [ə] in the late-fourteenth and early-fifteenth centuries, the surviving Late ME ISs of the strong- and weak-adjective paradigms were lost by the EModE period. For example, ME (strong) sg.

swēt–e, pl. *swēt–e* and (weak) sg. *swēt–e*, pl. *swēt–e* > all EModE *sweet*. Consequently, by the EModE period the adjective had lost all strong and weak ISs, and has since been marked only by comparative-degree and superlative-degree PoBs, as in these EModE sets:

1. The /ər/, /əst/–set.
   {'hard'} = /hɔ́rd ~ hǽrd/.
   hard   /hərd ~ hærd/
   harder   /hərd ~ hærd/+/ər/
   hardest   /hərd ~ hærd/+/əst/
   {'long'} = /láŋ/.[6]
   long   /laŋ/
   longer   /laŋ/+/ər/
   longest   /laŋ/+/əst/

2. The /ər/, /st/–set.
   {'good'} = /gúd/, /bɛ́t–/, /bɛ́–/.
   good   /gud/
   better   /bɛt/+/ər/
   best   /bɛ/+/st/

3. The /Ø ~ ər/, /t/–set.
   {'little'} = /lítəl/, /lɛ́s–/.
   little   /lɪtəl/
   lesse ~ lesser   /lɛə/ | /Ø ~ ər/
   lost ~ least   /lɛs/+/t/

LModE Adjectives

Apart from some phonetic differences in stem nuclei, such as EModE *hard* [hɔ́ɹd ~ háɹd] > AmE *hard* [hárd], the adjective sets of LModE are morphologically the same as those previously cited for EModE, with one exception: the set of *little* has variant comparative and superlative forms.

1. The /ər/, /əst/–set.
   {'hard'} = /hárd/.
   hard   /hard/
   harder   /hard/+/ər/
   hardest   /hard/+/əst/

{'long'} = /lɔ́ŋ/.
long   /lɔŋ/
longer   /lɔŋ/+/ər/
longest   /lɔŋ/+/əst/

2. The /ər/, /st/–set.
   {'good'} = /gʊ́d/, /bɛ́t–/, /bɛ́–/.
   good   /gʊd/
   better   /bɛt/+/ər/
   best   /bɛ/+/st/

3. The /Ø ~ ər/, /ɪst ~ t/–set.
   {'little'} = /lítəl/, /lítl–/, /lɛ́s/, /lís–/.
   little   /lɪtəl/
   littler ~ less ~ lesser   /lɪtl/+/ər/, /lɛs/+/Ø ~ ər/
   littlest ~ least   /lɪtl/+/ɪst/, /lis/+/t/

SUMMARY

OE adjectives had three stems: positive, comparative, and superlative. The last two were formed by the comparative PoBs –r, /Ø/ and the superlative PoBs –ost, –est, –st, –t. To the positive, comparative, and superlative stems were added ISs (indicating case, number, and sometimes gender) of the strong- and weak-adjective paradigms.

In the ME period the comparative PoBs were –er and /–Ø/, and the superlative PoBs were –est, –st, –t, and so they remained in EModE and generally in LModE. Also in the ME period, the ISs of the strong- and weak-adjective paradigms were reduced to –e [–ə], with the loss of all OE gender and case distinctions. The only remaining grammatical contrast in ME was between singular and plural number as in strong gōd, gōde.

With the loss of –e [–ə] by the time of EModE, the strong and weak adjective ISs of ME were lost. Thereafter, adjective sets were marked only by comparative- and superlative-degree PoBs as in hard, hard-er, hard-est.

NOTES

[1] Constituents of other OE adjective stems, as well as other OE noun and verb stems, include these examples:

OE adjectives: (B+PoB) *menn-isċ* 'human,' (B+PoB+PoB) *menn-isċ-liċ* 'human,' (PB+B) *niþer-weard* 'turned downward,' (PB+B+PoB+PoB) *un-menn-isċ-liċ* 'inhuman,' (B+B) *ealdor-lang* 'life-long,' (B+B+PoB) *ēaδ-mōd-liċ* 'humble,' etc.

OE nouns: (B+PoB) *blind-nes* 'blindness,' (PB+B) *fram-cynn* 'progeny,' (PB+B+PoB) *on-flǣsċ-nes* 'incarnation,' (B+B) *æppel-wīn* 'cider,' (B+B+PoB) *mild-heort-nes* 'mercy,' (B+PoB+PoB+PoB) *menn-isċ-liċ-nes* 'human nature,' (PB+PB+B+PoB+PoB) *un-ġe-lēaf-sum-nes* 'unbelief,' etc.

OE verbs: (PB+B) *fore-bod-* 'to announce,' (B+PoB) *lāδ-ett-* 'to loathe,' (PB+PB+B) *ġe-ān-lǣc-* 'to unite,' (B+B) *mān-swer-* 'to perjure,' (PB+B+PoB) *mis-crōc-ett-* 'to croak horribly,' etc.

[2] There are two good reasons for labeling the OE comparative and superlative suffixes as postbases rather than as inflectional suffixes: 1) The comparative and superlative morphemes do not characterize all OE adjectives, as in the case of OE positive-degree adjectives. Instead, OE adjectives were characterized by ISs of the OE strong and weak paradigms. 2) ISs usually have a connection with sentence concord, but the OE comparative and superlative suffixes were not so involved. Therefore, we have labeled them PoBs rather than ISs here, and in our OE adverb sets.

[3] Sometimes OE present participles also became morphological adjectives when adjective ISs were added to them, as in *singende* 'singing' > strong sg. n. *singend-ne* and *weallende* 'boiling' > weak sg. a. *weallend-an*. OE past participles frequently were not inflected like adjectives, but when they were, adjective ISs (usually strong) were added to them, as in *ofslæġen* 'slain' > strong sg. a. *ofslæġen-ne*. Less often weak adjective ISs were added, as in *ongunnen* 'begun' > weak pl. *ongunnen-an*.

Similarly, adjective ISs, usually weak, were added to OE ordinal numerals (*fyrst* 'first,' *ōδer* 'second,' *þridd* 'third,' etc.). In contrast, adjective ISs were not usually added to OE cardinal numerals (*ān* 'one,' *twā* 'two,' *þrēo* 'three,' etc.).

[4] Adjectives with comparative-degree stems, however, were always inflected with the weak paradigm as in (weak neut. pl. n.) *bēoδ heardran* 'are harder.'

[5] In ME the possessive forms of first- and second-person personal pronouns that ended in a consonant continued sometimes to be inflected as adjectives with *-e* [-ə] in the plural, as in *δīne cherles* 'your churls.'

[6] [-ó:-] in ME *lǫng-* /lɔ́:ng/ > shortened [-ó-] in EModE *long* /láŋ/.

Historical Adverbs

OE adverbs, unlike OE nouns, pronouns, verbs, and adjectives, lacked ISs; OE adverbs were a PoB class of words. Most OE adverbs consisted of a lexical morpheme and a positive-, comparative-, or superlative-degree PoB. Some OE adverbs, however, lacked a positive-degree PoB.

OE Adverb Sets

The positive-degree form of most OE adverbs was formed by adding the PoB *-e* /-ɛ/ to the positive-degree stem of an OE adjective, as in these examples:

OE Adjective	OE Adverb
heard– /hǽaɪ̈d/ 'severe'	+/-ɛ/ > *hearde* /hǽaɪ̈dɛ/ 'severely'
heardliċ– /hǽaɪ̈dlɪč/ 'severe'	+/-ɛ/ > *heardliċe* /hǽaɪ̈dlɪčɛ/ 'severely'

Not all positive-degree adverbs in OE had the PoB *-e*; some lacked a positive-degree PoB. For example, the positive-degree OE adverb *wel* /wɛl/ 'well' lacked a positive-degree PoB, as did all OE positive-degree adjective stems.

The comparative PoBs of some OE adverbs differed from those of OE adjectives. However, the superlative PoBs of OE adverbs and adjectives were alike:

	Comparative	Superlative
OE Adjectives	/-r̈ ~ -Ø/	/-ɔst ~ -ɛst ~ -st ~ -t/
OE Adverbs	/-ɔr̈ ~ -Ø/	/-ɔst ~ -ɛst ~ -st ~ -t/

Examples of OE adverb sets include the following:

1. The /ɔ̈r/, /ɔst/–set.
   {'severe'} = /hǽɑr̈d–/.
   hearde   /hǽɑr̈d/+/ɛ/
   heardor   /hǽɑr̈d/+/ɔ̈r/
   heardost   /hǽɑr̈d/+/ɔst/
2. The /Ø/, /ɛst/–set.
   {'long'} = /lɑ́ng–/, /lɛ́ng–/.
   lange   /lɑng/+/ɛ/
   leng   /lɛng/+/Ø/
   lengest   /lɛng/+/ɛst/
3. The /Ø/, /st/–set.
   {'well'} = /wɛ́l/, /bɛ́t–/.
   wel   /wɛl/
   bet   /bɛt/+/Ø/
   betst   /bɛt/+/st/
4. The /Ø/, /t/–set.
   {'little'} = /lʉ́:t/, /lǽ:s–/.
   lȳt   /lü:t/
   lǣs   /læ:s/+/Ø/
   lǣst   /læ:s/+/t/

ME Adverbs

Adverbs underwent the following developments in the ME period:

1. OE positive-degree PoB *-e* [-ɛ] > ME *-e* [-ə], as in OE *hearde* [hǽɑr̈dɛ] > ME *harde* [hár̈də], and also OE *openliče* 'openly' [ɔ́penlɪčɛ] > ME *ǭpenliche* [ɔ́:penlɪčə]. After c. 1350 in East Midland, forms ending in *–liche* [-lɪčə] > progressively *–lȳ* [-li:], as in ME *ǭpenliche* [ɔ́:penlɪčə] > Late ME *ǭpynlȳ* [ɔ́:penli:]. The origin of Late ME *–lȳ* is not known. It may have developed from ME *–lich* [-lɪč] with loss of [-č], as in *ǭpenliche* > *ǭpenlich* > *ǭpenlȳ*, or it may have developed from OScand *–ligr*, *–liga*. Thus, in Late ME there were two kinds of positive-degree adverb PoBs: *-e* [-ə] as in *harde* [hár̈də] and *–lȳ* as in *ǭpenlȳ* [ɔ́:penli:].

2. The comparative- and superlative-degree forms of some OE adverb sets did not survive past the OE period. For example,

OE *hearde, heardor, heardost* > *harde*, *harder, *hardest, of which only positive-degree *harde* 'severely' survived in Early ME. On the other hand, some OE adverb sets did pass over into ME without loss of forms, as in OE *wel, bet, betst* > ME *wel, bet, best*.

ME Adverb Sets

Of the OE adverb sets we previously listed, only the following forms survived in ME:

1. {'severe'} = /hárd–/.

  harde   /haɪ̆d/ + /ə/

2. {'long'} = /lɔ:ng–/, /lɛ́ng/.

  lǫnge   /lɔ:ng/ + /ə/

  leng   /lɛng/

3. {'well'} = /wɛ́l/, /bɛ́t/, /bɛ́–/.

  wel   /wɛl/

  bet   /bɛt/

  best   /bɛ/ + /st/

4. {'little'} = /lí:t ~ lítəl/, /lɛ́s/.

  līt ~ litel   /li:t ~ lɪtel/

  less   /lɛs/[1]

  lest   /lɛs/ + /t/

EModE Adverbs

These changes took place in the adverb system of English by the EModE period:

1. ME positive-degree PoB *–lȳ* [–li:] > EModE *–ly* [–li ~ –lɪ], as in ME *ǭpenlȳ* [ɔ́:penli:] > EModE *openly* [ópenli ~ ópenlɪ].

2. Loss of ME positive-degree PoB *–e* [–ə], as in ME *harde* > EModE *hard*, and ME *lǫnge* > EModE *long*. Thus, morphologically, EModE *hard* and *long* became EModE positive-degree adjectives of the EModE sets *hard, harder, hardest* and *long, longer, longest*.

3. Loss of some ME comparative-degree forms such as ME *leng* and *bet*.

As a result, only ME *well-best* and ME *less-lest*, of the ME adverb forms we previously examined, survived in EModE.

EModE *well* was a FW, and EModE *best* was morphologically an adjective (EModE *good, better, best*), as were EModE *less* and *lest* (EModE *little, lesse ~ lesser, lest ~ least*).

In short, some ME positive-degree adverbs and all ME comparative- and superlative-degree adverbs were lost by the time of EModE. Some simply disappeared from use, and others became morphologically EModE adjectives. The only ME adverb forms that survived in EModE as adverbs were those in ME *-lȳ*, as in ME *ǭpenlȳ* > EModE *openly*.

LModE Adverbs

In LModE, as in EModE, all adverbs end in *-ly* and, unlike adjectives, are not capable of comparison.[2] As in EModE, adverbs in LModE are formed by adding the PoB *-ly* to a positive-degree adjective stem, as in these examples:

quick /kwík/+*-ly* /li/ > *quickly* /kwíkli/[3]
short /šɔ́rt/+*-ly* /li/ > *shortly* /šɔ́rtli/
swift /swíft/+*-ly* /li/ > *swiftly* /swíftli/

Although all LModE adverbs end in *-ly*, not all words that end in *-ly* are adverbs. For example, *quickly* is an adverb consisting of positive-degree adjective *quick*+adverb PoB *-ly*. *Friendly* is not an adverb, but the positive-degree adjective form of the adjective set *friendly, friendlier, friendliest*. On the other hand, *rapidly* is neither an adverb nor an adjective but a FW, because there is no adjective set *rapid, *rapider, *rapidest*.

SUMMARY

OE adverbs were a PoB class of words, not an IS class of words. Most OE adverbs consisted of a lexical base plus the positive PoB *-e*, the comparative PoBs *-or*, /-Ø/, or the superlative PoBs *-ost, -est, -st, -t*. Some positive-degree adverbs like *wel* 'well' lacked a positive-degree PoB.

In the ME period, alternate positive-degree PoB *-lȳ* developed, possibly from ME *-lich* or OScand *-ligr, -liga*. Some comparative- and superlative-degree adverbs were lost in ME.

In the EModE period, some positive-degree adverbs and all

comparative- and superlative-degree adverbs were lost. Some disappeared from use and others became morphological adjectives. Only the adverb forms in *–ly* remained.

Since the EModE period, adverbs are words that are formed by adding the PoB *–ly* to the positive-degree stem of an adjective, as in quick+*–ly* > quickly. Unlike adjectives, they cannot be used to make comparisons.

NOTES

[1] OE *lǽs* [lǽ:s] > ME [lέ:s] > [lέs] through shortening of nucleus.

[2] See James Sledd, *A Short Introduction to English Grammar* (Chicago, 1959), p. 187.

[3] LModE (AmE) *–ly* /–li/ may become /–lɪ/ in rapid speech.

Mood, Case, Aspect

In examining historical English nouns, pronouns, verbs, adjectives, and adverbs, we were engaged in the study of morphology — the arrangement and interrelationship of morphemes in words. As we turn now to consider grammatical signals, such as case, we pass from the study of morphology to the study of syntax — the arrangement and interrelationship of words in phrases and sentences.

In this chapter we are going to examine the syntactic signals of mood and case, and such related grammatical matters as aspect, voice, concord, and government. As a preliminary to the discussion of mood, let us examine what is meant by a verb phrase.

Verb Phrase

A verb phrase is a linguistic construction consisting of at least one auxiliary verb, such as *be, have, shall,* or *ought (to),* plus either 1) the base form of a verb (as in *shall sing, ought to sing*), 2) present participle (*is singing, has been singing*), or 3) past participle (*has sung, should have sung*).

Auxiliaries

There are two kinds of auxiliaries: modal auxiliaries (or simply modals), and primary auxiliaries.

Modals

There are four paired modals in AmE, and two unpaired ones:[1]

>can shall will may ought (to) must
>could should would might

Modals do not have a present tense third singular form in
−s, nor present participle, past participle, or infinitive forms.
However, some analysts loosely refer to *could, should, would,
might* as the past forms of *can, shall, will, may*.

The paired modals do not co-occur: *might could*.

Primary Auxiliaries

The primary auxiliaries are *have, do*, and *be*. Unlike the
modals, the primary auxiliaries have a present tense third
singular form in −s, as well as present participle, past participle,
and infinitive forms. They also show concord (agreement) with
subjects.

In verb phrases in which both a modal and a primary auxiliary
occur, the modal precedes the primary auxiliary, as in *should
be going, may be going*.

Mood

Mood is a set of the inflectional forms of a verb, or a set of
modal auxiliaries whose selection depends either on stylistic
convention or on whether the speaker regards the action or state
denoted by the verb as an actual fact (indicative mood), as
possibility, doubt, desire, supposal (subjunctive mood), or as
command, entreaty, exhortation (imperative mood). Therefore,
mood is indicated in two ways: morphologically and phrasally.

Morphological Mood

In OE there were morphologically distinct subjunctive verb
forms, like plural *singen* and *cyssen*. Sometimes they indicated
that the speaker's attitude was one of potentiality or unrealiza-
tion. Sometimes, however, the use of the morphological subjunctive was determined by syntactic convention instead of the

"attitude" of the speaker. For example, in OE the morphological subjunctive was used after verbs expressing command, statement, thought, advice; in constructions containing a subjunctive verb; in constructions beginning with *ġif* 'if,' *būtan* 'unless,' *ðēah* 'although,' etc.; in constructions whose contexts expressed purpose or result, and so on. In other words the use of the morphological subjunctive in OE was often syntactically dictated. It would therefore be erroneous to interpret the morphological subjunctive in OE as always expressing a non-factual mood or attitude.

It is sometimes said of LModE that a verb form like *sing* in (I) *sing* is indicative, that *sing* in (If he) *sing* is subjunctive, and that *sing* in (Now) *sing!* is imperative. But, *sing-sing-sing* have no mood because they show no morphological distinctions in form.

In regard to (Now) *sing!* the so-called imperative is indicated not by the verb *sing* but by the exclamation mark *!*, a graphemic signal of forceful utterance or strong feeling. Indeed, we can turn any LModE verb base into a so-called imperative by the addition of *!*. On the other hand, the verb form *sing* in OE was an imperative which was morphologically distinct from all other forms of the verb *singan* 'sing' (*singe, singest, singeð, singað, singen, singende*). As for the so-called LModE subjunctive verb forms *sing* and *were* in (If he) *sing* and (If I) *were*, they do not differ morphologically from the so-called indicatives *sing* and *were* in (They) *sing* and (They) *were*.

Actually, the use of *sing* and *were* in *If he sing* and *If I were* is governed by *If*. LModE style is such that we use verb forms like *sing* or *were* with *If*, instead of *sings* or *was*. That is, the use of verb forms such as *sing* or *were* in LModE is a matter of stylistic convention, not morphological mood, because LModE verbs are morphologically moodless, as we explained in the chapter about English verbs.

Phrasal Mood

In addition to morphological mood, or mood expressed by the form of a verb, as in OE, mood in English is also indicated in verb phrases by means of modal auxiliaries (AmE *can/could, shall/should, will/would, may/might, ought to, must*). Such mood is called phrasal mood.

The moods indicated in such LModE verb phrases as *shall go, will go, can go, could go, might go, ought to go*, etc., have no names, but are sometimes referred to as the *can*-mood, *could*-mood, *shall*-mood, *ought to*-mood, and so on. The modals in AmE express various shades of meaning, but that subject is outside the scope of this book.[2]

Phrasal mood also occurred in OE. Some OE modal auxiliaries were *magan* 'be able, may, can,' *mōtan* 'be permitted, compelled, must,' *sċulan* 'shall, must, ought to,' and *willan* 'be willing, wish.' They expressed mood in such OE verb phrases as *wille . . . onsendan* 'wish . . . to send,' *sċeall habban* 'shall have,' *mæġ . . . oferfēran* 'can . . . cross.' The ellipsis . . . in these examples indicates that intervening words have been omitted.

Aspect

In addition to mood, verb phrases in English indicate aspect: the status or category of an action. For example, continuing or durative aspect indicates that the action or state denoted by the verb has begun and is continuing. In contrast, completed aspect indicates that the action or state denoted by the verb has been completed.

Continuing aspect in LModE is indicated by a form of the verb *be* plus present participle, as in *is singing, is going*. Completed aspect is indicated by a form of the verb *have* plus a past participle, as in *have/has/had sung* and *have/has/had gone*. Such constructions do not indicate tense (time) but aspect — the status of an action.

OE verb phrases also indicated continuing aspect and completed aspect. For example, continuing aspect was indicated by a form of the combined verb *bēon, wesan* 'be' plus a present participle, as in *is iernende* 'is flowing' and *wǽron biddende* 'were asking.' Completed aspect in OE was indicated by a form of the verb *habban* 'have' or *āgan* 'have' plus a past participle of a transitive verb, as in *ġeseten hæfdon* 'sat down had' and *āgon . . . ġewinnen* 'have . . . earned.' Sometimes completed aspect in OE was also indicated by a form of the verb *bēon, wesan* 'be' plus a past participle of an intransitive verb, as in *is . . . ġeworden* 'has . . . happened' and *wæs . . . āgān* 'had . . . gone.'

Voice

In addition to mood and aspect, verb phrases in English also indicate passive voice, which is indicated in LModE by a form of the verb *be* plus the past participle of transitive verbs, as in (He) *was shot*. In transforming a verb as *shot* in (*I*) *shot* (*him*) into a passive voice construction, there is a semantic change in which the so-called receiver of the action of the verb becomes the subject and thereby undergoes rather than performs the action denoted by the verb, as in *He was shot* (*by me*).

Similarly, passive voice in OE was indicated by a form of *bēon, wesan* 'be' or *weorðan* 'be' plus the past participle of a transitive verb. Examples are *ġewundad wæs* 'wounded was,' *wearð . . . ofslæġen* 'was . . . slain,' and *sind ġehātene* 'are called.'

Case

Case is a set of the inflectional forms of a noun, pronoun, or adjective which indicates the word's syntactic relationship (such as subject, object, possessor, thing possessed) to another word.[3] In English, case is determined by government or concord.

Government

Government is that system by which one word determines the case or mood of another word. We have already stated that certain verbs and other words in OE required the use of the subjunctive. In so doing, those OE words governed the mood of the verb that followed them.

Prepositions in OE were also governing words that governed the case of their noun or pronoun objects, as in (genitive) *wið exanċeastres* 'towards Exeter,' (accusative) *wið alne ðone here* 'against all the army,'' (dative) *tō him* 'to him.' Prepositions in LModE also govern or determine the case of their pronoun objects. For example, in LModE *to him* the preposition *to* requires the use of the object-case pronoun *him* instead of the subject-case form *he* or the possessive-case form *his*.

Verbs in OE governed the case of their objects. In the examples that follow the OE verbs govern the case of the object of person or the object of thing, as in (genitive) *ǣlċes cræftes bedǣled* 'of all ability deprived,' (dative) *him ... answarode* 'him ... answered,' (accusative) *ofslōg ðone aldormon* 'killed the governor,' and (dative) *sealde ǣlċum* 'gave to each.'

When two objects occurred in OE, each was generally in a different case, as in these examples:

dat. of person and accus. of thing: *ðām folce ... ġerihta lǣrde* 'to the people ... laws taught.'

accus. of person and gen. of thing: *hine nānes ðinges ne lyste* 'him of no thing not desired.'

In LModE, verbs govern the case of pronouns and nouns. For example, *shot* requires *him* rather than *he* in *I shot him*. Similarly, *is* requires such pronoun forms as *she* and *he* in *This is she* and *This is he* for many standard speakers, although some use *her* and *him* in *This is her* and *This is him*.

Another type of government involves nouns that govern the case of their modifiers. For example, in LModE *his book*, *book* requires *his* rather than *he* or *him* because **he book* or **him book* is nonstandard English. The possessive case *his* in *his book* denotes possession, ownership, or a relation analogous to ownership.

More relationships were indicated by case in OE than in LModE because there were more ISs that indicated case in OE than in LModE. Moreover, case was more extensively governed in OE than in LModE. We have already illustrated how OE prepositions and verbs governed the case of their objects. Some additional examples of the relationships indicated by case in OE are presented below in summary form:

  A. *Nominative case.*
    1. Subject of a verb: *iċ eom* 'I am'
    2. Nouns of address: *lēofa cyning* 'dear king'
    3. Subjective complement: *iċ eom fisċere* 'I am (a) fisherman'[4]

  B. *Genitive case.*
    1. Partition: *fīftiġ wintra* 'fifty of winters'
    2. Description: *folces weard* 'of people protector'
    3. Instrument: *hyġesorga ofercumen* 'by means of sorrows overcome'

4. Possession: *hiora sċipu* 'their ships'
5. Origin: *ides sċyldinga* 'lady of (the) Scyldings'
6. Measure: *fōtes trym* 'of (a) foot the space'
C. *Dative case.*
   1. Instrument: *hondum ġebrōden* 'by hands woven'
   2. Location: *wīcum wunian* 'in (the) dwellings to live'
D. *Instrumental case.*
   1. Causality (with *þȳ, hwȳ*): *þȳ hē ðone fēond ofercwōm* 'for this reason (=therefore) he the devil defeated'; *hwȳ sċeal iċ . . . ðēowian* 'why must I . . . serve?'
   2. Expressions of comparison (with *þon*): *mǣrða þon mā . . . ġehedde* 'glorious deeds the more . . . perform (=perform more glorious deeds).'

Concord

Concord or grammatical agreement is a system of correspondence between two or more words in regard to gender, number, case, or person. It is a grammatical correlation that exists between two or more variable items.

For example, in LModE there is a correlation of number between *this* and *boy* and *these* and *boys* in *this boy* and *these boys*. There is a correlation of gender and number between *man* and *he, woman* and *she, stone* and *it* in *He is the man, She is the woman,* and *It is a stone.*

These are some features of concord in OE:

1. Correlation of gender, number, and case between adjectives, pronouns, and the nouns they modify, as in adjective-noun *gōd cyning* (both masculine, singular, nominative) 'good king' and pronoun-adjective-noun *ðǣre ylcan nihte* (all feminine, singular, dative) 'the same night.'

2. Correlation of number and person between subject and verb as in *ðā denisċan cōmon* (both plural, third person) 'the Danes came'; *iċ eom* (both singular, first person) I am.'

3. Correlation of gender, number, and case between pronouns and their noun antecedents, as in *sē hwæl . . . hē* (all masculine, singular, nominative) 'the whale . . . he'; *sum widewe . . . sēo* (all feminine, singular, nominative) 'a certain widow . . . she.'

4. Correlation of gender, number, and case between subjective complements and subjects, as between (adj.) *mǣre* and *sē god* (all masculine, singular, nominative) in *mǣre is sē god* 'glorious is (the) God'; and also between (noun) *man* and *hē* (both masculine, singular, nominative) in *hē wæs swiþe spēdiȝ man* 'He was a very wealthy man.'

SUMMARY

Mood, verb phrase, auxiliaries (modal and primary), aspect (continuing and completed), passive voice, government, case, and concord.

NOTES

[1] *Dare* and *need* function as unpaired modals but also as verbs.

[2] See further W. F. Twaddell, *English Verb Auxiliaries*, 2nd ed., rev. (Providence, 1963), pp. 13–15, and also Martin Joos, *The English Verb, Form and Meanings* (Madison, 1964), pp. 20–31, 147–153.

[3] LModE nouns and pronouns indicate case, but LModE adjectives do not. OE adjectives, however, did indicate case.

[4] The term complement refers to a word or phrase used after a verb to complete the predication. A subjective or predicate complement is said to identify or describe the subject of the verb, as *she* and *happy* in *I am she, Mary is happy.* An objective complement is said to identify or describe the direct object, as *secretary* and *green* in *They elected him secretary, He painted the house green.*

20

Greco-Roman Prescriptive Grammars

In this chapter we shall trace the development of what is called traditional English grammar, more accurately Greco-Roman prescriptive grammar, the kind of grammar usually taught in secondary schools. After that we shall examine some of the weaknesses of traditional grammar and then briefly discuss other theories of grammar.

Origin

The word grammar is derived from Latin *grammatica* < Greek *grammatikē* 'skilled in grammar' < *gramma* 'letter, piece of writing.' The study of Western grammar originated with philosophical inquiry by ancient Greeks into the nature of language. In the writings of such philosophers as Plato, Aristotle, Protagoras, and the Stoics, we find sporadic speculations about the nature of language and the properties of word classes, such as verbs and nouns.

Thrax

The first partial Western grammar was written about 100 B.C. by the Greek grammarian Dionysius Thrax (born c. 166 B.C.).[1] The title of his work is *Technē Grammatikē* 'art of grammar, art of letters.' Thrax's *Technē*, which codified earlier Greek philosophical speculation about language, was used for many generations as a school text in the Roman Empire.

In the *Techné*, a work intended for the elementary student, Thrax defines grammar as "an experimental knowledge of the usages of language as generally current among poets and prose writers."[2] He also discusses such matters as accents, syllables, letters, punctuation marks, and the eight parts of speech and their inflections. Thrax does not discuss syntax, except to define the sentence. Therefore, Thrax's *Techné* is only a partial grammar.

A short work of about a dozen pages in translation, the *Techné* has strongly influenced grammatical studies in the West for about two thousand years. For example, the following extracts from Thrax's *Techné* illustrate how similar many current school grammars are to this work written more than two millennia ago:

> A Sentence is [a] combination of words, either in prose or in verse, making complete sense. There are eight parts of speech: Noun, Verb, Participle, Article, Pronoun, Preposition, Adverb, and Conjunction. . . . A Noun is a declinable part of speech, signifying something either concrete or abstract . . . common or proper . . . A Verb is an indeclinable word, indicating time, person, and number, and showing activity or passivity. . . .
> A Participle is a word partaking of the nature both of nouns and verbs. It has all the accidents which belong to nouns as well as those which belong to verbs, except mood and person. . . . An Article is a declinable part of speech, prefixed or subjoined to the various cases of nouns . . . A Pronoun is a word assumed instead of a noun, and indicating definite persons. . . . A Preposition is a word placed before any of the parts of speech, both in Composition and in Syntax. . . . An Adverb is an indeclinable part of speech, said of a verb or added to a verb. . . . A Conjunction is a word binding together a thought in order and filling up the hiatuses of speech.

Dyscolus

The honor of producing the first complete Western grammar belongs to the Greek grammarian Apollonius Dyscolus (second century A.D.), a resident of Alexandria, the ancient Greek capital of Egypt founded by Alexander the Great. According to John E. Sandys, Dyscolus "was the founder of scientific grammar, and the creator of Greek Syntax."[3] Although most of Dyscolus' many works have been lost, his writings on the *Pronoun, Conjunction, Adverb,* and *Syntax* remain.

The writings of Thrax were known to Dyscolus, and apparently he was influenced by his predecessor in regard to the parts of speech. For example, both Thrax and Dyscolus list noun, verb, participle, article, pronoun, preposition, adverb, and conjunction; however, as Sandys points out, Dyscolus "was the only ancient grammarian who wrote a complete and independent work on Syntax. . . .[4]

Varro

Following the military and political conquest of Greece by Rome, teachers of Greek, some of them slaves, arrived in the Eternal City. Subsequently the grammatical works of the Greeks became known to the Romans, who modified them somewhat, amplified them as needed, and then applied them to Latin.

The first Roman writer and scholar to adapt the mass of Greek grammatical scholarship to Latin was the grammarian Marcus Terentius Varro (166–27 B.C.).[5] His *De Lingua Latina* 'About the Latin Language' (47–45 B.C.) was a monumental work in twenty-five books, of which only six survive. Clearly, Varro was indebted to the Greeks, but his treatment of Latin grammar shows originality, especially his morphological classification of Latin words into nouns (including adjectives), verbs, adverbs, and participles.

However, later Roman grammarians (first century A.D.) preferred a word class system based on Thrax's eight parts of speech, with one change. The interjection was added in place of the article.

Donatus and Priscian

Because of their influence upon later grammatical studies in England, especially during the OE and ME periods, two Roman grammarians stand out from all others. They are Aelius Donatus (c. 350 A.D.) and Priscianus Caesariensis (c. 500 A.D.), better known, respectively, as Donatus and Priscian.

Each wrote two Latin grammars, the larger of which are Donatus' *Ars Grammatica* 'Art of Grammar, Art of the Rudiments of Learning' and Priscian's *Institutiones Grammaticae* 'Institutes of Grammar' in eighteen books.

Donatus also wrote a shorter *Ars Minor*, which teaches the eight parts of speech. It was widely used as an elementary textbook by beginning students in Latin during the Middle Ages. In fact, the work was so popular that the labels *Donat ~ Donet* came to be applied to any elementary treatise.

Priscian also wrote a popular minor work entitled *Partitiones XII Versuum Aeneidos Principalium*. It taught Latin grammar through parsing. To parse is to break down a sentence into its parts, describing each part of speech and the function of each word in the sentence. That question-and-answer method of teaching grammar is still used in classrooms today.

Donatus, whose work shows little originality, listed the Greco-Roman eight parts of speech established by the late Roman grammarians. Priscian, a century and a half later, borrowed that classification from Donatus.

OE Period

Unlike today, few boys went to school during the OE period, and girls, apparently, not at all. The schools were religious institutions whose purpose was to prepare young clerics for service in the church.

The students in those monastic schools studied Latin, not English, for Latin was the language in which the mass was conducted and in which religious rites were performed. Latin was also the language in which religious records, such as the Bible, and classical writings were preserved. Furthermore, Latin was the international language of scholarship and diplomacy of medieval Europe. In English grammar schools, Latin, not English, was originally studied.[6]

During the OE period the English abbot and writer Aelfric Grammaticus (?955–?1020), now simply called Aelfric, wrote a Latin grammar based on the writings of earlier Roman grammarians.[7] Aelfric's grammar is essentially a paraphrase and translation of Priscian. From Priscian, Aelfric also borrowed Donatus' eight parts of speech: *Nomen, Pronomen, Verbum, Adverbium, Participium, Conjunctio, Praepositio, Interjectio.*[8]

Aelfric, however, was not the first Englishman in the OE period to rely on the authority of a Roman grammarian. Priscian, for example, was quoted by Aldhelm (c. 604–709) in the seventh century, and by Bede and by Alcuin (735–804) in the eighth century. Thus, in the works of the OE writers Aldhelm, Bede, Alcuin, and Aelfric, we see the influence of the classical grammatical descriptions found in the works of Donatus and Thrax.

ME, EModE Periods

Throughout the ME period and the EModE period, Latin remained influential in England. Schoolboys in grammar schools studied Latin, not English. During the Renaissance, students also studied Greek and sometimes Hebrew because of rising interest in ancient literature. It was then believed that the ancients had possessed vast knowledge and wisdom. Therefore, one studied Latin, then Greek, and possibly also Hebrew in order to read and to comprehend that literature.

Lily

In the sixteenth century, the study of Latin in English schools became so codified that all students had to study one text, William Lily's *A Short Introdvction of Grammar* (1540). That authorized wolk, actually the product of Erasmus, Dean Colet, Lily, and various revisers, was the only Latin text allowed in schools, including the Stratford Grammar School which William Shakespeare attended.[9] The dedication in the first part of the 1567 edition of Lily's *Grammar* contains this extract:[10]

> Kinge Henrye the eight ... did not forget, ne neglect, the good and vertuous education of the tender youth of this saide Realme, but hauing a feruent zeale, bothe towards the Godly bringing vp of the saide youth, and also a speciall regarde that they might attaine the Rudiments of the Latine tongue, with more facilitye then aforetime. And for auoyding of diuersitie and tediousnes of teaching, did cause one vniforme Grammar to be set forth, commaunding all Scholemasters & teachers within this saide Realme, to teache, vse and exercise the same.

Lily's *Grammar* consists of two parts, with the first part in English, entitled "An Introdvction of the Eyght Partes of Latine Speache." The eight parts listed are *Noune, Pronoune,*

Verbe, Participle, Aduerbe, Coniunction, Preposition, and *Interiection.* The classification is that of Donatus.

The second part of the 1567 edition of Lily's *Grammar* is written in Latin and bears the title *"Brevissima Institutio sev Ratio Grammatices Cognoscende"* ('A Very Brief Description or Account of Learning Grammar'). In it are discussed 'grammar and its parts.' The four parts of grammar are 'orthography, etymology, syntax, and prosody.'

Early English Grammars

In the latter portion of the sixteenth century, English came to be studied, not for its own intrinsic merit, but as a preliminary to the study of Latin. The new belief was that it would be preferable for students first to study English "grammar" to facilitate their later study of Latin. For example, William Bullokar (*A Short Introduction*, 1580) urged learning English before Latin, toward which end he directed his English *Pamphlet for Grammar.* Thus, in the late-sixteenth century, a knowledge of English "grammar" came to be a prerequisite to the study of Latin.[11]

As the grammatical study of English spread, there appeared on the market first one and then another English "grammar," some written in Latin, some in English. They included William Bullokar's *Pamphlet for Grammar* (1586), the first English grammar;[12] ?P[aul] ?Gr[eaves]' *Grammatica Anglicana* (1594); Alexander Gil's *Logonomia Anglica* (1619); Charls Butler's *The English Grammar* (1633); Ben Jonson's *The English Grammar* (1640); John Wallis' *Grammatica Linguae Anglicanae* (1653); Jeremiah Wharton's *The English Grammar* (1654); Christopher Cooper's *Grammatica Linguae Anglicanae* (1685); and Joseph Aickin's *The English Grammar* (1693).

Latinate Framework

As their titles indicate, these volumes were advertised as English grammars. In reality, they were not; they were works in which the grammatical categories and framework of Greco-Latin grammars, such as Lily's, were superimposed onto English. Here are some extracts from the first part of Lily's Latin *Grammar* (1567):

A Verbe is a parte of speache declined with Mode and tense & betokeneth doinge: as Amo, *I love*, or suffering: as Amor, *I am loved*, or being: as Sum, *I am*.

... There be fiue Tenses or Times: the Present tense, the Preterimperfect tense, the Preterperfect, the Preterpluperfect, and the Future tense.

The Present tense speaketh of the time that nowe is: as Amo, *I loue*.

The Preterimperfect tense speaketh of the time not perfectly past: as Amabam, *I loued or did loue*.

The Preterperfect tense speaketh of the time perfectly past, w[ith] this Signe *Haue*, as Amaui, *I haue loued*.

The Preterpluperfect tense speaketh of the time more the perfectly past, with this signe *Had*: as Amaueram, *I had loued*.

The Future tense speaketh of the time to come, with this signe *Shall* or *will*: as Amabo, *I shall or will loue*.

... *I loue. Thou louest. He loueth. We loue. ye loue. They loue.* Amo, amas, amat. Amamus, amatis, amant.

... Amaui, *I haue loved.*

... Amaueram, *I had loved.*

... Amabo, *I shall or will loue.*

... Amem, *I maie or can loue.*

... Amarem, *I might or coulde loue.*

... Amauerim, *I might, would, should, or ought to haue loved.*

... Amauissem, *I might, would, should, or ought to had loved.*

... Amauero, *I maie or can loue hereafter.*

Now, for the purpose of comparison, examine these extracts from Jonson's *English Grammar* (1640):[13]

A *Verbe* is a word of number, which hath both *Tyme*, and *Person Tyme* is the difference of a *Verbe*, by the *present*, *past*, and *future*, or *to come*. A *Verbe finite* therefore hath three only *Tymes*, and those alwayes *imperfect*.

The first is the *present*: as *Amo, Love.*

The second is the *Tyme past*: as *Amabam, loved.*

The third is the *Future*: as *Ama, amato: Love, love.*

The other *Tymes* both *imperfect*: as *Amem, amarem, amabo.* and also *perfect*: as *Amavi, amaverim, amaveram, amavissem, amavero.*

...

Pr.	*Love, lovest, loveth.*		Pl.	*Love, love, love.*	
Pa.	*Loved, loved'st, loved.*		Pl.	*Loved, loved, loved.*	
Fu.	*Love, love.*		Pl.	*Love, love.*	
	Inf.			*Love.*	
	Part. Pr.			*Loving.*	
	Part. past.			*Loved.*	

... The *Syntaxe* of *imperfect* Times in this manner:

The Presents by the *infinite*, and the Verbe, *may*, or *can*, as for, *Amem, Amarem: I* may *love: I* might *love.* And againe, *I* can *love: I* could *love.*

The *futures* are declared by the *infinite*, and the *Verbe, shall,* or *will*: as *Amabo: I* shall, or, will *love. Amavero* addeth thereunto, *have,* taking the nature of two divers Times; that is, of the *future,* and the Time *past: I shall* have *loved:* or, *I will* have *loved.*

The *perfect* Times are expressed by the Verbe, *have*: as, *Amavi. I* have *loved. Amaveram. I* had *loved.*

Amaverim, and *Amavissem* adde *might* unto the former Verbe: as, *I* might *have loved.*

As a comparison of the extracts from Lily and Jonson clearly shows, early English grammars, such as Jonson's, were close copies of Latin grammars. In fact, the English works were little more than attempts to find the equivalents in English of Latin constructions and categories.

A Dissenter

One partially dissenting voice was that of Wallis, who in a tract prefixed to his *Grammatica* (1653) complained of the attempt to impose the pattern of Greco-Latin grammar upon English. The writers of such grammars, he said, were wrong in yoking the English language to alien noun and verb paradigms, cases, genders, tenses, and moods. Such labels and categories, he stated, were "a fictitious and quite foolish collection."

Despite his legitimate complaint, Wallis himself essentially remained subservient to the Greco-Latin tradition and Greco-Latin descriptions. Wallis, for example, was the first English "grammarian" to offer rules concerning the use of *shall* and *will* to indicate what he incorrectly regarded as the "future tense" in so-called declarative sentences. Later, those rules were amplified by such grammarians as Robert Lowth and William Ward.

Prescriptive Grammar

In the first half of the eighteenth century, the belief emerged that English was a debased language, which had to be methodically and vigorously cleansed of its improprieties. This attitude was based upon a scholarly reverence for the classical languages and a strong desire to make English conform to the standards of Classical Latin.

According to the scholars' linguistic scale of values, the more remote the kinship of a language to Greek and Latin, the more debased and corrupt it was. Greek, for example, was regarded as pre-eminent among known languages. Second in rank of linguistic excellence and elegance was Latin.[14] Languages derived from Latin, such as Spanish, French, and Italian, were rated as less refined because they were considered vulgar corruptions of Latin. Other modern languages only distantly related to Latin, such as German and English, were held to be even more debased and inferior.

Impressed by the *Accademia della Crusa* (1582) and the *Salon de Rambouillet* (1635), dedicated, respectively, to the linguistic regulation of Italian and French, proponents in England advocated a similar academy to cleanse and refine English. Daniel Defoe, for example, in *An Essay Upon Several Projects* (1702), advocated that:

> The Work of this Society shou'd be to . . . polish and refine the English Tongue, and advance the so much neglected Faculty of Correct Language, to establish Purity and Propriety of Stile, and to purge it from all the Irregular Additions that Ignorance and Affection have introduc'd . . . in short, every thing that wou'd appear necessary to the bringing our English tongue to a due Perfection.

Some very determined efforts were made to purify and fix the English language. According to Sterling A. Leonard, "The prevailing view of language in the Eighteenth Century was that English could and must be subjected to a process of classical regularizing."[15] To achieve that end, English grammarians sought to refine the language through a marriage with logic and Greco-Latin grammar. In the process of their refining, the grammarians completely disregarded English usage, including that of the best authors.[16]

In the second half of the eighteenth century, various "new" English grammars were published, including Ann Fisher's *A New Grammar* (1750), Robert Lowth's *A Short Introduction to English Grammar* (1762), William Ward's *An Essay on Grammar* (1765), James Buchanan's *A Regular English Syntax* (1767), and Charles Coote's *Elements of the Grammar of the English*

Language (1788). Such grammars, and others like them, are called prescriptive, because they contain prescriptions for the regulation of English.

Ruled English

The prescriptive grammarians advised the English that they should study grammar to eliminate "errors" and to acquire "correct" English.[17] To the prescriptivists, however, the study of grammar meant the study of the "rules" of grammar, "rules" which the prescriptivists themselves devised. In time the list of "rules" grew, and the study of those "rules" spread, especially in the classroom.

A typical advocate of the study of grammar was Lowth, who in the second edition (1763) of his *Grammar* stated:

> The Truth is, Grammar is very much neglected among us . . . if children were first taught the common principles of Grammar by some short and clear System of English Grammar . . . they would have some notion of what they were going about, when they should enter into the Latin Grammar. . . .

Praising Lowth's work, "in which are shown the grammatic [sic] Inaccuracies that have escaped the Pens of our most distinguished Writers," Ward in his *Grammar* (1765) advocated "assisting children to comprehend the general Import and Advantage of Rules concerning Language."

Similarly, Buchanan said in his *Syntax* (1767):

> Considering the many grammatical Improprieties to be found in our best Writers, such as Swift, Addison, Pope, etc. a Systematical English syntax is not beneath the Notice of the Learned themselves. Should it be urged, that in the Time of these Writers, English was but a very little subjected to Grammar, that they had scarcely a single Rule to direct them, a question readily occurs: Had they not the Rules of Latin syntax to direct them?

Coote, in his *Grammar* (1788), in which he criticized the "grammatical propriety" of "learned professions," persons "of rank and fashion," as well as "Authors," suggested:

> This deficiency in grammatical precision may be obviated and supplied by a competent degree of attention, in the first place, to the fundamental principles of grammar, and, secondly to the particular rules of the language.

Some Prescriptions

James Greenwood, in *An Essay Towards a Practical English Grammar*, 4th ed. (1740), adequately summarized the prescriptive viewpoint that, "Grammar doth deliver the Rules." The arbitrary prescriptive rules that evolved, based on "logic," "reason," and the syntax of Classical Latin, eventually developed into a "fixed" standard of neo-classic correctness.[18] Needless to say, that eighteenth-century attitude, which associated correctness with grammatical rules, continues to be reflected in classrooms and in school handbooks of English.

Here are some of the "rules" that the prescriptivists put forth. Contrary to long-standing English usage, the authoritarians prohibited sentences containing double negatives, and they prohibited ending a sentence with a preposition. They also spoke against splitting an infinitive, and they restricted *it* and *which* as references to inanimate antecedents. They amplified the subjection of *shall* and *will* to the "rules" and made *lie* and *lay* distinct. They also made a distinction in use of *between* (two objects) and *among* (several objects). To make English conform more to Latin, they created such constructions as (I) *am being attacked.* In addition, they prohibited *they was, you was, of who, different than* or *to, had better, It is me, between you and I, more round, is wrote,* and *more* and *most* as modifiers, respectively, of comparative and superlative adjectives.

The rigorous application of such rules, especially when backed by the authority of the classroom teacher and the "grammar book," has since produced numerous changes in English usage. But some "rules" apparently have not prevailed, such as the injunction against ending a sentence with a preposition. One does not have to search very far to encounter a standard construction as *What's she up to?*

American Grammars

Prior to 1775 in America, few private schools taught English grammar, and the public schools apparently not at all. In the latter, instruction was confined largely to reading and writing. Schoolbooks were scarce, and "Handwritten texts and other prepared-at-home substitutes were in widespread use."[19] On the other hand, students from families of means attended Latin grammar schools where they read Latin and Greek works.

The first English grammars used in Colonial America were British imports of the Greco-Roman-prescriptive type, the most popular of which was Thomas Dilworth's *New Guide to the English Tongue* (1740), which was reprinted by many American publishers.[20] Other British imports included Greenwood's *Essay* (1711); James Harris' *Hermes, a Philosophical Inquiry Concerning Grammar* (1751); and Lowth's *Short Introduction* (1762).

In the period following the Revolutionary War, a popular American work was Noah Webster's *A Grammatical Institute of the English Language, Part II: Containing, a plain and comprehensive grammar* (1784). Based largely on Lowth's *Short Introduction*, Webster's *Institute* also followed the pattern established by the Greco-Roman English grammarians.

Five years later, however, Webster reversed his course. In *Dissertations on the English Language* (1789), he complained:

> Most writers . . . lay down certain rules, arbitrary perhaps or drawn from the principles of other languages, and then condemn all English phrases which do not coincide with those rules . . . Instead of examining to find what the English language is, they endeavor to show what it ought to be according to their rules. It is for this reason that some of the criticisms of the most celebrated philologers are so far from being just, that they tend to overthrow the rules, and corrupt the true idiom of the English tongue.

Murray

Unquestionably the most popular and most influential grammar in America for decades after the Revolutionary War was Lindley Murray's *English Grammar*, printed in England in 1795. In various abridgements and revisions, Murray's *Grammar* "in its field ranked in popularity with that of Webster's Spelling book."[21] Following the familiar pattern of English "grammarians," Murray, a Pennsylvanian who emigrated to England, made generous use of the works of writers who preceded him, including Lowth, Ward, and Webster. Murray's *Grammar*, as such, was Greco-Roman and prescriptive.

However, unlike several earlier English grammarians who borrowed Lily's eight parts of speech, Murray adopted Robert

Lowth's classification, which included the article but not the participle, and which split the Greco-Roman noun (+adjective) class into separate noun and adjective groups. The result is known as the neo-traditional nine parts of speech: article, noun, adjective, pronoun, verb, adverb, conjunction, preposition, and interjection.

Later some traditionalist grammarians reduced the nine word classes to eight by reclassifying the article as a subclass of adjectives. Other traditionalists further reduced the number to seven by reclassifying the interjection as a subclass of adverbs or by eliminating the interjection as a part of speech. Thus, over the centuries the Greco-Roman English grammarians have variously advocated nine, eight, and seven parts of speech.

Nineteenth Century

With increasing elaboration of "rules," the English grammar books of nineteenth-century America imitated the grammars of the earlier period. Works such as Samuel Kirkham's *English Grammar* (1825), Peter Bullion's *Principles of English Grammar* (1844), William Wells' *School Grammar* (1846), and Goold Brown's *Grammar of English Grammars* (1851) continued the Greco-Roman-prescriptive tradition. In these and similar later works, one finds a strong dependence on authority.

Twentieth Century

The development of Greco-Roman English grammar reached its apex in the early-twentieth century in the works of university scholars, mostly European. Major writers of that period include the Dutch scholars Etsko Kruisinga and Henrik Poutsma, the Dane Otto Jespersen, and the American George O. Curme. Their publications include Kruisinga's *A Handbook of Present-Day English*, 3 vols., 5th ed. (1931); Poutsma's *A Grammar of Late Modern English*, 5 vols. (1904–29); Jespersen's *A Modern English Grammar*, 7 vols. (1909–49); and Curme's *A Grammar of the English Language*, 2 vols. (1931–35).

Unlike their predecessors, whose studies were based on a

limited sample of English sentences, the twentieth-century scholars compiled a large number of literary citations, from which they made many syntactic and other observations. To their credit, they also asked many questions, probed into various areas that were uncertain or unexplored, and offered new terminology. Their works are accurate within the limitations of their grammatical framework, and are quite thorough in matters of detail. Nevertheless, despite rather wide differences in their interpretation of data, the scholars were basically conservative and basically dependent on the Greco-Roman model of description. Their definitions and classifications also show a heavy dependence on either function or meaning or both. The main criticism against them is that their works lack the foundation of an adequate theory of grammar, and that they fail to outline the principles upon which English sentences are organized. For these reasons, and because their works contain a mass of often unrelated details, their analyses are considered highly inefficient as descriptions of the grammar of English. Also, the scholars confined their analyses largely to written English and essentially neglected the analysis of the spoken forms of English.

At present, many Greco-Roman English prescriptive grammars, which are actually handbooks of English rather than grammars, continue to be published and continue to be used in schools. Such works are little more than repetitious echoes of those of the preceding century. Historically, their nomenclature and classifications date back to Thrax and Donatus. Their prescriptive rules date from the eighteenth century. From that time to the present, such authoritarian rules have found favor with lower social-economic groups seeking a quick guide to linguistic propriety.

As an illustration of the dependence of present-day traditional grammars upon earlier ones, the following extracts may recall to the reader somewhat similar if not identical dictates from his own days in secondary school. The material is taken from *English Exercises adopted to Murray's English Grammar: Consisting of Exercises in Parsing . . . Violations of the Rules of Syntax . . . and Violations of the Rules respecting perspicuous and accurate Writing . . .* by Lindley Murray from the fourteenth English edition . . . Baltimore, 1815.

Specimen of Etymological Parsing
"A peaceful mind is virtue's reward"

A is the indefinite article. *Peaceful* is an adjective. (Repeat the degrees of comparison.) *Mind* is a common substantive of the neuter gender, the third person, in the singular number, and the nominative case. (Decline the substantive.) *Is* is an irregular verb neuter, indicative mood, present tense, and the third person singular. (Repeat the present tense, the imperfect tense, and the participle; and occasionally conjugate the verb entirely.) *Virtue's* is a common substantive, of the neuter gender, the third person, in the singular number, and the possessive case. (Decline the substantive.) *Reward* is a common substantive, of the neuter gender, the third person, in the singular number, and the nominative case.

Rule XVI

Two negatives, in English, destroy one another, or are equivalent to an affirmative: *I am resolved not to comply with the proposals, neither at present, nor at any other time.*

A fifth rule for the strength of sentences, is, to avoid concluding them with an adverb, preposition, or an inconsidereble (sic) word. *Generosity is a showy virtue, which many persons are very fond of.*

Major Weaknesses

As a description of LModE, traditional or Greco-Roman-prescriptive grammar may be criticized for these major weaknesses:

1. It fails to describe. A primary weakness of traditional grammar is the attempt to impose the categories and framework of Greco-Roman grammar onto English, which is as erroneous as attempting to squeeze English into the grammatical framework of Hottentot or Japanese. The simple truth is that a universal grammar does not exist because the grammar of each language is unique. A description of the grammar of English, therefore, is to be obtained from an analysis of the structure of English, not from a model based on the structure of some other language.

2. It attempts to prescribe. Traditional grammar sets up an artificial standard of usage by means of numerous, inflexible rules based on "logic" and Latin syntax. As we stated in Chapter One, standard English is determined from the actual practices of speakers of standard English. Standard usage cannot be prescribed by self-appointed linguistic legislators. Thus, in

matters of usage, the rules of traditional grammar frequently fail to reflect reality, or actual standard usage.

3. It analyzes writing, not speech. Traditional descriptions of English grammar fail to acknowledge that language is speech and base their analyses entirely on written or printed materials. As a result, traditional grammar does not describe the phonemic system of English nor does it provide a phonemic transcription of linguistic constructions, such as words.

4. It gives definitions usually based entirely on meaning or function, not form. For example, definitions of the parts of speech are based on meaning (a noun *is the name of* . . .) or function (a pronoun *takes the place of* . . .). Such definitions completely overlook the grammatical signals of inflected word classes. Recognition of the latter would permit a LModE noun to be more accurately described as, say, 'a word that patterns as *man, man's men, men's* /mǽn mǽnz mɛ́n mɛ́nz/.'

5. It employs overlapping categories. For example, *stone* in *stone wall* is said to be a noun used as an adjective.

6. It is not explicit. For example, different grammatical structures are diagrammed as being grammatically identical in structure. In traditional grammar, the constructions *Often he danced* and *He danced often* both = *He/danced* ← *often*. In reality, however, the structures are different. *Often he danced* = *Often* → *he danced* and *He danced often* = *He danced* ← *often*.

7. It fails to show the actual working processes of the language. Traditional grammar does not describe the ordered procedures by which one sentence may be transformed into other sentences. For example, it does not show how *Mary ate the pie* may be transformed into *The pie was eaten by Mary* or *Did Mary eat the pie?*

8. It is a limited or bound grammar. Traditional grammar, for example, can analyze only specific sentences. It cannot generate sentences.

Structural Grammar

The grammatical description that one offers of a language or a period of a language depends upon the theory of grammar that one adopts for the analysis of that language or period of a language. One theory of grammar is the traditional or Greco-Roman model we have discussed.

In the present century some analysts have reacted against the inadequacies of traditional grammar and have formulated new theories of grammar in order to provide more efficient descriptions of the structure of English. One of these new theories is the theory of descriptive or structural grammar, also called IC (immediate constituent) grammar. We employed IC analysis, you will recall, in our description of historical English morphology.

IC grammar has been in the process of formulation for several decades. Although the pioneer work of Edward Sapir, Franz Boas, and others is recognized,[22] it is generally held that structural or IC analysis attained recognition in America with the publication in 1933 of Leonard Bloomfield's *Language,* a synthesis of American linguistics up to that time.[23] A later and more complete synthesis of American linguistic methodology was set forth by Zellig S. Harris in *Methods in Structural Linguistics* (1951).

Some descriptions of the structure of American English based on the theory of structural or IC grammar are given in such works as *An Outline of English Structure* (1951) by George L. Trager and Henry L. Smith, Jr., and in various texts by Paul Roberts, such as *Patterns of English* (1956). Additional publications are *American English in Its Cultural Setting* by Donald J. Lloyd and Harry R. Warfel (1956); *The Structure of American English* (1958) by W. Nelson Francis; Archibald A. Hill's *An Introduction to Linguistic Structures: From Sound to Sentence in English* (1958); James Sledd's *A Short Introduction to English Grammar* (1959); and Eugene A. Nida's *A Synopsis of English Syntax* (1960). A more extensive list would be outside the scope of this book.

Structural grammars of American English, such as those cited above, provide a relatively accurate and detailed description of the structure of American English phonology and morphology. They are less successful with respect to syntax, because of certain descriptive limitations inherent in the theory of IC analysis, but we shall not enter into the details of those limitations here.

Transformational Grammar

Attempts to overcome the deficiencies of structural or IC grammar in describing the syntax of American English have resulted in various new analytic procedures and theories of grammar, one of which is called tagmemic or slot-filler grammar.[24] Another is the theory of generative-transformational grammar, initially outlined in Noam Chomsky's *Syntactic Structures* (1957).[25]

At the present time, generative-transformational grammar, often called simply transformational grammar, is undergoing intensive investigation in America.[26] Its popularity may be attributed to the fact that the theory of generative-transformational grammar has certain merits over IC grammar in the analysis of American English syntax. For one thing, transformational grammar gives more explicit, more clearly stated descriptions than does IC grammar. Furthermore, transformational grammar can do things that IC grammar cannot, such as generate sentences and show how one sentence may be transformed into other sentences. As a result, transformational grammar provides a better and more efficient description of syntax.

More works may be expected in the future, but to date only a few partial descriptions of American English based on the theory of transformational grammar have been published. They include *The Grammar of English Nominalizations* (1960) by Robert B. Lees; *English Syntax* (1964) by Paul Roberts; and Syrell Rogovin's *Modern English Sentence Structure* (1964). Noam Chomsky's *Aspects of the Theory of Syntax* (1965) deals with a reformulation of the theory of generative-transformational grammar.[27]

In succeeding chapters of this book we shall employ the theory of generative-transformational grammar to describe briefly OE and LModE (AmE) syntax.

SUMMARY

Greek grammars, such as those of Thrax and Dyscolus, served as models of description for later Latin grammatical works, such as those of Donatus and Priscian. In England there was an ancient tradition of Latin grammar studies extended from the OE period to Lily's Latin *Grammar*. Beginning in the sixteenth century, there was a direct superimposition of a Greco-Roman grammatical framework onto English by writers of the first English grammars. In the eighteenth century there was a growth of strong pseudo-scientific influences that sought to codify and purify English usage through prescriptive rules. Greco-Roman English grammar reached its zenith in the early-twentieth century. In the middle of the twentieth century IC (immediate constituent) and transformational descriptions of American English, based on new theories of grammar, emerged.

NOTES

[1] Information about Greek and Latin grammarians is taken from John E. Sandys, *A History of Classical Scholarship*, 1 (New York, 1964), *passim*, and R. H. Robins, *Ancient & Mediaeval Grammatical Theory in Europe* (London, 1951), *passim*.

[2] All extracts from Thrax are taken from "The Grammar of Dionysios Thrax," trans. Thomas Davidson, *Journal of Speculative Philosophy*, VIII (1874), 326–339.

[3] *Scholarship*, p. 319.

[4] *Scholarship*, p. 321.

[5] Karl W. Dykema, "Where Our Grammar Came From," *College English*, 22 (April, 1961), 460.

[6] After elementary studies (*credo, paternoster*, letters of the Latin alphabet, *Psalter*, elementary reading and writing), the student went on to study the seven liberal arts, divided into the *trivium* (Latin grammar, logic, rhetoric) and *quadrivium* (arithmetic, geometry, astronomy, music.).

[7] See J. Zupitza, *Aelfrics Grammatik und Glossar* (Berlin, 1880).

[8] George K. Anderson, *The Literature of the Anglo-Saxons* (Princeton, 1949), p. 314.

[9] For an account of school studies in Shakespeare's day, see T. W. Baldwin, *William Shakespeare's Small Latine & Lesse Greeke* (Urbana, 1944), I, 94–98; II, 690–701.

[10] All extracts from Lily are taken from William Lily, *A Short Introdvction of Grammar*, ed. Vincent J. Flynn (New York: Scholars' Facsimiles & Reprints, 1945).

[11] Later, Joshua Poole, preface, *The English Accidence: or, a short, plaine and easie way, for the more speedy attaining to the Latine tongue, by the helpe of the English*, edition of 1655, stated: "My drift and scope . . . is, to have a

child, so well verst in his Mothers toungue, before he meddle with Latine, that . . . he shall know from his English both what part of Speech every word is, And what Syntaxis . . . it should have in Latine, though in the mean time he never heard of one Latine word." See Richard F. Jones, *The Triumph of the English Language* (Stanford, 1953), p. 280.

[12] Usually but erroneously called *Bref Grammar for English.* See R. C. Alston, *English Grammars Written in English* (Leeds, 1965), p. 2.

[13] Ben Jonson, *The English Grammar* (1640), ed. C. H. Herford, Percy and Evelyn Simpson (Oxford, 1954), viii, 505, combined the morphological classifications of both Thrax and Dyscolus: "In our *English* speech, we number the same parts with the *Latines. Noune. Pronoune. Verbe. Participle. Adverbe. Conjunction. Præposition. Interjection.* Only, we add a ninth, which is the *Article*: And that is two-fold, *Finite.* as *The. Infinite.* as *A.*"

[14] Roger Ascham, *The Scholemaster* (1570), ed. Edward Arber (Boston, 1898), p. 275, said:

But yet, bicause the prouidence of God hath left vnto vs in no other tong, saue onelie in the Greke and Latin tong, the trew preceptes, and perfite examples of eloquence, therefore must we seeke in the Authors onelie of those two tonges, the trewe Paterne of Eloquence, if in any other mother tonge we looke to attaine, either to perfit vtterance of it our selues, or skilfull iudgement of it in others.

[15] *The Doctrine of Correctness in English Usage, 1700–1800,* Univ. of Wisconsin Studies in Lang. and Lit., 25 (Madison, 1929), p. 14.

[16] Joseph Priestly, *The Rudiments of English Grammar,* 2nd ed. (1771), preface and *passim,* advocated usage as the "norm of speech." A similar view was expressed by George Campbell, *The Philosophy of Rhetoric* (1776), ed. Lloyd F. Bitzer (Carbondale, 1963), pp. 141–145.

[17] The belief in the salutary character of grammar was not new. For example, Charls Butler, *English Grammar* (Oxford, 1633), p. 1, said: "Grammar is the Art of writing and Speaking wel." Jonson, *Grammar* (1640), Herford and Simpson, viii, 467, said: "*Grammar* is the art of true, and well speaking a Language: the writing is but an Accident." Also, Lily, Latin *Grammar* (London, 1567), fol. 2v, said: "*Grammatica est recte scribendi atque loquendi ars*" or, 'Grammar is the art of right writing and speaking.'

[18] See Joan Platt, "The Development of English Colloquial Idiom During the Eighteenth Century," *Review of English Studies,* II (1926), 72–73, 196; Albert C. Baugh, *A History of the English Language* (New York, 1957), pp. 335–340; Charles C. Fries, *American English Grammar* (New York, 1940), pp. 15, 20–23.

[19] Charles Carpenter, *History of American Schoolbooks* (Philadelphia, 1963), p. 16.

[20] See Rollo L. Lyman, *English Grammar in the American Schools Before 1850,* U. S. Bureau of Education Bulletin No. 12 (Washington: Government Printing Office), 1921.

[21] Carpenter, *History,* p. 97.

[22] See Edward Sapir's *Language* (New York, 1921).

[23] For an account of the development of linguistics from ancient times to the nineteenth and twentieth centuries, see John T. Waterman, *Perspectives in Linguistics* (Chicago, 1963).

[24] See Kenneth L. Pike, *Language in Relation to a Unified Theory of the Structure of Human Behavior* (Glendale, Calif.) Part I (1954); Part II (1955); Part III (1960).

[25] Between IC analysis and transformational analysis there is another sort called string analysis. See, for example, Zellig S. Harris, *String Analysis of Sentence Structure* (The Hague, 1962). In addition, there is the theory of stratificational grammar as advocated by Sydney M. Lamb and also by Henry A. Gleason, Jr.

[26] Transformational grammar developed in part from attempts to analyze language samples larger than the sentence. See, for example, Zellig S. Harris, "Discourse Analysis," *Language*, 28 (1952), 18–23, and "Discourse Analysis: A Sample Text," *Language*, (1952), 474–498. See also Harris, "Co-occurrence and Transformation in Linguistic Structure," *Language*, 33 (1957), 283–340.

[27] In addition to the linguistic movements and scholars cited in the text and footnotes of this chapter, the following also may be noted:

1. The rationalist movement — based on R. Descartes' assertion of human reason — reflected in the "universal" or "general" grammar of the 17th-cent. French Port Royal grammarians, whose influence continued in various 18th cent. *grammaires raisonnées* and is reflected also in the 20th-cent. work of the transformationalists (cf. Chomsky's *Cartesian Linguistics*: New York, 1966).

2. Historical scholars — including advocates of the neogrammarian or *Junggrammatiker* doctrine — such as F. Bopp, M. Bréal, K. Brugmann, C. D. Buck, W. Carey, S. Feist, J. Fourquet, E. Hermann, W. von Humboldt, Sir W. Jones, G. W. Leibnitz, A. Leskien, A. Martinet, A. Meillet, W. Meyer Lübke, M. Müller, H. Osthoff, H. Paul, S. Pop, J. J. and J. C. Scaliger, A. Schleicher, E. Sievers, E. H. Sturtevant, H. Sweet, F. and A. W. von Schlegel, W. D. Whitney, C. Wilkins, J. Wright, and others.

3. The "Copernicus" of modern linguistics, Ferdinand de Saussure, a Swiss; L. Hjelmslev and others of the Danish glossematics school; Prince N. S. Trubetzkoy and others of the Prague school, including R. Jakobson; British linguists as Daniel Jones, J. R. Firth, and neo-Firthians as M. A. K. Halliday, A. McIntosh, and P. D. Strevens; many Americans as H. B. Allen, E. B. Atwood, E. Bach, B. Bloch, D. L. Bolinger, J. B. Carroll, F. G. Cassidy, C. C. Fries, J. Fodor, P. Garvin, I. J. Gelb, J. H. Greenberg, R. A. Hall, Jr., M. Halle, E. Haugen, C. F. Hockett, H. Hoenigswald, H. Hoijer, F. W. Householder, Jr., D. H. Hymes, M. A. Joos, J. J. Katz, J. S. Kenyon, S. M. Kuhn, H. Kurath, W. P. Lehmann, R. E. Longacre, A. H. Marckwardt, R. W. McDavid, Jr., S. B. Meech, S. Moore, W. G. Moulton, D. L. Olmsted, P. M. Postal, E. Pulgram, T. Pyles, C. Reed, R. P. Stockwell, M. Swadesh, C. K. Thomas, W. F. Twaddell, C. F. Voeglin, R. S. Wells, H. Whitehall, B. F. Whorf, and many others.

Old English Syntax: I

As we turn to a description of the historical syntax of English, we find ourselves faced with certain restrictions. The limitations of space in this book prevent us from examining the historical syntax of each period of English; thus our descriptions of historical syntax must be brief. We shall therefore examine some features of OE syntax in this chapter and some additional features in the next. In a following chapter we shall look at some similarities and differences between the syntax of OE and LModE, after which we shall conclude with a chapter describing some features of LModE syntax, specifically that of AmE.

The Sentence

From the various methods by which it is possible to describe the syntax of OE, we choose the theory of generative-transformational grammar.

Our unit of analysis shall be the sentence. Thus, we turn from a "word grammar," as in our description of English morphology, to a "sentence grammar," as in this chapter.

A generative-transformational description of the sentence in OE consists of a series of ordered rules that predict and evaluate the grammaticality of any and all OE sentences. A listing of the rules by which any sentence is generated constitutes an analysis of the structure and items of that sentence.

Unfortunately, we cannot offer rules that will generate and predict any and all OE sentences because such rules have yet to be worked out by analysts. Even if they were available, we would not be able to include them all and explain them adequately in a few short chapters. We must therefore restrict ourselves to a small number of rules that will account for some features of OE prose non-question sentences. Our description is intended to be suggestive and illustrative of a method of description rather than a definitive treatment of all the features of OE syntax.

Form of Rules

We begin our description of OE syntax with a set of symbols related by a set of rules. All rules are of the form $A \rightarrow B$ or $C \rightarrow D+E$. These are instructions to rewrite A as B and to rewrite C as $D+E$.

The abstract symbols and abbreviated notations that appear in our rules are more or less arbitrary. Some represent classes, but others are abstractions leading to lower-level abstractions in a machine-like process. Symbols with subscripts represent subclasses.

Kinds of Rules

We shall speak of four different kinds of rules:
1. Phrase-structure or P-rules.
2. Lexical or L-rules.
3. Transformation or T-rules.
4. Morphophonemic or M-rules.

P-Rules

Phrase-structure or P-rules are rules that replace one symbol by another symbol or by a sequence of more than one symbol, as in this example:

Initial string: X

P-rule 1: $X \rightarrow Y+C$

P-rule 2: $Y \rightarrow A+B$

P-rule 3: $C \rightarrow c$

P-rule 4: $A \rightarrow a$

P-rule 5: $B \rightarrow b$

The application of P-rules to an initial string produces a derivation called a terminal string, in which the items themselves and the order of the items constitute a description of its structure.

Applying P1–5 above to X gives us the following:

$$
\begin{array}{ll}
& \text{Given: X} \\
\text{P1} & \text{Y}+\text{C} \\
\text{P2} & \text{A}+\text{B}+\text{C} \\
\text{P3} & \text{A}+\text{B}+\text{c} \\
\text{P4} & \text{a}+\text{B}+\text{c} \\
\text{P5} & \text{a}+\text{b}+\text{c}
\end{array}
$$

L-Rules

Lexical or L-rules specify lexical items, as in these few examples:

L1 a → {dog, cat, boy . . .}
L2 b → {sing, run, dance . . .}
L3 c → {green, yellow, blue . . .}

The ellipsis . . . in these examples indicates that additional items follow but have been omitted for simplicity. As we stated earlier, our illustrations are intended to be suggestive rather than detailed and complete.

T-Rules

Transformation or T-rules apply to strings at a certain stage of generation, specifically after all P-rules and L-rules have been applied.

T-rules consist of two strings (of one or more items) separated by a double arrow ⇒ . The string to the *left* of ⇒ is the string to be transformed, and the string to the *right* of ⇒ specifies the items and the order of items in the transform string, which is the product of the transformation.

T-rules, which may apply to whole strings or to parts of strings, may be optional (OPT) or obligatory (OBL). Such rules may rearrange the order of items in a string, delete items, add items, combine two strings, insert one string into another string, or do several of these things at once.

There are various ways of symbolizing items and their order in T-rules. In the two examples below, a simple form of representation is used to suggest the nature of T-rules.

Transform

T2 OPT $a+b+c \Rightarrow b+c+a+g$ (addition and rearrangement)

T9 OBL $d+e+f \Rightarrow d+f$ (deletion)

M-Rules

M-rules in a generative-transformational description relate to morphology and phonology and are called morphophonemic rules, but as we shall not enter into phonology, our M-rules are morphographemic. An elementary form of such rules is presented here to suggest their nature:

$eat+$Pres $\rightarrow$ *eats*	$eat+$Past $\rightarrow$ *ate*
talk $+$ Pres $\rightarrow$ *talks*	*talk* $+$Past $\rightarrow$ *talked*
be $+$ Pres $\rightarrow$ *is*	*be* $+$Past $\rightarrow$ *was*
$eat+$Part $\rightarrow$ *eaten*	$eat+-ing \rightarrow$ *eating*
$talk+$Part $\rightarrow$ *talked*	$talk+-ing \rightarrow$ *talking*
$be+$Part $\rightarrow$ *been*	$be+-ing \rightarrow$ *being*
man $+-$'s $\rightarrow$ *man's*	*man* $+-m \rightarrow$ *man*
he $+-$'s $\rightarrow$ *his*	$he+-m \rightarrow$ *him*
they $+-$'s $\rightarrow$ *their(s)*	*they* $+-m \rightarrow$ *them*

OE P-Rules

We begin our description of the OE sentence with the symbol S, which we shall use to represent *Sentence*. Given S, our first P-rule for OE is:

P1 $S \rightarrow NP+VP$

This may be interpreted roughly as S consists of noun phrase (NP) plus verb phrase (VP). It is an instruction to rewrite S as NP+VP. What NP and VP represent shall be described later.

At this point we should provide some means for obtaining numerical agreement between NP and VP. Actually the matter is quite complex in OE, but two recurring patterns of numerical agreement between NP and VP are (1) *NP singular+VP singular*, and (2) *NP plural+VP plural*. One way of providing such agreement is to rewrite our first P-rule so that its form is as follows, with braces to enclose and indicate a choice of alternative items:

$$P1 \; S \rightarrow \left\{ \begin{array}{l} NP_{sg}+VP_{sg} \\ NP_{pl}+VP_{pl} \end{array} \right\}$$

Another way of providing numerical agreement is to introduce Number (No) in P1 this way:

$$P1 \; S \rightarrow (No+NP)+(No+VP)$$

In a lower-level P-rule, we can then allow a choice for No of *sg* or *pl*, as in P9 $No \rightarrow \left\{ \begin{array}{l} sg \\ pl \end{array} \right\}$

There are more efficient ways than the ones we have illustrated to provide agreement of number between NP and VP. But, to employ any one method here would require the introduction of complexities beyond the scope of this elementary description. Instead, we shall assume the convenient fiction that our rules will automatically provide the agreement of number, as well as the agreement of case, gender, etc., required in our sample OE sentences.

We now proceed from our original P-rule P1 $(S \rightarrow NP+VP)$ to our next P-rule, P2. It is one that must begin either $NP \rightarrow$ or $VP \rightarrow$.

Let us first look at some elementary rules for NPs.

OE NPs

Some possibilities for NP in OE are these:

NP may be a pronoun (Pro). We write this $NP \rightarrow Pro$.

NP may be a proper noun (N-prop). A determiner (Det) may precede N-prop. What Det represents will be explained later. Because Det is optional before N-prop, we enclose Det in parentheses and write $NP \rightarrow (Det+)$ N-prop.

A third possibility for NP is $(Det+) \; N_1$. N_1, as in the case of Det, will be explained later.

In summary, the alternatives we have listed for NP are:

$$NP \rightarrow Pro$$
$$NP \rightarrow (Det+) \text{ N-prop}$$
$$NP \rightarrow (Det+) \; N_1$$

One additional qualification is this: to N-prop we add X. In this chapter we shall let X symbolize those grammatical features of case, gender, and number required to obtain the necessary morphological (morphographemic) forms in our sample OE NPs. In the next chapter we shall further discuss X.

For brevity, we now combine the three possibilities for NP into one rule (P2), and we use braces to enclose and to indicate these alternatives:

$$\text{P2 NP} \rightarrow \begin{cases} \text{Pro} \\ (\text{Det}+) \ \text{N-prop}+\text{X} \\ (\text{Det}+) \ \text{N}_1 \end{cases}$$

Additional P-rules for items of NP are these:

$$\text{P3 Det} \rightarrow \begin{cases} \text{NP} \\ \text{Nu} \end{cases}$$

Nu: numeral

$$\text{P4 N}_1 \rightarrow \begin{cases} \text{AP}+\text{N}_1 \\ \text{N-c}+\text{X} \end{cases}$$

AP: adjective phrase
N-c: noun-count[1]

$$\text{P5 AP} \rightarrow \begin{cases} \text{Adj} \\ \text{Int}+\text{Adj} \end{cases}$$

Adj: adjective
Int: intensifier[2]

$$\text{P6 Pro} \rightarrow \begin{cases} \text{Pers}+\text{X} \\ \text{Dem}+\text{X} \\ \text{Inter}+\text{X} \end{cases}$$

Pers: personal
Dem: demonstrative
Inter: interrogative

$$\text{P7 Adj} \rightarrow \begin{cases} \text{Adj-pos} \\ \text{Adj-comp} \\ \text{Adj-super} \end{cases} + \begin{cases} \text{Sn} \\ \text{W} \end{cases} + \text{X}$$

Adj-pos: adj. stem-positive
Adj-comp: adj. stem comparative
Adj-super: adj. stem-superlative
Sn: strong paradigm adj.
W: weak paradigm adj.
X: (number) (+gender)+case

L-Rules for NPs

We add here some unnumbered L-rules for items in OE NPs, although L-rules properly follow all P-rules, including those we shall add later in this and in the next chapter.

L N-prop → {*ecgbryht* 'Egbert,' *æþelwulf* 'Athelwulf,' *ælfred* 'Alfred' . . .}

L Nu → {*i* 'one,' *ii* 'two,' *iii* 'three' . . .}

L N–c → {*cyning* 'king,' *ġēar* 'year,' *þeġen* 'thane' . . .}

L Int → {*fela* 'much, many,' *full* 'very,' *tō* 'too' . . .}

L Pers → {*iċ* 'I,' *þū* 'thou,' *hē* 'he' . . .}

L Dem → {*sē*, *þæt*, *sēo* 'the, that'; *þes*, *þis*, *þēos* 'this' . . .}

L Inter → {*hwā* 'who,' *hwæt* 'what'}

L Adj-pos → {*gōd–* 'good,' *ilca–* 'same,' *denisċ–* 'Danish' . . .}

L Adj-comp → {*betr–* 'better,' *heardr–* 'harder,' *lengr–* 'longer' . . .}

L Adj-super → {*heardost–* 'hardest,' *betst–* 'best,' *lengest–* 'longest' . . .}

M-Rules for NPs

Our unnumbered M-rules for items of NP are cast in a simple form. We shall later revise them, but for the moment we shall assume that an adjective stem, noun, or pronoun plus X will give us the proper (number) (+gender)+case to obtain the grammatical forms we need in our sample OE NPs. A few examples of such simplified M-rules follow:

$$M \; gōd\text{–}+X → gōde$$
$$M \; sē+X → þæm$$
$$M \; mann+X → menn$$

NP Examples

P-, L-, and M-rules for OE NPs are illustrated in the following examples.

I: *hine* 'him'

Given: S

P1 S → NP+VP	NP+VP
P2 NP → Pro	Pro
P6 Pro → Pers+X	Pers+X
L Pers → *hē* 'he'	*hē*+X
M *hē*+X → *hine*	*hine*

II: *þȳ ilcan ġēare* 'that same year'

Given: S

P1 S → NP+VP	NP+VP
P2 NP → Det+N₁	Det+N₁
P3 Det → NP	NP+N₁
P2 NP → Pro	Pro+N₁
P4 N₁ → AP+N₁	Pro+AP+N₁
P4 N₁ → N–c+X	Pro+AP+N–c+X
P5 AP → Adj	Pro+Adj+N–c+X
P6 Pro → Dem+X	Dem+X+Adj+N–c+X
P7 Adj → Adj-pos+W+X	Dem+X+Adj-pos+W+ X+N–c+X
L Dem → *sē* 'that'	*sē*+X+Adj-pos+W+X+ N–c+X
L Adj-pos → *ilca-* 'same'	*sē*+X+*ilca-*+W+X+ N–c+X
L N–c → *ġēar* 'year'	*sē*+X+*ilca-*+W+X+ *ġēar*+X
M *sē*+X → *þȳ*	*þȳ*+*ilca-*+W+X+*ġēar*+X
M *ilca-*+W+X → *ilcan*	*þȳ*+*ilcan*+*ġēar*+X
M *ġēar*+X → *ġēare*	*þȳ*+*ilcan*+*ġēare*

III: *fela gōde menn* 'many good men'

Given: S

P1 S → NP+VP	NP+VP
P2 NP → N₁	N₁
P4 N₁ → AP+N₁	AP+N₁
P4 N₁ → N–c+X	AP+N–c+X
P5 AP → Int+Adj	Int+Adj+N–c+X
P7 Adj → Adj-pos+Sn+X	Int+Adj-pos+Sn+X+ N–c+X
L Int → *fela* 'many'	*fela*+Adj-pos+Sn+X+ N–c+X
L Adj-pos → *gōd-* 'good'	*fela*+*gōd-*+Sn+X+N–c+X
L N–c → *mann* 'man'	*fela*+*gōd-*+Sn+X+ *mann*+X
M *gōd-*+Sn+X → *gōde*	*fela*+*gōde*+*mann*+X
M *mann*+X → *menn*	*fela*+*gōde*+*menn*

Recursion

An important feature contained in our P-rules for OE NPs is recursion, which means 'to run back, return.' Recursion occurs in strings in which the same item appears on both sides of the arrow, as the first option in P4: $N_1 \rightarrow AP + N_1$. For example, study the following derivation of NP:

	Given: S
P1 $S \rightarrow NP + VP$	$NP + VP$
P2 $NP \rightarrow N_1$	N_1
P4 $N_1 \rightarrow AP + N_1$	$AP + N_1$

At this point we must make another choice for N_1, and we may again choose

P4 $N_1 \rightarrow AP + N_1$ $\qquad AP + AP + N_1$

It is possible for us to "reloop" again by electing $N_1 \rightarrow AP + N_1$, but this time we choose the second option in P4, as below.[3]

P4 $N_1 \rightarrow N-c + X$ $\qquad AP + AP + N-c + X$

Having chosen $N_1 \rightarrow N-c + X$, we cannot further "reloop" because we no longer have N_1 in the string.

Such recursion or "relooping," as illustrated above, permits us to increase the variety and length of sentences that may be generated. In a given language, however, recursion cannot ordinarily be reapplied without limit because otherwise relooping would continue to infinity. Thus, if this were a detailed description of OE, it would contain a statement of the permissible limit of recursion for N_1. If the limit were, for instance, four permissible recursions, there would be a statement to the effect that after the maximum four recursions the choice $N_1 \rightarrow N-c + X$ would be obligatory on the fifth reloop, thus ending the recursion.

More About Recursion

Options contained in P-rules 3 and 2 also permit a form of recursion, but only through the reapplication of those two P-rules. As such, the recursive element entails a two-rule reloop, not a one-rule reloop as in P4. Note the reapplication of P3 and P2 in the following example:

Given: S

P1 S → NP+VP	NP+VP
P2 NP → Det+N₁	Det+N₁
P3 Det → NP	NP+N₁

Through the option Det → NP, there is a reintroduction of NP into the string. We now reloop to P2 to elect an option for NP. Let us choose, for example,

P2 NP → Pro	Pro+N₁

or

P2 NP → Det+N₁	Det+N₁+N₁

after which we may expand further to the permissible limit by again electing

P3 Det → NP	NP+N₁+N₁

Desirability of T-Rules

It is convenient at this point, before we examine OE VPs, to demonstrate the limitations of P-rules in general and the desirability of formulating T-rules to effect, for example, a different order of items in a string.

For example, suppose that we wanted to generate the NP string N-prop+X+Pers+X+N–c+X, specifically *ælfred his brōþor* 'Alfred his brother.' The steps, according to our P-rules, would be as follows:

Given: S

P1 S → NP+VP	NP+VP
P2 NP → Det+N-prop+X	Det+N-prop+X
P3 Det → NP	NP+N-prop+X
P2 NP → Det+N₁	Det+N₁+N-prop+X
P3 Det → NP	NP+N₁+N-prop+X
P2 NP → Pro	Pro+N₁+N-prop+X
P4 N₁ → N–c+X	Pro+N–c+X+N-prop+X
P6 Pro → Pers+X	Pers+X+N–c+X+ N-prop+X
L Pers → *hē* 'he'	*hē*+X+N–c+X+ N-prop+X
L N–c → *brōþor* 'brother'	*hē*+X+*brōþor*+X+ N-prop+X
L N-prop → *ælfred* 'Alfred'	*hē*+X+*brōþor*+X+ *ælfred*+X

Examination of this string shows that the order of items is not N-prop+X+Pers+X+N–c+X as needed for our sample NP, but our P-rules and L-rules can take us no further. To obtain the desired order, we formulate and apply a transformation or T-rule, such as T2 OPT, which "preposes" N-prop+X to the front of the string, as below:

T2 OPT: Pers+X+N–c+X+N-prop+X ⇒ N-prop+X+Pers+X+N–c+X

T2 $h\bar{e}$+X+$br\bar{o}\text{þor}$+X+$\text{æ}lfred$+X ⇒ $\text{æ}lfred$+X+$h\bar{e}$+X+$br\bar{o}\text{þor}$+X

M $\text{æ}lfred$+X → $\text{æ}lfred$ $\text{æ}lfred$+$h\bar{e}$+X+$br\bar{o}\text{þor}$+X

M $h\bar{e}$+X → his $\text{æ}lfred$+his+$br\bar{o}\text{þor}$+X

M $br\bar{o}\text{þor}$+X → $br\bar{o}\text{þor}$ $\text{æ}lfred$+his+$br\bar{o}\text{þor}$

As this example illustrates, the advantages of T-rules are greater than those of P-rules. T-rules not only permit that which P-rules do not, but they add immeasurably to the explicitness, efficiency, and integrated apparatus of a generative description.

We shall examine OE NPs again in the next chapter. We turn here to some P-rules for OE VPs.

P-Rules for VPs

VP must have tense (Present or Past) plus a verbal element, which we label V_4. Our first P-rule (P9) for OE VP, therefore, is:[4]

$$P9 \; VP \rightarrow \begin{Bmatrix} Pres+V_4 \\ Past+V_4 \end{Bmatrix}$$

For V_4 our next rule allows a choice of V_3 or a choice of modal (Mod) plus V_3. Two OE modals, for example, are $\dot{s}culan$ 'shall, must, ought to' and $willan$ 'be willing, wish.' To Mod we add optional (Y), which in this chapter symbolizes those grammatical features of mood, person, and number required to obtain the grammatical forms needed in our OE VPs.

$$P10 \; V_4 \rightarrow \begin{Bmatrix} V_3 \\ Mod \; (+Y)+V_3 \end{Bmatrix}$$

For V_3, rule P11 offers the alternatives V_2 or the past participle of V_2 preceded by $habban$ 'to have' plus Y. For past participle we write Part, which may be interpreted as 'whatever is done to make V_2 a past participle.'

$$P11 \ V_3 \rightarrow \left\{ \begin{array}{l} V_2 \\ habban + Y + Part + V_2 \end{array} \right\}$$

For V_2, our next rule P12 allows a choice of V_1 or present participle of V_1 preceded by *bēon* 'to be.' For present participle we write OE *–ende*, which may be interpreted as 'whatever is done to make V_1 a present participle.'

$$P12 \ V_2 \rightarrow \left\{ \begin{array}{l} V_1 \\ b\bar{e}on + -ende + V_1 \end{array} \right\}$$

Finally, the possibilities for V_1 must include $(+Y)$ and at least verb-intransitive (V-i), NP plus verb-transitive (V-t), verb-*bēon* (V-b) plus NP or AP, and NP plus verb-*habban* (V-h), as follows:

$$P13 \ V_1 \rightarrow \left[\begin{array}{l} \text{V-i } (+Y) \\ \text{NP} + \text{V-t } (+Y) \\ \text{V-b } (+Y) + \left\{ \begin{array}{l} \text{NP} \\ \text{AP} \end{array} \right\} \\ \text{NP} + \text{V-h } (+Y) \end{array} \right]$$

L-Rules for VPs

These are the L-rules to account for items in OE VPs:

L Mod → {*sculan* 'shall, must, ought to,' *willan* 'be willing, wish,' *magan* 'be able, may, can,' *mōtan* 'be permitted, compelled, must' . . .}

L V–i → {*cuman* 'to come,' *rinnan* 'to run,' *swimman* 'to swim' . . .}

L V t → {*findan* 'to find,' *niman* 'to take, win,' *onginnan* 'to begin,' (*ge*)*lystan* 'to desire, please' . . .}

L V–b → {*bēon, wesan* 'to be,' *weorðan* 'to be, become' . . .}

L V–h → {*habban* 'to have,' *āgan* 'to have, own' . . .}

M-Rules for VPs

In our M-rules for items of VP, we shall assume that a verb plus tense plus Y will give us the proper mood, person, and number that we need to obtain the grammatical forms required in our OE VPs. Three examples of such M-rules are these:

M *cuman*+Past+Y → *cuōm*
M *bēon*+Pres+Y → *eom*
M *willan*+Past+Y → *wolde*

VP Examples

P-rules for OE VPs are illustrated in the following examples.

I: *cuōm* 'came'

Given: S

P1 S → NP+VP	NP+VP
P9 VP → Past+V_4	Past+V_4
P10 V_4 → V_3	Past+V_3
P11 V_3 → V_2	Past+V_2
P12 V_2 → V_1	Past+V_1
P13 V_1 → V–i+Y	Past+V–i+Y
L V–i → *cuman* 'to come'	Past+*cuman*+Y

At this point we must pause to explain that in order to obtain the final string we need, it is necessary to introduce and apply and obligatory T-rule, which we label T-fix.

T-Fix

In P-rules, it is necessary to write the affixes we symbolized as tense, Part, and *–ende* before verbs to avoid various technical complications that we shall not discuss here. After all P-rules, L-rules, and all other T-rules have been applied, however, the affixes we have labeled tense, Part, and *–ende* must be put in their proper place at the end of a verb. To achieve that order, we must have T-fix OBL, the application of which produces a T-terminal string.

T-fix OBL: Fix+V+Y ⟹ V+Fix+Y. Remember that Fix is any tense, Part, or *–ende*. V is any modal, *habban*, *bēon*, or verb.

We now apply T-fix OBL to the string Past+*cuman*+Y as follows:

T-fix OBL: Past+*cuman*+Y ⟹ *cuman*+Past+Y

M *cuman*+Past+Y → *cuōm*   *cuōm*

Additional examples illustrating the application of P-rules to VP are these:

II: *wolde drīfan* 'wanted to drive'

Given: S

P1 S → NP+VP	NP+VP
P9 VP → Past+V₄	Past+V₄
P10 V₄ → Mod+Y+V₃	Past+Mod+Y+V₃
P11 V₃ → V₂	Past+Mod+Y+V₂
P12 V₂ → V₁	Past+Mod+Y+V₁
P13 V₁ → V–i	Past+Mod+Y+V–i
L Mod → *willan* 'to wish'	Past+*willan*+Y+V–i
L V–i → *drīfan* 'to drive'	Past+*willan*+Y+*drīfan*
T-fix OBL ⇒	*willan*+Past+Y+*drīfan*
M *willan*+Past+Y → *wolde*	*wolde*+*drīfan*

III: *sige nōm* 'victory won'

Given: S

P1 S → NP+VP	NP+VP
P9 VP → Past+V₄	Past+V₄
P10 V₄ → V₃	Past+V₃
P11 V₃ → V₂	Past+V₂
P12 V₂ → V₁	Past+V₁
P13 V₁ → NP+V–t+Y	Past+NP+V–t+Y
P2 NP → N₁	Past+N₁+V–t+Y
P4 N₁ → N–c+X	Past+N–c+X+V–t+Y
L N–c → *sige* 'victory'	Past+*sige*+X+V–t+Y
L V–t → *niman* 'to take, win'	Past+*sige*+X+*niman*+Y

We now introduce a T-rule, which we arbitrarily label T3 optional.

T3 OPT: Tense+Z+V ⇒ Z+Tense+V. In the preceding, Z symbolizes any items between Tense and V. We now apply T3 OPT, as follows:

T3 OPT ⇒	*sige*+X+Past+*niman*+Y
T-fix OBL ⇒	*sige*+X+*niman*+Past+Y
M *sige*+X → *sige*	*sige*+*niman*+Past+Y
M *niman*+Past+Y → *nōm*	*sige*+*nōm*

IV: *winnende wǣron* 'fighting were'

Given: S

P1 S → NP+VP	NP+VP
P9 VP → Past+V₄	Past+V₄
P10 V₄ → V₃	Past+V₃
P11 V₃ → V₂	Past+V₂
P12 V₂ → *bēon*+*-ende*+V₁	Past+*bēon*+*-ende*+V₁
P13 V₁ → V–i+Y	Past+*bēon*+*-ende*+V–i+Y
L V–i → *winnan* 'to fight'	Past+*bēon*+*-ende*+*winnan*+Y

To obtain the desired order of elements in the final string, we must introduce another T-rule, say T4 OPT, as follows:

T4 OPT: Tense + *bēon* + *-ende* + V–i + Y ⇒ *-ende* + V–i + Tense+*bēon*+Y

T4 OPT ⇒	*-ende*+*winnan*+Past+*bēon*+Y
T-fix OBL ⇒	*winnan*+*-ende*+*bēon*+Past+Y
M *winnan*+*-ende* → *winnende*	*winnende*+*bēon*+Past+Y
M *bēon*+Past+Y → *wǣron*	*winnende*+*wǣron*

V: *ġewicod hæfdon* 'encamped had'

Given: S

P1 S → NP+VP	NP+VP
P9 VP → Past+V₄	Past+V₄
P10 V₄ → V₃	Past+V₃
P11 V₃ → *habban*+Y+Part+V₂	Past+*habban*+Y+Part+V₂
P12 V₂ → V₁	Past+*habban*+Y+Part+V₁
P13 V₁ → V–i	Past+*habban*+Y+Part+V–i
L V–i → *wician* 'to encamp'	Past+*habban*+Y+Part+*wician*

Again we introduce another T-rule: T5 OPT, as below:

T5 OPT: Tense + *habban* + Y + Part + V–i ⇒ Part + V–i + Tense+*habban*+Y

T5 OPT ⇒	Part+*wician*+Past+*habban*+Y
T-fix OBL ⇒	*wician*+Part+*habban*+Past+Y
M *wician*+Part → *ġewicod*	*ġewicod*+*habban*+Past+Y
M *habban*+Past+Y → *hæfdon*	*ġewicod*+*hæfdon*

SUMMARY

P-rule	P: phrase structure
L-rule	L: lexical
M-rule	M: morphographemic
T-rule	T: transformation

P-, L-, and M-rules have →, but T-rules have ⇒

T OPT	OPT: optional
T OBL	OBL: obligatory

P1 S → NP+VP

P2 NP → $\begin{cases} \text{Pro} \\ (\text{Det}+)\ \text{N-prop}+X \\ (\text{Det}+)\ N_1 \end{cases}$
    Pro: pronoun
    N-prop: noun-proper
    Det: determiner

P3 Det→ $\begin{cases} \text{NP} \\ \text{Nu} \end{cases}$
    X: (number) (+gender) +case
    Nu: numeral

P4 N_1 → $\begin{cases} AP+N_1 \\ \text{N-c}+X \end{cases}$
    AP: adjective phrase
    N-c: noun-count

P5 AP → $\begin{cases} \text{Adj} \\ \text{Int}+\text{Adj} \end{cases}$
    Int: intensifier
    Adj: adjective

P6 Pro → $\begin{cases} \text{Pers}+X \\ \text{Dem}+X \\ \text{Inter} \mid X \end{cases}$
    Pers: personal
    Dem: demonstrative
    Inter: interrogative

P7 Adj→ $\begin{cases} \text{Adj-pos} \\ \text{Adj-comp} \\ \text{Adj-super} \end{cases} + \begin{cases} \text{Sn} \\ \text{W} \end{cases} +X$

Adj-pos: adj. stem-positive
Adj-comp: adj. stem-comparative
Adj-super: adj. stem-superlative
Sn: strong paradigm adj.
W: weak paradigm adj.

P9 VP → $\begin{cases} \text{Pres}+V_4 \\ \text{Past}+V_4 \end{cases}$
    Pres: present tense
    Past: past tense

P10 V_4 → $\begin{cases} V_3 \\ \text{Mod}\ (+Y)+V_3 \end{cases}$
    Mod: modal
    Y: (mood) (+person) (+number)

P11 V_3 → $\begin{cases} V_2 \\ habban+Y+\text{Part}+V_2 \end{cases}$
    Part: past participle

P12 $V_2 \rightarrow$ $\begin{cases} V_1 \\ b\bar{e}on+-ende+V_1 \end{cases}$ *-ende*: present participle

P13 $V_1 \rightarrow$ $\begin{bmatrix} \text{V-i } (+Y) \\ \text{NP}+\text{V-t } (+Y) \\ \text{V-b } (+Y)+\begin{cases} \text{NP} \\ \text{AP} \end{cases} \\ \text{NP}+\text{V-h } (+Y) \end{bmatrix}$

V-i: verb-intransitive
V-t: verb-transitive
V-b: verb-*bēon*
V-h: verb-*habban*

T-fix OBL: Fix$+$V$+$Y $\Rightarrow$ V$+$Fix$+$Y. Fix$=$tense, Part, or *-ende*. V$=$modal, *habban*, *bēon*, or verb.

T3 OPT: Tense$+$Z$+$V $\Rightarrow$ Z$+$Tense$+$V

T4 OPT: Tense$+bēon+-ende+$V–i$+$Y $\Rightarrow -ende+$V–i$+$Tense $+bēon+$Y

T5 OPT: Tense $+$ *habban* $+$ Y $+$ Part $+$ V–i $\Rightarrow$ Part $+$ V–i $+$ Tense$+habban+$Y

NOTES

[1] A count noun is one that refers to things which can be counted, as in LModE *one boy, two boys*, etc. In contrast, a mass or noncount noun is one that refers to that which cannot be counted, as LModE *wheat, courage, mush*. Thus, count nouns (N-c) have sg. and pl. forms. Mass nouns (N-m) have only one form that is numberless.

[2] Intensifiers, as LModE *very, rather, quite*, modify adjectives (*very tall, rather tall, quite tall*) and adverbs (*very slowly, rather slowly, quite slowly*), but not verbs (*ran very, *ran rather, *ran quite).

[3] In our brief sketch of OE syntax, AP is an item in P-rules. In a definitive grammar of OE, however, it would be preferable to handle AP on the T-rule level.

[4] Missing P-rule P8 occurs in the next chapter.

Old English Syntax: II

In the last chapter we briefly examined OE NPs and VPs; in this chapter we shall examine them both more closely, and also discuss subordination, negation, clause, adverbial, and relative. We also shall look at some additional transformations, including what are known as double-base transformations.

More About NPs

In our earlier examples of NPs, we let X symbolize number, gender, and case, so that we might obtain the necessary noun, pronoun, and adjective forms we required in our examples. We now discard X and add these revised P-rules (P2, P4, P6, P7), and one new P-rule (P8), as follows:

$$P2\ NP\ \rightarrow \left\{ \begin{array}{l} Pro \\ (Det+)\ N\text{-prop}\ (+pl)+Case \\ (Det+)\ N_1 \end{array} \right\}^1$$

$$P4\ N_1\ \rightarrow \left\{ \begin{array}{l} AP'+N_1 \\ N\text{-c}\ (+pl)+Case \end{array} \right\}$$

$$P6\ Pro\ \rightarrow \left\{ \begin{array}{l} Pers+\left\{ \begin{array}{l} dual \\ pl \end{array} \right\}+Case \\ Dem\ (+pl)+Case \\ Inter+Case \end{array} \right\}$$

$$P7\ Adj\ \rightarrow \left\{ \begin{array}{l} Adj\text{-pos} \\ Adj\text{-comp} \\ Adj\text{-super} \end{array} \right\}+\left\{ \begin{array}{l} Sn \\ W \end{array} \right\}(+pl)+\left\{ \begin{array}{l} M \\ F \\ N \end{array} \right\}+Case$$

M: masculine
F: feminine
N: neuter

P8 Case → $\begin{cases} \text{Nom} \\ \text{Acc} \\ \text{Gen} \\ \text{Dat} \\ \text{Instr} \end{cases}$

OE NPs

The following examples illustrate our new and revised P-rules for OE NPs:

I: *hine* 'him'

Given: S

P1 S → NP+VP	NP+VP
P2 NP → Pro	Pro
P6 Pro → Pers+Case	Pers+Case
P8 Case → Acc	Pers+Acc
L Pers → *hē* 'he'	*hē*+Acc
M *hē*+Acc → *hine*	*hine*

II: *þȳ ilcan ġēare* 'that same year'

Given: S

P1 S → NP+VP	NP+VP
P2 NP → Det+N₁	Det+N₁
P3 Det → NP	NP+N₁
P2 NP → Pro	Pro+N₁
P4 N₁ → AP+N₁	Pro+AP+N₁
P4 N₁ → N–c+Case	Pro+AP+N–c+Case
P5 AP → Adj	Pro+Adj+N–c+Case
P6 Pro → Dem+Case	Dem+Case+Adj+N–c+Case
P7 Adj → Adj-pos+W+ M+Case	Dem+Case+Adj-pos+W+ M+Case+N–c+Case
P8 Case → Instr	Dem+Instr+Adj-pos+W+ M+Case+N–c+Case
P8 Case → Dat	Dem+Instr+Adj-pos+W+ M+Dat+N–c+Case
P8 Case → Dat	Dem+Instr+Adj-pos+W+ M+Dat+N–c+Dat

L Dem → *sē* 'that'   *sē*+Instr+Adj-pos+W+
                       M+Dat+N–c+Dat

L Adj-pos → *ilca*- 'same'   *sē*+Instr+*ilca*-+W+M+
                             Dat+N–c+Dat

L N–c → *ġēar* 'year'   *sē*+Instr+*ilca*-+W+M+
                        Dat+*ġēar*+Dat

M *sē*+Instr → *þȳ*   *þȳ*+*ilca*-+W+M+Dat+
                      ġēar+Dat

M *ilca*-+W+M+Dat →   *þȳ*+*ilcan*+*ġēar*+Dat
  ilcan

M *ġēar*+Dat → *ġēare*   *þȳ*+*ilcan*+*ġēare*

Note: Instrumental *þȳ* appears instead of dative *þǣm* above with the datives *ilcan ġēare*.

III: *fela gōde menn* 'many good men'

Given: S

P1 S → NP+VP   NP+VP
P2 NP → N₁   N₁
P4 N₁ → AP+N₁   AP+N₁
P4 N₁ → N–c+pl+Case   AP+N–c+pl+Case
P5 AP → Int+Adj   Int+Adj+N–c+pl+Case
P7 Adj → Adj-pos | Sn | Int | Adj-pos+Sn+pl+M+
  pl+M+Case   Case+N–c+pl+Case
P8 Case → Nom   Int+Adj-pos+Sn+pl+M+
                 Nom+N–c+pl+Case
P8 Case → Nom   Int+Adj-pos+Sn+pl+M+
                 Nom+N–c+pl+Nom
L Int → *fela* 'many'   *fela*+Adj-pos+Sn+pl+M+
                         Nom+N–c+pl+Nom
L Adj-pos → *gōd*- 'good'   *fela*+*gōd*-+Sn+pl+M+
                            Nom+N–c+pl+Nom
L N–c → *mann* 'man'   *fela*+*gōd*-+Sn+pl+M+
                        Nom+*mann*+pl+Nom
M *gōd*-+Sn+pl+M+   *fela*+*gōde*+*mann*+pl+Nom
  Nom → *gōde*
M *mann*+pl+Nom → *menn*   *fela*+*gōde*+*menn*

More About VPs

In the last chapter we let Y symbolize mood, person, and number. Thus, Verb+Y gave us the proper verb forms we needed in our examples. To account for items represented by Y, we now add these three new P-rules (P14–16):

P14 $Y \rightarrow$ Mood $(+$Person$)$ $(+$pl$)$

P15 Mood $\rightarrow \begin{Bmatrix} \text{Indic} \\ \text{Subj} \\ \text{Imper} \end{Bmatrix}$
Indic: indicative
Subj: subjunctive
Imper: imperative

P16 Person $\rightarrow \begin{Bmatrix} 1 \\ 2 \\ 3 \end{Bmatrix}$

OE VPs

These examples illustrate the new P-rules for OE VPs:

I: *cuōm* 'came'

Given: S

	NP+VP
P1 $S \rightarrow NP+VP$	NP+VP
P9 $VP \rightarrow Past+V_4$	$Past+V_4$
P10 $V_4 \rightarrow V_3$	$Past+V_3$
P11 $V_3 \rightarrow V_2$	$Past+V_2$
P12 $V_2 \rightarrow V_1$	$Past+V_1$
P13 $V_1 \rightarrow V\text{-}i+Y$	$Past+V\text{-}i+Y$
P14 $Y \rightarrow Mood+Person$	$Past+V\text{-}i+Mood+$ Person
P15 Mood $\rightarrow$ Indic	$Past+V\text{-}i+Indic+$ Person
P16 Person $\rightarrow$ 3	$Past+V\text{-}i+Indic+3$
L $V\text{-}i \rightarrow cuman$ 'to come'	$Past+cuman+Indic$ $+3$
T-fix OBL $\Rightarrow$	$cuman+Past+Indic$ $+3$
M $cuman+Past+Indic+$ $3 \rightarrow cuōm$	$cuōm$

II: *winnende wǣron* 'fighting were'

Given: S

P1 S → NP+VP	NP+VP
P9 VP → Past+V₄	Past+V₄
P10 V₄ → V₃	Past+V₃
P11 V₃ → V₂	Past+V₂
P12 V₂ → *bēon*+*-ende*+V₁	Past+*bēon*+*-ende*+V₁
P13 V₁ → V–i+Y	Past+*bēon*+*-ende*+ V–i+Y
P14 Y → Mood+Person+pl	Past+*bēon*+*-ende*+ V–i+Mood+Person +pl
P15 Mood → Indic	Past+*bēon*+*-ende*+ V–i+Indic+Person +pl
P16 Person → 3	Past+*bēon*+*-ende*+ V–i+Indic+3+pl
L V–i → *winnan* 'to fight'	Past+*bēon*+*-ende*+ *winnan*+Indic+ 3+pl
T4 OPT ⇒	*-ende*+*winnan*+Past +*bēon*+Indic+ 3+pl
T-fix OBL →	*winnan*+*-ende*+*bēon*+ Past+Indic+3+pl
M *winnan*+*-ende* → *winnende*	*winnende*+*bēon*+Past +Indic+3+pl
M *bēon*+Past+Indic+3+ pl → *wǣron*	*winnende*+*wǣron*

III: *ġewicod hæfdon* 'encamped had'

Given: S

P1 S → NP+VP	NP+VP
P9 VP → Past+V₄	Past+V₄
P10 V₄ → V₃	Past+V₃
P11 V₃ → *habban*+Y+ Part+V₂	Past+*habban*+Y+ Part+V₂
P12 V₂ → V₁	Past+*habban*+Y+ Part+V₁

P13 $V_1 \rightarrow$ V–i

Past+*habban*+Y+
Part+V–i

P14 Y $\rightarrow$ Mood+Person

Past+*habban*+Mood
+Person+Part+V–i

P15 Mood $\rightarrow$ Indic

Past+*habban*+ Indic+
Person+Part+V–i

P16 Person $\rightarrow$ 3

Past+*habban*+ Indic+
3+Part+V–i

L V–i $\rightarrow$ *wician* 'to encamp'

Past+*habban*+ Indic+
3+Part+*wician*

T5 OPT $\Rightarrow$

Part+*wician*+Past+
habban+ Indic+3

T-fix OBL $\Rightarrow$

wician+Part+*habban*
+Past+Indic+3

M *wician*+Part $\rightarrow$ *ġewicod*

ġewicod+*habban*+
Past+Indic+3

M *habban*+Past+ Indic+
3 $\rightarrow$ *hæfdon*

ġewicod+*hæfdon*

OE Adverbials

Having examined in slightly more detail some expanded P-rules for OE NPs and VPs, we now turn to OE adverbials, after which we shall look at some additional T-rules for OE, and then describe the syntactic structure called the clause.

Adverbials are single words or groups of words that appear in VPs. Adverbials include these main types:

1. Adverbs, a class of uninflected words marked by characteristic PoBs. Example: (comparative) *swīþor* 'more severely' as in *swīþor ġebrocede* 'more severely afflicted.'

2. Uninflected FWs not marked by PoBs. Example: *hider* 'hither' in *cōmon hider* 'came hither.'

3. NPs. Example: (gen. sg.) *dæġes* 'by day' in *sæt . . . dæġes* 'sat . . . by day.'

4. Adjectives. Example: (dat. pl.) *miclum* 'greatly' in *miclum . . . weorðude* 'greatly . . . honored.'

5. Prepositional phrases consisting of a preposition plus NP. Example: *æt hamtune* 'at Southampton' in *ġefeaht æt hamtune* 'fought at Southampton.'

Any of the above — adverb, FW, NP, adjective, prepositional phrase — may function in OE as an:

Adverbial of time	(Adv-t)
Adverbial of place	(Adv-p)
Adverbial of manner	(Adv-m)
Adverbial of frequency	(Adv-f)

Examples of these are as follows:

Adv-t+V	*sume dæ̆ge rād* 'one day rode'
V+Adv-p	*ġedydon æt cwātbrycġe* 'arrived at Quat-bridge'
Adv-m+V	*swīðlīċe ġedrefed* 'severely troubled'
Adv-f+V	*oft . . . feaht* 'often . . . fought'
Mod+V+Adv-p	*wolde drīfan tō ðæs cyninges tūne* 'wanted to drive to the king's town'
V+Adv-m	*fōron ānstreċes* 'traveled continuously'

We have illustrated some OE adverbials, but we have not provided for them in our P-rules, mainly because the best way of handling such adverbials in expanded P-rules of an OE generative-transformational grammar remains to be worked out. Another difficult problem concerns the T-rules that will be needed to obtain the desired order of adverbials in derived sentences. In this book we can only point out that OE adverbials existed.

T-Neg

All OE VPs in our examples so far have been affirmative, although negative OE VPs also occurred. One way to handle negation in OE VPs is by adding the negator *ne* 'no, not' in P9:

$$P9 \; VP \rightarrow \left\{ \begin{array}{l} \text{Pres } (+ne)+V_4 \\ \text{Past } (+ne)+V_4 \end{array} \right\}$$

In the interests of simplicity, however, it is preferable to handle negation on the T-level, which permits us the option of transforming any affirmative VP into a negative one by means of T-neg:

T-neg OPT: $NP+V \Rightarrow NP+ne+V$

Examples

hē+wiste ⟹ *hē+ne+wiste* 'He not knew'
hīe+mehton+ūt bringan ⟹ *hīe+ne+mehton+
ūt bringan* 'They not might out bring'

T-neg would have to be expanded in a larger OE grammar to handle different kinds of Vs, but the process of T-neg is essentially that which we have illustrated here.[2]

T-Pass

To transform strings with V–t from active to passive voice, we apply T-pass, a simplified version of which is presented here:

T-pass OPT: NP_1+V–t+NP_2 ⟹ NP_2+*weorðan* 'be, become' +Part+V–t

A slightly more detailed version of one form of T-pass is as follows:

T-pass OPT: NP_1+X+Tense+V–t+Y+NP_2+X ⟹ NP_2+ Nom+Tense+*weorðan*+Y+Part+V–t

To illustrate T-pass, suppose that we wished to transform the OE construction *hīe ofslōgon hine* 'They killed him' into the passive voice construction *hē wearð ofslǣgen* 'He was killed.' To do so, we proceed like this:

T-pass OPT: *hē*+pl+Nom+Past+*ofslēan* 'to kill'+Indic+ 3+pl+*hē*+Acc ⟹ *hē*+Nom+Past+*weorðan*+Indic+3+Part +*ofslēan*

(Note: 3+pl ⟹ 3 because *hē*+Nom is singular.)

T-fix OBL ⟹ *hē*+Nom+*weorðan*+Past+Indic+3+*ofslēan*+ Part

M *hē*+Nom → *hē*   *hē*+*weorðan*+Past+Indic+3+*ofslēan*+ Part

M *weorðan*+Past+Indic+3 → *wearð*   *hē*+*wearð ofslēan*+ Part

M *ofslēan*+Part → *ofslǣgen*   *hē wearð ofslǣgen*

Clause

A clause is a structure that contains tense, meaning that a clause contains a verb that indicates tense. A clause may be a sentence. In English a clause may also be a subordinate clause or a relative clause. Thus, there are sentence clauses, subordinate clauses, and relative clauses.

Sentence Clauses

There were two types of sentence clauses in OE.

Type I consisted of NP+VP as in *hē ārās* 'He arose' and *hē rīcsode v ġear* 'He ruled five years.'

Type II consisted of VP, as in *fōron* 'traveled (they),' in which 'they' is indicated by the inflectional suffix *-on*. An NP that occurs in a type II clause is part of the VP, as the NP *hine* 'him' in *hine ðǣr berād* 'him there pursued (He).'

T-Sub

A clause that is subordinated in a sentence is a subordinate clause. For example, the structure of the sentence *ðā onġet sē here ðæt hīe ne mehton ðā sċipu ūt bringan* 'then perceived the army that they not might the ships out bring' is *ðā onġet sē here*+Subordinator+Clause. In that sentence the clause *ðæt hīe ne mehton ðā sċipu ūt bringan* 'that they not might the ships out bring' is a subordinate clause. It is subordinated in the sentence by the subordinator (Sub) *ðæt* 'that.'

Any clause can be made into a subordinate clause by the addition of a Sub. The function of Sub is to subordinate a clause in a larger sentence clause.

To provide for subordinate clauses in OE sentences, we need T-sub. Our earlier T-rules were single-base transformations that involved one base sentence. T-sub, a double-base transformation, differs in that it involves two base sentences. The first is called the insert sentence, and the second the matrix sentence. The product of the transformation is called the result. The general nature of T-sub is presented here in an elementary form.

T-sub OPT: Insert: S (1)
Matrix: A (2) − NP (3) − B (4)
Result: A (2) + Sub + S (1) + B (4)

A and B stand for whatever occurs in those positions. For example, suppose that we wanted to obtain the result: *ðā onġet sē here ðæt hīe ne mehton ðā sċipu ūt bringan* 'then perceived the army that they not might the ships out bring.' According to T-sub:

Insert: *hīe ne mehton ðā sċipu ūt bringan* (1)
Matrix: *ðā onġet sē here* (2) − NP (3) − Ø (4)
Result: *ðā onġet sē here* (2)+*ðæt* (Sub)+*hīe ne mehton ðā sċipu ūt bringan* (1)+Ø (4).

Note: In *ðā onġet sē here* (2) — NP (3), NP is the object of the V–t *onġet* 'perceived.' Thus, in the result the subordinate clause *ðæt* (Sub)+*hīe ne mehton ða sċipu ūt bringan* is also an NP that functions as the object of *onġet.*

T-Rel

In the OE construction *sē micla here ðe wē ġefyrn ymbe sprǣcon* 'the large army which we formerly about spoke,' the structure is NP+Relative+Clause. The NP is *sē micla here.* The relative (Rel) is *ðe* 'which,' and the clause is *wē ġefyrn ymbe sprǣcon.* Thus, *ðe wē ġefyrn ymbe sprǣcon* 'which we formerly about spoke' is a relative clause with the Rel *ðe* in initial position in the clause. To provide for relative clauses in OE constructions, we need T-rel.

T-rel is like T-sub in that there is an insert, matrix, and result, but T-rel produces relative clauses, whereas T-sub produces subordinate clauses.

According to the version of T-rel below, the relative clause modifies an NP, while a subordinate clause is one that is subordinated in a sentence clause.

T-rel OPT: Insert: A (1) − NP$_1$ (2) − B (3)
Matrix: C (4) − NP$_1$ (2) − D (5)
Result: $4+2+ \begin{Bmatrix} sē \text{ 'who'} \\ ðǣt \text{ 'that'} \\ ðe \text{ 'which'} \end{Bmatrix} +1+3+5$

The positional symbols A, B, C, D signify whatever occurs in those positions.

If we wished to obtain the result, *fōr sē micla here ðe wē ġefyrn ymbe sprǣcon* 'traveled the large army which we formerly about spoke,' we would apply T-rel as follows:

T-rel OPT: Insert: *wē ġefyrn ymbe sprǣcon* (1) — *sē micla here* (2) — Ø (3)

Matrix: *fōr* (4) — *sē micla here* (2) — Ø (5)

Result: *fōr* (4) + *sē micla here* (2) + *ðe* 'which' + *wē ġefyrn ymbe sprǣcon* (1) + Ø (3) + Ø (5)

Coordination

Coordination between elements and clauses in OE was indicated by the coordinate conjunction (conj) *and ~ ond* 'and,' as in these examples:

and stuf and wihtgār fuhton wið brettas and hīe ġeflīemdon

'And Stuf and Wihtgar fought against the Britons, and them put to flight (they)'

and ðǣr wearð sidroc eorl ofslæġen sē alda and sidroc eorl sē ġioncga and ōsbearn eorl and frǣna eorl and hareld eorl

'and there was Sidroc Earl slain the old and Sidroc Earl the young and Osborn Earl and Frǣna Earl and Harold Earl'

Correlation

Correlation between clauses in OE was signaled by pairs of correlative conjunctions, such as *þā . . . þā* 'when . . . then,' *ne . . . ne* 'neither . . . nor,' and *ġe . . . ġe* 'both . . . and.'[3]

Examples

1. *þā/þā: þā hē forð on ðæt lēoht cōm ðā beseah hē hine under bæc wið ðæs wīfes*

'When he forth to that light came, then looked he himself back towards his wife'

2. *ne/ne: ne ġeseah nān ċepa ēaland ne weroð*

'Neither saw (he) no trader, island, nor shore'

3. *ġe/ġe: ond ġenāmon eal þæt þǣr binnan wæs ġe on fēo ġe on wīfum ġe ēac on bearnum*

'And took (they) all that there within was both in riches and in women and also in children'

Prose Extract

We conclude this chapter with an excerpt from a lawsuit about wood pasture, as an example of OE prose (c. 825):

Ðy gere þe wæs from cristes geburde agæn · eahta hund winter ·]
XXV ·] æfterre indictio wæs in rime ·] wæs beornwulfes rice mercna
cyninges · þa wæs sinodlic gemot on þære meran stowe ðe mon hateþ
clofeshous on þam se siolfa cyning biornwulf ·] his biscopas ·] his aldormen ·] alle þa wioton þisse þiode þær gesomnade weron · þa wæs tiolo
micel sprec ymb wuduleswe to suþtune ongægum west on scirhylte · waldon
þa swangerefan þa leswe forður gedrifan] þone wudu geþiogan · þonne
hit ald geryhta weron · þonne cuæð se biscop] þara hira wiotan þæt hio
him neren maran ondeta þonne hit aræded wæs on æþelbaldes dæge þrim
hunde swina mæst ·] se biscop] ða higen ahten twæde þæs wudu] þæs
mæstes : · Ða geræhte wulfred arcebiscop ·] alle þa wiotan þet se biscop]
þa higen moston mid aþe gecythan þet hit sua aræden were on æþelbaldes
dage him mare to ne sohte : · And he þa sona se biscop bewæddade eadwulfe
ðæm aldormen þæs aþes biforan allum þæm wiotum ·] him mon þone gelædde
ymb XXX næhta to þæm biscopstole æt wigoernaceastre : · In þa tiid
wæs hama suangerefa to suðtune ·] he ræd ðæt he wæs æt ceastre and þone
aað gesæh ·] gesceawade sua hine his aldormon heht eadwulf ·] he hine
hweþre ne grette.[4]

'In the year which was from christ's birth since · eight hundred winters · and 25 · and after the indication was in course · and was in beornwulf's reign of mercia king · there was a council meeting in the famous place which one calls clofesho at which the same king beornwulf · and his bishops · and his aldermen · and all the councilors of this nation there assembled were. then was a very great suit about woodpasture at sinton toward the west in scirhylte. desired the swineherd-reeves the pasture farther to extend and the wood take in · than it the old rights were. then said the bishop and their counselors that they to them not were more to acknowledge than it appointed was in athelbald's day for three hundred swine mast · and the bishop and the inhabitants had two thirds of the wood and of the mast. Then directed wulfred archbishop · and all the counselors that the bishop and the inhabitants must with oath declare that it so decided was in athelbald's day and for themselves more not sought. And he then soon the bishop gave security to eadwulf the alderman of the oath before all the counselors · and it one then brought after 30 nights to the bishop's seat at worcester. At that time was hama the swineherd-reeve at sinton · and he rode until he was at worcester and the oath saw · and observed as him his alderman ordered eadwulf · but he himself however not challenged (it).'

SUMMARY

P2 NP $\rightarrow \left\{ \begin{array}{l} \text{Pro} \\ (\text{Det}+)\text{N-prop}(+\text{pl})+\text{Case} \\ (\text{Det}+)\text{N}_1 \end{array} \right\}$

P4 N_1 $\rightarrow \left\{ \begin{array}{l} \text{AP}+\text{N}_1 \\ \text{N-c}(+\text{pl})+\text{Case} \end{array} \right\}$

P6 Pro $\rightarrow \left\{ \begin{array}{l} \text{Pers}+\left\{ \begin{array}{l} \text{dual} \\ \text{pl} \end{array} \right\}+\text{Case} \\ \text{Dem}(+\text{pl})+\text{Case} \\ \text{Inter}+\text{Case} \end{array} \right\}$

P7 Adj $\rightarrow \left\{ \begin{array}{l} \text{Adj-pos} \\ \text{Adj-comp} \\ \text{Adj-super} \end{array} \right\}+\left\{ \begin{array}{l} \text{Sn} \\ \text{W} \end{array} \right\}(+\text{pl})+\left\{ \begin{array}{l} \text{M} \\ \text{F} \\ \text{N} \end{array} \right\}+\text{Case}$

P8 Case $\rightarrow \left\{ \begin{array}{l} \text{Nom} \\ \text{Acc} \\ \text{Gen} \\ \text{Dat} \\ \text{Instr} \end{array} \right\}$

P14 Y $\rightarrow \text{Mood}(+\text{Person}))(+\text{pl})$

P15 Mood $\rightarrow \left\{ \begin{array}{l} \text{Indic} \\ \text{Subj} \\ \text{Imper} \end{array} \right\}$

P16 Person $\rightarrow \left\{ \begin{array}{l} 1 \\ 2 \\ 3 \end{array} \right\}$

Adv-t, Adv-p, Adv-m, Adv-f

T-neg OPT: $\text{NP}+\text{V} \Rightarrow \text{NP}+ne+\text{V}$

T-pass OPT: $\text{NP}_1+\text{X}+\text{Tense}+\text{V-t}+\text{Y}+\text{NP}_2+\text{X} \Rightarrow \text{NP}_2+\text{Nom}+\text{Tense}+weor\eth an+\text{Y}+\text{Part}+\text{V-t}$

Clause

Sentence clause: type I (NP+VP), type II (VP)

T-sub OPT: Insert: S (1)
Matrix: A (2) $-$ NP (3) $-$ B (4)
Result: A (2) $+$ Sub $+$ S (1) $+$ B (4)
T-rel OPT: Insert: A (1) $-$ NP$_1$ (2) $-$ B (3)
Matrix: C (4) $-$ NP$_1$ (2) $-$ D (5)
Result: $4+2+\left\{\begin{array}{l} s\bar{e} \text{ 'who'} \\ \eth\ae t \text{ 'that'} \\ \eth e \text{ 'which'} \end{array}\right\} +1+3+5$

Coordination and correlation

NOTES

[1] We have provided choices in P-rules for case, but in a more detailed grammar that feature is best handled on the transformational level. See Noam Chomsky, *Aspects of the Theory of Syntax* (Cambridge, Mass., 1965), pp. 170–175.

In addition to P-, L-, T-, and M-rules, a detailed grammar of OE would describe the relations and restrictions of occurrences of items in certain contexts. For example, in some contexts item A may require item B, or A and B may require each other, or the presence of A may exclude the presence of B, and so on.

In some cases it may be best to handle certain selectional or occurrence relations in what are called context-sensitive or CS-rules. Such rules specify the kinds of items that appear in specific environments and are of the form $X \to Y$ in env. A+____. For example, there must be a CS-rule for OE Y that excludes Person if pl is selected. There also must be a CS-rule for OE case that excludes Instr if the stem of Dem is Feminine.

[2] Optional negative, passive, and question transformations in a more detailed grammar would be reformulated as obligatory transformations that apply to Phrase-markers in strings. See Chomsky, *Aspects of the Theory of Syntax*, pp. 132, 223, n. 3; Jerrold J. Katz and Paul M. Postal, *An Integrated Theory of Linguistic Descriptions* (Cambridge, Mass., 1964), pp. 71–74, 79–117.

[3] Coordination is the relation of being coordinate or equal. Correlation is a reciprocal or mutual relation, an interdependence.

[4] The OE text has been collated from *Anglo-Saxon Charters*, ed. A. J. Robertson, 2nd ed. (Cambridge, 1956), p. 8, and G. Hicks, *Linguarum Veterum Septentrionalis Thesaurus* (London, 1705), I, 80–81. OE] = 'and.' Macrons and other graphemic marks have been omitted to illustrate that OE MSS were not so marked. For a description of the OE punctuation marks, see Chapter 26 of this book. In the translation the punctuation and capitalization parallel those in the OE test. OE *clofeshous* > LModE *Clofesho.*

Comparative Historical Syntax

In the last two chapters we examined a generative-transformational grammar of OE, and in the next chapter we shall examine a similar grammar of LModE. Before we go on to that subject, we shall look at some similarities and differences between the syntax of former periods of English and that of the modern period.

The material that follows is intended only as an elementary introduction to a comparative syntax of historical English. Description is limited to non-question, non-imperative sentence clauses that occur in prose. Because of the wide variety of positions of adverbials in English, particularly in OE, no account will be given of them here.

The OE material is taken primarily from the *OE Annals* or *Anglo-Saxon Chronicle*, a chronological prose history of England in Old English from early Christian times to 1154. Examination of that material was limited mostly to entries before c. 1000.

Similarities

1. In OE sentence clauses without initial adverbial *þā* 'then,' FW negator *ne* 'not,' or FW conjunction *and* 'and,' the most common orders of major items appear to have been these:

a. $NP+V-i$
b. $NP_1+V-t+NP_2^1$
c. $NP_1+V-b+NP_2$
d. $NP+V-b+AP$
e. $NP_1+NP_2+V-t+NP_3$

Examples

a. *hē ārās* 'He arose'
b. *hī ǧesāwon ðone steorran* 'They saw the star'
c. *iċ eom fisċere* 'I am a fisherman'
d. *þæt is sārliċ* 'That is sad'
e. *iċ ēow secge þæt . . .* 'I you tell that . . .'

Of the five orders of items listed above, the orders *a, b, c, d* are identical to those that commonly occur in ModE:

a. NP+V–i: *He arose*
b. NP₁+V–t+NP₂: *They saw the star*
c. NP₁+V–b+NP₂: *I am a fisherman*
d. NP+V–b+AP: *That is sad*

The order of items in OE pattern *e* (NP₁+NP₂+V–t+NP₃: 'I you tell that . . .' in ModE shows a change in the position of V–t, namely NP₁+V–t+NP₂+NP₃: *I tell you that. . .*

Various other orders of items occurred in OE, mainly as a result of placing an item in string-initial position for rhetorical emphasis. Two examples are NP₂+NP₁+V–t (*maneǧa þing iċ dyde* 'Many a thing I did') and AP+V–b+NP (*swīðe waxǧeorn eart ðū* 'Very greedy are you'). Such variations are a matter of style rather than syntax.

Other variations in orders, such as those after initial adverbial *þā*, FW negator *ne*, FW conjunction *and*, as well as orders in subordinate and relative clauses, will be described later in this chapter.

2. Prepositions in OE regularly preceded their noun objects (*tō lundene* 'to London') and the modifiers of those objects (*on þissum ǧēare* 'in this year'). Prepositions also preceded their pronoun objects (*tō him* 'to him'), but sometimes occurred in postposition (*him tō*), particularly when a verb immediately followed (*him wið ǧefeaht* 'them with fought'). In contrast, prepositions in ModE normally precede their noun and pronoun objects, as in *to him* and *fought with them*.

3. As in ModE, determiners in OE as *sē, sēo, þæt* 'the, that' regularly preceded nouns (*sē bisċop* 'the bishop') and noun modifiers (*sē hālga beda* 'the holy Bede'). Although determiners regularly occurred in OE, as *sum* 'some, a certain' in *sum man* 'a certain man' and *ān* 'one, a certain, a, an' in *ānne æþeling* 'an atheling,' sometimes an OE determiner did not occur in an

environment which in ModE requires a determiner. One example is the absence of OE 'the' before *wælstōwe* in *āhton wælstōwe ġewald* 'had of (*the*) battlefield mastery.' In contrast, in OE a determiner sometimes occurred in an environment which in ModE does not require a determiner, as in *þā ġefeaht sē cyning æþered* 'Then fought *the* King Athered.'

4. Also as in ModE, predeterminers occurred before determiners in expanded OE NPs, as the predeterminer *eall* 'all' before the determiner *ðā* 'the' in *ealle ðā tīd* 'all the time.' Another OE predeterminer was *bēġen* 'both' as in *bēġen þā ġebrōþru*.

ModE predeterminers, in addition to *all* and *both*, include *half* (*half the men*), *nearly all* (*nearly all the men*), and *such* (*such a man*).

5. A fifth feature of similarity between OE and ModE concerns the position of OE genitive-case and ModE possessive-case nouns and pronouns. In OE such nouns and pronouns usually preceded the words to which they were related, as in *iōhannes fōtum* 'John's feet' and *hira land* 'their land.' In ModE an identical order is found in *John's feet* and *their land.*

6. As in ModE, appositives in OE regularly followed words with which they were in apposition, as in *iōsepe ðæs ċildes fōsterfæder* 'Joseph, the child's fosterfather,' *ēadweard his sunu* 'Edward, his son,' and *ēadmund sē ēadiga* 'Edmund the blessed (one).'

Differences

Having examined some syntactic similarities between OE and ModE, we now turn to some syntactic differences among the various periods of English.

1. An important difference between the syntax of OE and that of ModE is the emergence by the time of EModE of a more rigid order of items in English sentences. This followed the loss of many inflections which had indicated the relation of items to one another in OE sentences.

The relationship of a noun, pronoun, or adjective to another word in an OE construction was indicated primarily by its inflection rather than its position in the construction. For example,

in OE it was theoretically possible to write a sentence, like ModE
The good queen struck the blind man, in these ways:

> ðone blindan mann slōg sēo gōde cwēn
> ðone blindan mann sēo gōde cwēn slōg
> sēo gōde cwēn ðone blindan mann slōg
> sēo gōde cwēn slōg ðone blindan mann
> slōg ðone blindan mann sēo gōde cwēn
> slōg sēo gōde cwēn ðone blindan mann

Despite the different orders of items in these OE sentences,
the grammatical inflections of the items indicate that each
sentence is to be read as 'The good queen struck the blind man.'
For example, the NP of each OE sentence above is *sēo gōde cwēn*
'the good queen,' in which the singular feminine nominative
items Pro+Adj *sēo gōde* 'the good' go with the singular feminine
nominative N–c *cwēn* 'queen.' The VP of each sentence consists
of the past tense V–t *slōg* 'struck' plus the NP *ðone blindan mann*
'the blind man.' The latter consists of the singular masculine
accusative items Pro+Adj *ðone blindan* 'the blind' and the
singular masculine accusative N–c *mann* 'man' which it modifies.

The theoretical variety of the orders of items in OE sentences
is not a feature of well-formed ModE sentences, in which the
order of items is more rigid than it was in OE. For example,
in ModE the meaning of the sentence *The good queen struck the
blind man* is totally different from that of *The blind man struck
the good queen.* The difference in meaning between the two
ModE sentences is based entirely on the difference in the order
of items in the two sentences. That is so because in ModE
the normal order of many non-question, non-imperative sentences
containing a transitive verb is $NP_1+V–t+NP_2$, in which NP_1
is normally regarded as the subject of the sentence, and NP_2
as the object of the V–t.

2. Another syntactic difference is the occurrence in OE of
long strings of sentence clauses linked together by the FW
conjunction *and ~ ond* 'and,' as in this example:

> *and þæs ymb ii mōnaþ ġefeaht æþered cyning and ælfred his brōþur wiþ
> þone here æt meretūne and hīe wǣrun on tuǣm ġefylcium and hīe būtū
> ġeflīemdon and longe on dæġ siġe āhton and þǣr wearþ miċel wælsliht on
> ġehwæþere hond and þā denisċan āhton wælstōwe ġewald*
>
> 'and after two months fought Athered King and Alfred his brother
> against the army at Merton, and they were in two bands, and they both

were put to flight, and far on in the day victory had (they), and there was much slaughter on either hand, and the Danes had of (the) battlefield mastery.'

In ModE long strings of sentence clauses linked together by *and* are not common.

3. A third syntactic difference between OE and ModE involves the expanded use of prepositions in ModE to make explicit some syntactic relationships indicated in OE by noun inflections. For example, one OE construction is dative plural *mannum* 'to men.' The equivalent of the OE one-item construction *mannum* in ModE is the two-item construction *to men*, in which the preposition *to* conveys the dative relationship indicated in OE by the case-number suffix *-um* in *mannum*.

4. OE phrases consisting of the preposition *of* 'of, from' plus a noun to indicate a genitive relationship (*menn of lundenbyriġ* 'men of London') were not common. Usually a genitive relationship was indicated by an inflection, as in *fōtes trym* 'foot's space' and *seaxes ecg* 'sword's edge.' But, in the ME period, and thereafter, there was an increase in the use of *of*-phrases, perhaps from the influence of Latin *de* and French *de*, which in *de*-phrases indicated a genitive relationship. Thus, the equivalents of OE *fōtes trym* 'foot's space' and *seaxes ecg* 'sword's edge' in ModE are *space of a foot* and *edge of the sword*, respectively, in which there is a transposition of the order of the OE words and the insertion of the preposition *of* plus a determiner.[2] In other genitive constructions, however, the order of OE *iohannes fōtum* and *hira land* remains in ModE, as in *John's feet* and *their land*, in which the possessive precedes the noun.

5. A feature of ModE rarely found in earlier periods of English is the so-called group or phrase possessive, such as the *Lord Mayor of London's house*, the *King of Sweden's throne*, and *somebody else's glove*. In such constructions the possessive *-'s* is added to the last unit of the phrasal noun, and the phrasal noun is an attribute modifier of the noun that follows it.

6. In OE verb phrases there was no fixed order of auxiliary and verb. The auxiliary could precede the verb (*hafde ġeworden* 'had fared') or follow it (*ofslæġenne hæfdon* 'killed had'). In ModE, on the other hand, auxiliaries regularly precede the verb, as in *should have been baked*.

7. Another feature of ModE is the occurrence of expanded verb groups, particularly since the eighteenth century, such as *is going to sing, is to be painted, is being painted, would have liked to have been asked, am about to be shown,* and others. In the earlier periods of English, expanded verb groups corresponding to those in the examples above were either nonexistent or uncommon.

8. The *get*-passive is also a ModE development. Some examples are (He) *gets killed,* (He) *got killed,* and (The work) *got finished.* The ModE *get*-passive occurs in addition to the historical *be*-passive, as in (He) *is killed,* (He) *was killed,* and (The work) *was finished.*

9. Use of the auxiliary *dōn* 'to do, cause, make, perform' was rare in OE verb phrases. One example is *ġymenne dyde* 'care did (he).' In ME there was an increase in the use of the auxiliary 'do,' but such practice did not become common until the ModE period, as in (I) *did go,* (I) *do enjoy* (movies), and *Do stay.*

10. From the time of ME there has developed a tendency, particularly in LModE, to cast pronouns that precede verbs in the subjective case, and to cast pronouns that follow verbs in the objective case.

In OE we find constructions in which dative-case pronouns precede the verb, as in *mē þyncþ* 'to me it seems' and *him þūhte* 'to him it seemed.' In ME we find objective-case pronouns as in *mē thinketh* 'to me it seems,' *mē thoghte* 'to me it seemed,' *ūs thynketh* 'to us it seems,' *hem thoghte* 'to them it seemed,' and *hym thoughte* 'to him it seemed.' Such constructions are reflected in ModE (archaic) *methinks* and *methought.*

Converse to the OE construction *iċ hit eom* 'I it am' we find in ME *hit am I,* in which *iċ* is placed after the verb. Later in EModE there developed the variant construction *It is me* beside the older *It is I,* both of which remain in LModE. *It is me,* which is standard colloquial English, shows that *me* is in the objective case on the basis of its position after the verb, in imitation of the common ModE pattern subject-verb-object. Thus, word order has effected changes in the use of pronoun forms.

Position also has brought about a decrease in the use of the object pronoun *whom* in the normal subject position in LModE, as in *Who did you give it to?* for more formal *Whom did you give it to?*

11. Another difference between OE and ModE concerns the ModE increased use of the intensifiers *more* and *most*. Intensifiers (*more, most, very, rather, less, least, really*) in English precede adjectives (*more kind, most kind*) and adverbs (*more quickly, most quickly*).

In Late OE such constructions as *þæt mǣre lēoht* 'the greater light' and *þā mǣstan swētnesse* 'the most sweetness' occurred but were not common. In ME from c. 1300 there was an increase in the use of the intensifiers *more* and *most*, perhaps from the influence of French comparative *plus* (*plus grand*) and superlative *le plus* (*le plus grand*). Two ME examples are *mǫre bysie* 'more busy' and *the mǭǭste preciouse stǭǭn* 'the most precious stone.' A further increase in such use occurred in ModE, as is clear from such common constructions as *more beautiful, most beautiful*, and so on.

In ME and EModE the intensifiers 'more' and 'most' also occurred before comparative and superlative adjectives, as in ME *the mǫst fairest damyselles* 'the most fairest damsels' and Shakespeare's *more kinder, more fairer*, and *the most unkindest cut*. Now, the classroom prescription against the use of such so-called double comparatives and superlatives has eliminated their occurrence in standard usage.

A final point about intensifiers concerns the development and use in ME of the intensifiers *full* and *ryght* as in *full cǭld* 'very cold' and *ryght yǒng* 'very young.' Use of these intensifiers continued in the EModE period, and *right* continues to be commonly used as an intensifier in the southern United States today, as in *We had a right good time*.

12. Multiple negation was more frequent in OE and ME than it is today. For example, in OE negative clauses the FW negator *ne* generally was prefixed to every word with which it could form a contraction, as in *nān < ne ān* 'none, no' *nyste < ne wiste* 'not knew' and *næfdon < ne hæfdon* 'not had (they).' Thus, negation occurs five times in the OE construction *nis nān wīsdōm ne nān rǣd nāht onġēan god* 'Not is no knowledge nor no understanding not towards God.'

To a lesser degree, such multiple negation also occurred in ME, as in *hē myghte not seye nǫ thing* 'He might not say no thing.' Today multiple negation is uncommon in ModE, largely as a result of the grammar-school prescription against the use of double negatives.

13. In the last chapter we stated that in some OE sentences a covert or hidden subject occurred, indicated by the person-number verb suffix as in *tū folcǧefeoht ǧefuhton* 'Two battles fought (they).' In most OE sentences, however, both a covert or hidden subject and an overt or observable subject occurred, as in *hī ǧesāwon ðone steorran* 'They saw (they) the star.' In ModE, following the loss of many historical verb inflections, overt NP subjects occur, as in *They fought two battles* and *They saw a star*, but not in subjectless sentences as *Stop!*

14. In OE the FW *þe* was used as a genderless, numberless relative, as in *mīnre ǣhte þe mē tō ǧebyreþ* 'of my property which belongs to me.' Also used as relatives were the demonstrative pronouns *sē, sēo,* and *þæt*. Two examples are *sē his hūs ofer stān ǧetimbrode* 'who his house on (a) rock built' and *þæt lȳtle þæt hē erede* 'the little that he ploughed.' With the loss of OE *sē* and *sēo*, the form *þat* became the ME common relative. Me *þē* also occurred, but disappeared early.

In Late ME some use is found of *whōs, whōm,* and *which*, but not *whō*, as relatives. In ModE the use of *who, whose,* and *whom* became common.

Which in EModE was used in reference to persons, as *The Amorites which dwelt in the land* and *Our Father, which art in heaven*. Later in the ModE period the relative *which* came to be restricted to inanimate objects, and *who* to humans, as is the practice today.

15. In OE relative clauses the verb was usually separated from its auxiliary and occurred last in the clause, as in *sē wæs on rōme ǧelǣred* 'who was in Rome educated.' In the ME period the verb was shifted from clause-final position to position after the auxiliary, and this same order is normal in ModE, as in *who was educated in Rome*.

Similarly, in OE sentence clauses with initial FW conjunction *and* 'and,' the verb frequently occupied clause-final position, as in *and hē hine tō cyninge ǧehālgode* 'and he him as (a) king consecrated.' In ME the verb increasingly occurred after the subject NP, as in *And hē had alsǫ in his gardyn all maner of fōūles and of bęstes* 'And he had also in his garden all manner of fowls and of beasts.' In ModE that same order occurs.

16. In an OE clause with initial FW adverbial *þā* 'then' or the FW negator *ne* 'not,' the verb usually followed *þā* and *ne*. Examples are *þā ēode sē here tō hiera scipum* 'Then went the army to their ships' and *Ne cōm sē here oftor eall ūte of þǣm setum þonne tuwwa* 'Not came the army more often entirely out of the entrenchments than twice.' In contrast, in ModE the verb normally occurs after the subject NP, as in *Then the army went to their ships* and *No miracles were performed at their tombs.*

17. An expletive is a "filler word" — one added to complete a syntactic pattern, as *it* in *It is fun to play tag* and *there* in *There is bread on the table.* The order in ModE is Expletive+ VP+NP.

The expletives *þǣr* 'there' and *hit* 'it' also occurred in OE, but not frequently. Two examples are *þǣr bið swȳðe mycel gewinn* 'There is very much strife' and *Hit ġelamp on sumne sǣl þæt hī sǣton ætgædere* 'It happened at a certain time that they sat together.' In ME the use of *þēr* 'there' and *(h)it* 'it, there' was also minimal, but in ModE the use of both expletives is common.

18. The final syntactic difference we describe concerns the position of titles in relation to N-props in OE and ModE.

In OE, as in ModE, a title, when preceded by a determiner, occurred before N-prop, as in *sē apostol iohannes* 'the Apostle John.' Sometimes, however, the OE use does not correspond to modern practice, as in *þam cyninge ælfrede* 'to *the* King Alfred.'

Unlike ModE, in OE when a determiner was absent, the title followed N-prop, as in *ælfred cyning* 'Alfred King' and *æþelwulf aldormon* 'Athelwulf Alderman.' In ModE the order is title+ N-prop: *King Alfred.*

SUMMARY

A. OE and ModE syntactic similarities:

1. Orders of major items in sentence clauses, except OE $NP_1+ NP_2+V-t+NP_3$, which in ModE is $NP_1+V-t+NP_2+NP_3$.

2. The order *preposition+object*, except that OE pronoun objects sometimes occurred before prepositions.

3. The order *determiner+noun* and *determiner+modifier+ noun*, with some minor differences in the use of determiners in OE.

4. The order *predeterminer+determiner*.

5. The order *genitive-case modifier+noun*.

6. The order *N-prop+appositive*.

B. OE and ModE syntactic differences:

1. More rigid word order in ModE following the loss of many historical English inflections.

2. Long strings of sentence clauses in OE linked by 'and' not common in ModE.

3. Increased use in ModE of prepositions following the loss of OE noun dative inflections.

4. Increased use in ModE of *of*-phrases to indicate a possessive relationship.

5. Increased use in ModE of group possessives.

6. Development in ModE of the order *auxiliary+verb*.

7. Development in ModE of expanded verb groups.

8. Development in ModE of the *get*-passive.

9. Increased use in ModE of the auxiliary *do*.

10. Decrease in use in ModE of object-case pronouns in subject position in a sentence clause, but an increase in object position.

11. Increased use in ModE of the intensifiers *more* and *most*.

12. OE multiple negation not common in OE.

13. Loss in ModE of OE covert subjects following the disappearance of many historical verb suffixes.

14. Development and restricted use in ModE of the relatives *who* (*whose*, *whom*), *that*, and *which*.

15. ModE change of OE verb position in relative clauses and also in clauses with initial conjunction 'and.'

16. ModE change of OE verb position in clauses with initial adverbial 'then' and negator 'not.'

17. Increased use in ModE of expletives *there* and *it*.

18. Development in ModE of the order *title+N-prop*.

NOTES

[1] The order $NP_1+NP_2+V\text{-}t$ also occurred frequently in OE besides $NP_1+V\text{-}t+NP_2$. For various reasons, it appears that OE P-rule 13 in Chapter 21 is best set up to provide the order $NP_2+V\text{-}t$ rather than $V\text{-}t+NP_2$, although additional experimentation may reverse that tentative conclusion. At any rate, in order to obtain $V\text{-}t+NP_2$, it is necessary to apply an optional T-rule, say T-12, that would change $NP_2+V\text{-}t \Rightarrow V\text{-}t+NP_2$.

[2] The *of*-possessive in ModE is relatively common with nouns denoting inanimate objects (*the horn of the car*), but the *s*-possessive is also used (*the car's horn*). The *s*-possessive is most commonly used in ModE with nouns denoting persons (*Ellen's book*).

24

Late Modern English Syntax

In this chapter, the final portion of our brief survey of the historical syntax of English, we shall examine some features of LModE sentences. The samples of grammar we shall use are based on the theory of generative-transformational grammar. As in the case of our previous OE grammatical samples, the material that follows is intended to be suggestive and illustrative of a method of description rather than a definitive study of all the features of LModE syntax.

LModE P-Rules

LModE P-rules, like OE P-rules, are applied to a given initial string. We shall therefore begin our description of LModE syntax with the sentence (S), to which we apply our first P-rule: S→NP+VP.

As in the case of our OE strings, we shall assume the convenient fiction that our LModE P-rules will automatically provide the agreement of number, person, and gender needed in our sample LModE sentences. The P-rules for LModE NPs and VPs that we shall present are approximately the same in number as those for OE, but are less complex than those for OE because fewer inflections occur in LModE.

We now turn to some P-rules for LModE NPs and then VPs, after which we shall examine some T-rules for LModE.

LModE NPs

Given P1 S → NP+VP, some simplified P-rules and some un-numbered L-rules for LModE NPs are as follows:

$$\text{P2 NP} \rightarrow \left\{ \begin{array}{l} \text{Pro} \\ \text{N-prop} \\ \text{(Det+)N}_3 \end{array} \right\}$$

$$\text{P3 Det} \rightarrow \left\{ \begin{array}{l} \text{(PreD+)D(+pl)} \\ \text{NP+-'}s \end{array} \right\}$$

$$\text{P4 N}_3 \rightarrow \left\{ \begin{array}{l} \text{N}_2 \\ \text{Nu+N}_2 \end{array} \right\}$$

$$\text{P5 N}_2 \rightarrow \left\{ \begin{array}{l} \text{N}_1 \\ \text{AP+N}_2 \end{array} \right\}$$

$$\text{P6 N}_1 \rightarrow \left\{ \begin{array}{l} \text{N} \\ \text{N}_2\text{+N}_1 \end{array} \right\}$$

$$\text{P7 N} \rightarrow \left\{ \begin{array}{l} \text{N-c(+pl)} \\ \text{N-m} \end{array} \right\}$$

$$\text{P8 AP} \rightarrow \left\{ \begin{array}{l} \text{Adj} \\ \text{Int+Adj} \end{array} \right\}^1$$

$$\text{P9 Adj} \rightarrow \left\{ \begin{array}{l} \text{Adj-pos} \\ \text{Adj-comp} \\ \text{Adj-super} \end{array} \right\}$$

L Pro → {*I, you, they, some(one), nobody* . . .}
L N-prop → {*Ellen, Audrey, Stuart, Elizabeth, Canada* . . .}
L PreD → {*several of, a lot of, a certain, many of* . . .}
L D → {*a, the, every, this, some, several* . . .}
L Nu → {*one, two, three, first, second, third* . . .}
L N–c {*dog, man, house, table, girl* . . .}
L N–m → {*furniture, wheat, mush, sarcasm* . . .}
L Adj-pos → {*blue, good, young, new, beautiful* . . .}[2]
L Adj-comp → {*bluer, better, younger, newer* . . .}
L Adj-super → {*bluest, best, youngest, newest* . . .}
L Int → {*very, rather, too, quite, pretty* . . .}

Examples

I: *John's aunts*[3]

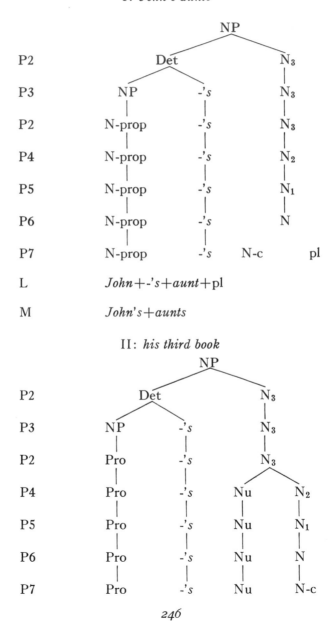

P2	Det		N₃	

L   *John+-'s+aunt+*pl

M   *John's+aunts*

II: *his third book*

246

L   *he+-'s+third+book*

M   *his+third+book*

III: *the stone furniture*

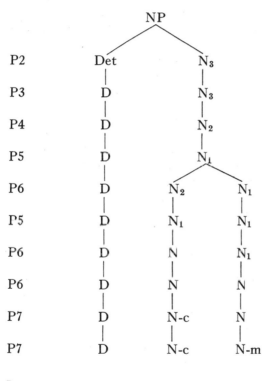

L   *the+stone+furniture*

IV: *many of those very young men*

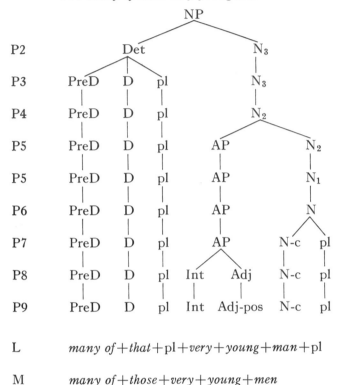

P2		Det				N₃	

L   *many of+that+*pl*+very+young+man+*pl

M   *many of+those+very+young+men*

LModE VPs

Some simplified P-rules and unnumbered L-rules for LModE VPs are these:

$$\text{P10 VP} \rightarrow \begin{Bmatrix} \text{Pres}+V_4 \\ \text{Past}+V_4 \end{Bmatrix}$$

$$\text{P11 } V_4 \rightarrow \begin{Bmatrix} V_3 \\ \text{Mod}+3 \end{Bmatrix}$$

$$\text{P12 } V_3 \rightarrow \begin{Bmatrix} V_2 \\ have+\text{Part}+V_2 \end{Bmatrix}$$

$$\text{P13 } V_2 \rightarrow \begin{Bmatrix} V_1 \\ be+\text{-}ing+V_1 \end{Bmatrix}$$

Part may be interpreted as 'whatever is done to a V to make it a past participle,' and *-ing* as 'whatever is done to a V to make it a present participle.'

$$\text{P14 } V_1 \rightarrow \left\{ \begin{array}{l} \text{V-i}(+\text{pl})(+\text{Adv}_1) \\ \text{V-t}(+\text{pl})+\text{NP}+\text{-}m \left(+\left\{ \begin{array}{l} \text{NP} \\ \text{AP} \end{array} \right\} \right) (+\text{Adv}_1) \\ \text{V-l}(+\text{pl})+\text{AP}(+\text{Adv}_1) \\ be(+\text{pl})+\text{Adv}_1 \\ \text{V-b}(+\text{pl})+\left\{ \begin{array}{l} \text{NP} \\ \text{AP} \end{array} \right\}(+\text{Adv}_1) \\ \text{V-h}(+\text{pl})+\text{NP}+\text{-}m(+\text{Adv}_1) \end{array} \right\}^4$$

$$\text{P15 Adv}_1 \rightarrow \left\{ \begin{array}{l} \text{Adv} \\ \text{Adv}_1+\text{Adv} \end{array} \right\}$$

$$\text{P16 Adv} \rightarrow \left\{ \begin{array}{l} \text{Adv-t} \\ \text{Adv-p} \\ \text{Adv-m} \\ \text{Adv-f} \\ \text{Prep}+\text{NP}+\text{-}m \end{array} \right\}$$

L Mod → {*shall, will, may, can* . . .}
L V–i → {*sleep, walk, work, run* . . .}
L V–t → {*see, give, elect, consider* . . .}
L V–l → {*look, feel, seem, taste* . . .}
L V–b → {*be, become, remain* . . .}
L V–h → {*have, weigh, cost* . . .}
L Adv–t → {*today, now, yesterday, then* . . .}
L Adv–p → {*here, there, upstairs, out* . . .}
L Adv–m → {*quickly, soundly, happily, willingly* . . .}
L Adv–f → {*frequently, sometimes, often, seldom* . . .}
L Prep → {*in, on, by, with, at* . . .}

Examples

In all the examples of VPs that follow, we shall apply T-fix. A simplified form of that obligatory transformation for LModE is this:

T-fix OBL: Fix+V ⇒ V+Fix

Fix stands for any tense, Part, or *-ing*. V stands for any modal, *have*, *be*, or verb.

I: *saw him*

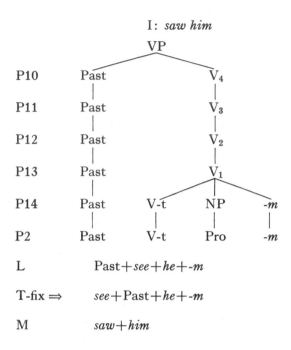

P10	Past		V₄	

$$\text{P10} \quad \text{Past} \qquad V_4$$

L Past+*see*+*he*+*-m*

T-fix ⟹ *see*+Past+*he*+*-m*

M *saw*+*him*

II: *should have been working*

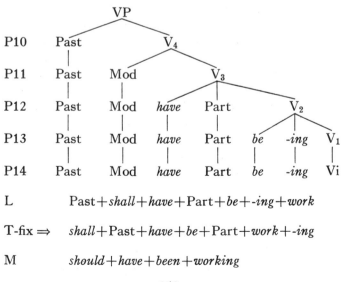

L Past+*shall*+*have*+Part+*be*+*-ing*+*work*

T-fix ⟹ *shall*+Past+*have*+*be*+Part+*work*+*-ing*

M *should*+*have*+*been*+*working*

III: *sat with them frequently*

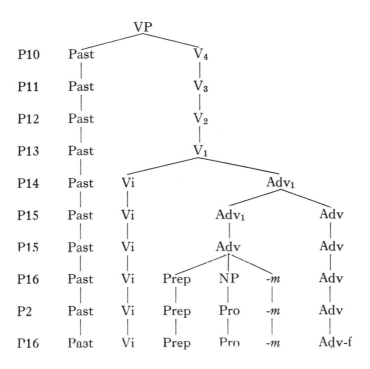

P10	Past		V₄		
P11	Past		V₃		
P12	Past		V₂		
P13	Past		V₁		
P14	Past	Vi		Adv₁	
P15	Past	Vi		Adv₁	Adv
P15	Past	Vi		Adv	Adv
P16	Past	Vi	Prep	NP -*m*	Adv
P2	Past	Vi	Prep	Pro -*m*	Adv
P16	Past	Vi	Prep	Pro -*m*	Adv-f

L   Past+*sit*+*with*+*they*+-*m*+*frequently*

T-fix ⇒   *sit*+Past+*with*+*they*+-*m*+*frequently*

M   *sat*+*with*+*them*+*frequently*

IV: *has been happy often*

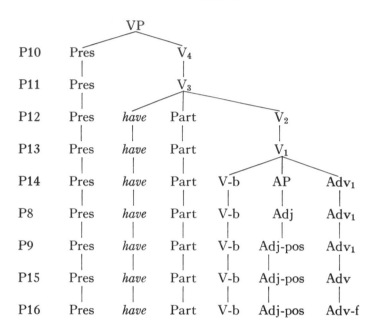

		VP			
P10	Pres		V₄		
P11	Pres		V₃		
P12	Pres	*have*	Part		V₂
P13	Pres	*have*	Part		V₁
P14	Pres	*have*	Part	V-b	AP	Adv₁
P8	Pres	*have*	Part	V-b	Adj	Adv₁
P9	Pres	*have*	Part	V-b	Adj-pos	Adv₁
P15	Pres	*have*	Part	V-b	Adj-pos	Adv
P16	Pres	*have*	Part	V-b	Adj-pos	Adv-f

L   Pres+*have*+Part+*be*+*happy*+*often*

T-fix ⟹ *have*+Pres+*be*+Part+*happy*+*often*

M   *has*+*been*+*happy*+*often*

V: *gave him a book*

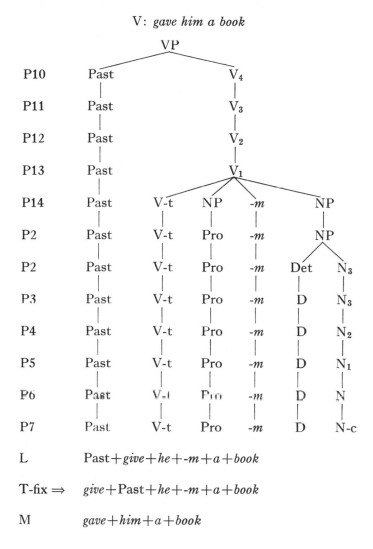

P10	Past			V_4		
P11	Past			V_3		
P12	Past			V_2		
P13	Past			V_1		
P14	Past	V-t	NP	-*m*		NP
P2	Past	V-t	Pro	-*m*		NP
P2	Past	V-t	Pro	-*m*	Det	N_3
P3	Past	V-t	Pro	-*m*	D	N_3
P4	Past	V-t	Pro	-*m*	D	N_2
P5	Past	V-t	Pro	-*m*	D	N_1
P6	Past	V-t	Pro	-*m*	D	N
P7	Past	V-t	Pro	-*m*	D	N-c

L   Past+*give*+*he*+-*m*+*a*+*book*

T-fix ⇒ *give*+Past+*he*+-*m*+*a*+*book*

M   *gave*+*him*+*a*+*book*

T-Rules

There are many LModE T-rules, but because of the limited scope of our study, only a few simplified T-rules are illustrated in this chapter. In the form in which they are given, many of the T-rules are limited in their application. Many restrictions

and variations apply to them, but we have omitted these complexities here. We shall examine these six single-base and
double-base transformations:

1. T-neg
2. T-pass
3. T-sub
4. T-rel
5. T-phrase
6. T-conj

T-Neg

The negative transformation T-neg transforms affirmative
strings into negative ones through the addition of a negator
(Neg), such as *not*. The following version of T-neg applies to
strings containing V–h.

T-neg OPT: NP+Tense+V–h+A $\Rightarrow$ NP+Tense+V–h+*not*
+A

Example

Mary has a cold $\Rightarrow$ *Mary hasn't a cold*
T-neg OPT: NP+Tense+V–h+A $\Rightarrow$ NP+
                  Tense+V–h+*not*+A
                  Mary+Pres+*have*+*a cold* $\Rightarrow$
                  Mary+Pres+*have*+*not*+*a cold*
T-fix $\Rightarrow$ *Mary*+*have*+Pres+*not*+*a cold*
M   *Mary*+*hasn't*+*a cold*

T-Pass

The passive transformation T-pass applies only to strings
containing V–t.

T-pass OPT: NP_1+Tense+V–t+NP_2 $\Rightarrow$ NP_2+Tense+*be*+
Part+V–t (+*by*+NP_1)

NP_2, the object of V–t in the given string, is transformed by
means of T-pass to become the subject of the transform string.
The prepositional phrase (+*by*+NP_1) in the transform string is
optional.

For example, if we wished to transform *Mary washed the lamb* into *The lamb was washed by Mary*, we would apply T-pass as follows:

T-pass OPT: NP_1+Tense+V–t+NP_2 $\Rightarrow$ NP_2+Tense+*be*+
Part+V–t (+*by*+NP_1)
Mary+Past+*wash*+*the lamb* $\Rightarrow$ *the lamb*+Past
+*be*+Part+*wash*+*by*+*Mary*

T-fix $\Rightarrow$ *the lamb*+*be*+Past+*wash*+Part+*by*+*Mary*

M   *The lamb*+*was*+*washed*+*by*+*Mary*

T-Sub

The subordination transform T-sub subordinates a clause in a string. The subordinate clause is introduced by a subordinator (Sub), such as *that*. In the version of T-sub presented below, the subordinate clause is the object of V–t.

T-sub OPT: Insert: S (1)
Matrix: A (2) − NP (3) − B (4)
Result: A (2)+Sub+S (1)+B (4)

To obtain *Tom believed that Mary bought the lamb*, we apply T-sub as follows:

T-sub OPT: Insert: *Mary bought the lamb* (1)
Matrix: *Tom believed* (2) − NP (3) − Ø (4)
Result: *Tom believed* (2) | *that*+ *Mary bought
the lamb* (1)+Ø (4) or *Tom be-
lieved that Mary bought the lamb*

T-Rel

The following version of the relative transform T-rel produces relative clauses that are modifiers of NPs.

T-rel OPT: Insert: A (1) − NP_1 (2) − B (3)
Matrix: C (4) − NP_1 (2) − D (5)
Result: $4+2+\begin{Bmatrix} who \\ that \\ which \end{Bmatrix}+1+3+5$

For example, the result *Tom gave the lamb that Mary bought yesterday a bath* may be obtained thus:

T-rel OPT: Insert: *Mary bought* (1) — *the lamb* (2) — *yesterday* (3)

Matrix: *Tom gave* (4) — *the lamb* (2) — *a bath* (5)

Result: *Tom gave* (4) + *the lamb* (2) + *that* + *Mary bought* (1) + *yesterday* (3) + *a bath* (5) or *Tom gave the lamb that Mary bought yesterday a bath*

The following example is one in which Ø occurs in some positions:

Insert: *Mary bought* (1) — *the lamb* (2) — Ø (3)

Matrix: Ø (4) — *the lamb* (2) — *was black* (5)

Result: Ø (4) + *the lamb* (2) + *that* + *Mary bought* (1) + Ø (3) + *was black* (5) or *The lamb that Mary bought was black*

T-Phrase

T-phrase may be applied to the result of T-rel if the relative clause of the result contains *be*, according to one version of T-phrase. T-phrase transforms such relative clauses into phrase modifiers of NPs.

For example, *who was bathing her lamb* is the relative clause in *Mary knew the man who was bathing her lamb*. The relative clause contains *be*. T-phrase may be applied to that clause as follows:

T-phrase OPT: $Y+NP+Rel+Tense+be+Z \Rightarrow Y+NP+Z$

Mary knew (Y) + *the man* (NP) + *who* + Past + *be* + *bathing her lamb* (Z) $\Rightarrow$ *Mary knew* (Y) + *the man* (NP) + *bathing her lamb* (Z) or *Mary knew the man bathing her lamb*

In effect, by means of T-phrase the items Rel + Tense + *be* in the given string are deleted in the transform.

T-Conj

The result of the conjunction transform T-conj may contain a coordinating conjunction or a pair of correlative conjunctions. Some coordinating conjunctions are *and, or, but*. Correlative conjunctions are conjunctions that occur in pairs, such as *either/or, not (only)/ but (also)*, etc.

Conjs join structures called conjuncts. Those conjuncts, which fill positions 2 and 5 in the formula below, must have the same grammatical structure. For example, they must both be coordinate NPs, VPs, subordinate clauses, sentences, etc.

The following formulation for T-conj is but one of various possible symbolizations. It is restricted to results that contain coordinating Conjs.

$$\text{T-conj OPT: Insert: } A\ (1) - B\ (2) - C\ (3)$$
$$\text{Matrix: } D\ (4) - E\ (5) - F\ (6)$$
$$\text{Result: } 4 + 2 + \text{Conj} + 5 + 6$$

Example

Insert: *She likes men* (1) *— that dance* (2) *— well* (3)

Matrix: *She likes men* (4) *— that ski* (5) *— well* (6)

Result: *She likes men* (4) *+that dance* (2) *+and+that ski* (5) *+well* (6) or *She likes men that dance and that ski well.*

Ø occurs in some positions in this example:

Insert: Ø (1) *— Jack* (2) *— went up the hill* (3)

Matrix: Ø (4) *— Jill* (5) *— went up the hill* (6)

Result: Ø (4) *+Jack* (2) *+and+Jill* (5) *+went up the hill* (6) or *Jack and Jill went up the hill*

Question Transforms

In our brief sketch of OE syntax we purposely avoided question sentences in the interest of simplicity. In connection with LModE, however, it is appropriate that we examine some question sentences for the insight they provide into the structure of English.

In English all question sentences are transforms. We shall examine three optional question transforms:

1. T-ques$_1$
2. T-ques$_2$
3. T-ques$_{who}$

T-Ques₁

T-ques₁, our first question transform, reads:

T-ques₁ OPT: NP+Tense+Mod+Z ⇒ Tense+Mod+NP+Z

For example, *Mary could sing* is transformed into *Could Mary sing?* as follows:

T-ques₁ OPT: NP+Tense+Mod+Z ⇒ Tense+Mod+
NP+Z
Mary+Past+*can*+*sing* ⇒ Past+*can*+
Mary+*sing*

T-fix ⇒   *can*+Past+*Mary*+*sing*

M   *Could*+*Mary*+*sing?*

T-Ques₂

A variation of T-ques₁ is the question transform which we label T-ques₂:

T-ques₂ OPT: NP+Tense+V–t+Z ⇒ Tense+NP+V–t+Z

Note in the result that tense is not linked to V–t. To such transforms the obligatory transform T-verb must be applied. T-verb reads:

T-verb OBL: Tense ⇒ *do*+Tense

For example, suppose that from *Mary saw Tom* we wished to obtain the transform *Did Mary see Tom?* In order to obtain that transform, we first apply T-ques₂ to *Mary saw Tom* as follows:

T-ques₂ OPT: NP+Tense+V–t+Z ⇒ Tense+NP+V–t+Z
Mary+Past+*see*+*Tom* ⇒ Past+*Mary*+*see*
+*Tom*

To any tense not adjacent to a verb, we must apply the obligatory transform T-verb:

T-verb OBL: Tense ⇒ *do*+Tense
Past ⇒ *do*+Past

Applying T-verb to the transform of T-ques₂ we get:

T-verb OBL ⇒ *do*+Past+*Mary*+*see*+*Tom*

M   *Did*+*Mary*+*see*+*Tom?*

T-Ques_who

The last question transform that we shall examine is T-ques_who, which applies to transforms of T-ques₂.

Example

Mary asked Tom $\Rightarrow$ *Who asked Tom?*

To obtain that transform, we first apply T-ques$_2$ to *Mary asked Tom*.

T-ques$_2$ OPT: NP+Tense+V-t+Z $\Rightarrow$ Tense+NP+V-t+Z

$\qquad$ *Mary*+Past+*ask*+*Tom* $\Rightarrow$ Past+Mary+

$\qquad$ *ask*+*Tom*

We next apply T-ques$_{who}$:

T-ques$_{who}$ OPT: Y+NP+Z $\Rightarrow$ *who*+Y+Z

$\qquad$ Past (Y)+*Mary* (NP)+*ask Tom* (Z) $\Rightarrow$

$\qquad$ *who*+Past (Y)+*ask Tom* (Z)

T-fix $\Rightarrow$ $\qquad$ *who*+*ask*+Past+*Tom*

M $\qquad$ *Who*+*asked*+*Tom?*

A variation of T-ques$_{who}$ involves the application of T–*m*:

$\quad$ T–*m* OPT: NP $\Rightarrow$ NP+–*m*

Example

Mary sees Tom often $\Rightarrow$ *Whom does Mary see often?*

To obtain the desired transform, we apply the following T-rules to *Mary sees Tom often*.

T-ques$_2$ OPT: NP+Tense+V-t+Z $\Rightarrow$ Tense+NP+V-t+Z

$\qquad$ *Mary*+Pres+*see*+*Tom often* $\Rightarrow$ Pres+*Mary*

$\qquad$ +*see*+*Tom often*

T-ques$_{who}$ OPT: Y+NP+Z $\Rightarrow$ *who*+Y+Z

$\qquad$ Pres *Mary see* (Y)+*Tom* (NP)+*often* (Z)

$\qquad$ $\Rightarrow$ *who*+Pres *Mary see* (Y)+*often* (Z)

Next to *who* (NP) we apply T–*m* OPT: NP $\Rightarrow$ NP + *m*

T–*m* OPT: *who*+Pres+*Mary* | *see*+*often* $\Rightarrow$ *who*+–*m*+

$\qquad$ Pres+*Mary*+*see*+*often*

T-verb OBL: Tense $\Rightarrow$ *do*+Tense

T-verb OBL: *who*+–*m*+Pres+*Mary*+*see*+*often* $\Rightarrow$ *who*+

$\qquad$ –*m*+*do*+Pres+*Mary*+*see*+*often*

M $\qquad$ *Whom*+*does*+*Mary*+*see*+*often?*

Prose Extract

As an example of LModE (AmE) prose, of a period approximately between the earliest and present stages of LModE, we offer Abraham Lincoln's address at the dedication of the Gettysburg National Cemetery (19 November 1863):

Four score and seven years ago our fathers brought forth on this continent, a new nation, conceived in liberty, and dedicated to the proposition that all men are created equal.

Now we are engaged in a great civil war; testing whether that nation, or any nation so conceived and so dedicated, can long endure. We are met on a great battlefield of that war. We have come to dedicate a portion of that field as a final resting-place for those who here gave their lives that that nation might live. It is altogether fitting and proper that we should do this.

But, in a larger sense, we cannot dedicate — we cannot consecrate — we cannot hallow — this ground. The brave men, living and dead, who struggled here have consecrated it, far above our poor power to add or detract. The world will little note, nor long remember, what we say here, but it can never forget what they did here. It is for us the living, rather, to be dedicated here to the unfinished work which they who fought here have thus far so nobly advanced. It is rather for us to be here dedicated to the great task remaining before us — that from these honored dead we take increased devotion to that cause for which they gave the last full measure of devotion; that we here highly resolve that these dead shall not have died in vain; that this nation, under God, shall have a new birth of freedom; and that government of the people, by the people, for the people, shall not perish from the earth.

SUMMARY

P1 S $\rightarrow$ NP+VP

P2 NP $\rightarrow$ $\begin{cases} \text{Pro} \\ \text{N-prop} \\ (\text{Det}+)\text{N}_3 \end{cases}$

P3 Det $\rightarrow$ $\begin{cases} (\text{PreD}+)\text{D}(+\text{pl}) \\ \text{NP}+\text{-'s} \end{cases}$

P4 N$_3$ $\rightarrow$ $\begin{cases} \text{N}_2 \\ \text{Nu}+\text{N}_2 \end{cases}$

P5 N$_2$ $\rightarrow$ $\begin{cases} \text{N}_1 \\ \text{AP}+\text{N}_2 \end{cases}$

P6 N$_1$ $\rightarrow$ $\begin{cases} \text{N} \\ \text{N}_2+\text{N}_1 \end{cases}$

P7 N $\rightarrow$ $\begin{cases} \text{N-c}(+\text{pl}) \\ \text{N-m} \end{cases}$

P8 AP $\rightarrow$ $\begin{cases} \text{Adj} \\ \text{Int}+\text{Adj} \end{cases}$

P9 Adj $\rightarrow$ $\left\{ \begin{array}{l} \text{Adj-pos} \\ \text{Adj-comp} \\ \text{Adj-super} \end{array} \right\}$

P10 VP $\rightarrow$ $\left\{ \begin{array}{l} \text{Pres} + V_4 \\ \text{Past} + V_4 \end{array} \right\}$

P11 V_4 $\rightarrow$ $\left\{ \begin{array}{l} V_3 \\ \text{Mod} + V_3 \end{array} \right\}$

P12 V_3 $\rightarrow$ $\left\{ \begin{array}{l} V_2 \\ have + \text{Part} + V_2 \end{array} \right\}$

P13 V_2 $\rightarrow$ $\left\{ \begin{array}{l} V_1 \\ be + \text{-}ing + V_1 \end{array} \right\}$

P14 V_1 $\rightarrow$ $\left\{ \begin{array}{l} \text{V-i}(+\text{pl})(+\text{Adv}_1) \\ \text{V-t}(+\text{pl}) + \text{NP} + \text{-}m \left(+ \left\{ \begin{array}{l} \text{NP} \\ \text{AP} \end{array} \right\} \right) (+\text{Adv}_1) \\ \\ \text{V-1}(+\text{pl}) + \text{AP}(+\text{Adv}_1) \\ be(+\text{pl}) + \text{Adv}_1 \\ \text{V-b}(+\text{pl}) + \left\{ \begin{array}{l} \text{NP} \\ \text{AP} \end{array} \right\} (+\text{Adv}_1) \\ \text{V-h}(+\text{pl}) + \text{NP} + \text{-}m(+\text{Adv}_1) \end{array} \right\}$

P15 $\text{Adv}_1 \rightarrow$ $\left\{ \begin{array}{l} \text{Adv} \\ \text{Adv}_1 + \text{Adv} \end{array} \right\}$

P16 Adv $\rightarrow$ $\left\{ \begin{array}{l} \text{Adv-t} \\ \text{Adv-p} \\ \text{Adv-m} \\ \text{Adv-f} \\ \text{Prep} + \text{NP} + \text{-}m \end{array} \right\}$

T-fix OBL: $\quad$ Fix + V $\Rightarrow$ V + Fix. $\quad$ Fix = tense, Part, or -ing. V = modal, have, be, or verb.

T-neg OPT: $\quad$ NP + Tense + V-h + A $\Rightarrow$ NP + Tense + V-h + not + A

T-pass OPT: $\quad$ NP_1 + Tense + V-t + NP_2 $\Rightarrow$ NP_2 + Tense + be + Part + V-t(+by+NP_1)

T-sub OPT: $\quad$ Insert: $\quad$ S (1)
$\qquad\qquad$ Matrix: $\quad$ A (2) − NP (3) − B (4)
$\qquad\qquad$ Result: $\quad$ A (2) + Sub + S (1) + B (4)

T-rel OPT: $\quad$ Insert: $\quad$ A (1) − NP_1 (2) − B (3)
$\qquad\qquad$ Matrix: $\quad$ C (4) − NP_1 (2) − D (5)

$$\text{Result:} \quad 4+2+ \left\{ \begin{array}{l} who \\ that \\ which \end{array} \right\} +1+3+5$$

T-phrase OPT: $\quad$ Y+NP+Rel+Tense+be+Z $\Rightarrow$ Y+NP+Z

T-conj OPT: $\quad$ Insert: $\quad$ A (1)$-$B (2)$-$C (3)

$\qquad\qquad\qquad$ Matrix: $\quad$ D (4)$-$E (5)$-$F (6)

$\qquad\qquad\qquad$ Result: $\quad$ 4+2+Conj+5+6

T-ques$_1$ OPT: $\quad$ NP+Tense+Mod+Z $\Rightarrow$ Tense+Mod+ NP+Z

T-ques$_2$ OPT: $\quad$ NP+Tense+V-t+Z $\Rightarrow$ Tense+NP+ V-t+Z

T-verb OBL: $\quad$ Tense $\Rightarrow$ do+Tense

T-ques$_{who}$ OPT: $\quad$ Y+NP+Z $\Rightarrow$ who+Y+Z

T-m OPT: $\quad$ NP $\Rightarrow$ NP+-m

NOTES

[1] T-rules of an expanded grammar of LModE also would provide for post-NP modifiers (PNPM), such as those that follow *man* in *man of the house*, *man in the street*, and others.

[2] Adj → adjectives like *green* (*green, greener, greenest*) and certain FWs like *beautiful* and *ambitious*.

[3] The representation that follows of the phrase structure of the construction is called a tree of derivation. The phrase structures of subsequent examples are also presented in trees of derivation.

[4] In the interest of simplicity, we have omitted some subsets of V-i and V-t. For example, there is also V-i+Particle as in *ran+away* and V-t+ Particle as in *clean+out*.

Historical Vocabulary

The subject matter of this chapter is the historical vocabulary of English. We shall begin with an analysis of the word stock of OE, including its loanwords,[1] and then consider losses and additions in the vocabulary of English in the later periods. We shall also examine such closely related matters as the EModE controversy concerning the legitimacy of English as a vehicle of composition, the dispute over inkhorn terms, and the fixation of English spelling. We shall conclude with a brief discussion about how words are formed, and about variations and changes in the meanings of words.

OE Vocabulary

It is estimated that about eighty-five percent of the vocabulary of OE is no longer in use because of replacements over the centuries by Latin and French loanwords.[2] The derivatives of OE words that have come down to us, however, are basic elements in our vocabulary. For example, the major portion of our conjunctions, auxiliary verbs, prepositions, and pronouns are derivatives of OE words. So too are a number of words that express fundamental concepts such as *eat, fight, sleep, work, live, child, foot, house, land, meat,* and others.

OE Germanic Words

The bulk of the word stock of OE consisted of Germanic words that constituted the vocabulary of the Anglo-Saxons when they migrated from the Continent to Britain. They include such OE words as *bān* 'bone,' *ēare* 'ear,' *niht* 'night,' *ċealf* 'calf,' *grund* 'ground,' *steorra* 'star,' *dēað* 'death,' *hēafod* 'head,' and *woruld* 'world.'

Through the use of derivational prefixes and suffixes, the Anglo-Saxons formed a variety of derivative words from various parts of speech, as we do today. For example, from *wīs* 'wise' they derived *unwīs* 'unwise' and *wīsdōm* 'wisdom'; from *settan* 'to set' they derived *foresettan* 'to set before' and *onsettan* 'to set on'; from *wynn* 'joy' they derived *wynnlēas* 'joyless'; from *grǣd* 'greed' they derived *grǣdiġ* 'greedy'; and so on. Like us, the Anglo-Saxons also joined words together to form compounds, such as *giesthūs* 'guest house, inn,' *goldhord* 'gold hord, treasure,' *morgensteorra* 'morning star,' *stēopċild* 'stepchild, orphan,' *trēow-wyrm* 'tree worm, caterpillar,' etc.

OE Latin Loanwords

A large number of OE words were Latin loanwords. Some of those borrowings date back to the time when the Germanic Anglo-Saxons lived on the Continent and met Roman soldiers, merchants, and colonists. From them were borrowed such words as OE *wīn* 'wine' < Latin *vīnum*; OE *strǣt* 'street, road' < Latin *strāta*; OE *mīl* 'mile' < Latin *mīlle (passum)* 'thousand (paces)'; OE *panne* 'pan' < Latin *panna*; and OE *wall* 'wall' < Latin *vallum*.

But the majority of OE loanwords from Latin consisted of religious and learned words that the Anglo-Saxons adopted in Britain through the Church, following their conversion to Christianity by Roman and Irish missionaries. Examples are OE *apostol* 'apostle' < Latin *apostolus*; OE *dīacon* 'deacon' < Latin *dīaconus*; OE *dēmon* 'demon, devil < Latin *daemōn*; OE *pāpa* 'pope' < Latin *papa*; OE *scōl* 'school' < Latin *schola*; and OE *ymen* 'hymn' < Latin *hymnus*.[3]

OE Celtic Loanwords

In comparison to the number of OE words borrowed from Latin, those borrowed from Celtic in the OE period were a handful. They include such words as OE *binn* 'bin,' *bratt* 'cloak,' *brocc* 'badger,' place-names, such as Modern English *Avon, Dee, Thames,* (Isle of) *Wight,* and words introduced by Irish missionaries, such as OE *æstel* 'bookmark,' *clucge* 'bell,' and *drȳ* 'magician, sorcerer.'

ME Vocabulary

Many OE words did not survive the ME period. Some, such as OE *fina* 'woodpecker' and *wuldor* 'glory,' disappeared in the Early ME period, and others were displaced by loanwords from Scandinavian and Old French. For example, OE *æġ* 'egg,' pl. *æġru* became in ME sg. *ei*, pl. *eiren*, but in Late ME those words were progressively replaced by sg. *egg*, pl. *egges* from Scandinavian sg. and pl. *egg*. Similarly, OE *æðele* 'noble, excellent' passed into Early ME, but that word was subsequently replaced by ME *nǫble* 'noble, great' < OFr *noble*. Another example is OE *sweostor ~ suster* 'sister' > Early ME *suster*, which form was displaced by Scand. *systir* > ME *sister*.

Not all ME loanwords survived, however. Many became archaic or obsolete in Late ME and EModE and eventually vanished, such as (French) *simenels* 'bread made from fine flour,' *cēte* 'whale,' *flum* 'river,' and (Scandinavian) *dreng* 'warrior,' *hīðing* 'root,' and *orrest* 'battle.'

ME French Loanwords

About ten thousand French loanwords entered the language in the ME period, of which about seventy five percent are still in use.[4] At first only a few French loanwords entered English, but thereafter the number increased progressively until it reached a peak at the end of the fourteenth century. After 1400 the number of French loanwords declined, although borrowing from French has continued to the present century.[5]

French loanwords in ME reflect various aspects of French life introduced in England. For example, loanwords were drawn from government as ME *parlement* 'parliament,' from finance as ME *trẹsor* 'treasure,' from titles of nobility as ME *duc* 'duke,' from the military as ME *serjeaunt* 'sergeant,' from law as ME *juge* 'judge,' from art as ME *tragedye* 'tragedy,' from medicine as ME *surgien* 'surgeon,' from meal terms as ME *diner* 'dinner,' from the Church as ME *religioun* 'religion,' and from other aspects of French culture. LModE *beef, mutton, veal,* and *pork* also are from French, in contrast to LModE *ox, sheep, calf,* and *swine* from OE.

OFr Dialects

Loanwords from French were sometimes adopted into ME in more than one form. For example, Northern Old French frequently preserved [k] from Late Latin as in Northern OFr *cachier* > ME *cachen* 'to catch,' but Central Old French had [č] as in Central OFr *chacier* > ME *chāssen* 'to chase.' Also, Northern Old French preserved [w] in words borrowed from German as in Northern OFr *wardein* > ME *wardaine* 'warden,' but Central Old French had [g] as in Central OFr *guarden* > ME *gardein* 'guardian.'

ME Latin Loanwords

Latin loanwords in ME were adopted mainly from learned and religious sources, including the spoken Middle Latin of priests. Examples of such loanwords are Latin *sacramentum* > ME *sacramente* 'sacrament,' Middle Latin *desca* > ME *deske* 'desk,' and Latin *nervosus* > ME *nervous* 'nervous.' But since Old French developed from a dialectal variety of Vulgar or spoken Latin, not from Classical or literary Latin, it is sometimes difficult to determine if a ME loanword was borrowed from Old French or from Latin, as in the case of ME *disciplīne* from either OFr *disciplīne* or Latin *disciplīna*.

ME Nordic Loanwords

Loanwords from Old Scandinavian first appeared in Late OE writings, but Scandinavian borrowings did not become numerous until the thirteenth century, at which time hundreds were recorded for the first time. In the ME period such borrowings first appeared largely in Northern and East Midland dialects, undoubtedly as a result of the widespread Scandinavian settlements in those areas prior to the Norman Conquest.

Examples of loanwords from Old Scandinavian include OScand *taka* > ME *tāken* 'to take,' OScand *skȳ* > ME *skīē* 'sky,' OScand *vengr* > *winge* 'wing,' and OScand *systir* > ME *sister* 'sister.' As in the case of Old French and Latin, however, the linguistic similarity of Old Scandinavian and Old English sometimes makes it difficult to determine from which of those two sources a ME word was derived, as in the case of OE *siððan* ~OScand *siðan* > ME *siðen* 'then, since.'

Scandinavian influence is also evident in more than 1,400 place-names in England. Borrowings from Scandinavian include such place-name elements as *–by* 'town' in *Derby*; as *–thorp* 'village' in *Althorp*; and as *–toft* 'dwelling house with buildings, lands' in *Eastoft*.

ME Germanic Loanwords

Germanic loanwords in ME were borrowed primarily from Middle Dutch and Middle Low German. Such loanwords, which generally refer to seafaring, commerce, and industry, were a handful compared with those borrowed from French and Scandinavian.

Historically, there was a close connection between England and the Low Countries of northwestern Europe. Old Frisian and Old English were both descended from Proto-Anglo-Frisian. Frisians settled in England at the time of the Anglo-Saxon invasions, and OE missionaries traveled and taught in northern Germany. In addition, the important English wool trade in the ME period led to frequent trade with ports of the Hanseatic League (Bremen, Hamburg, etc.), and many Flemish weavers taught and worked throughout medieval England.[6]

ME Low German loanwords first entered the language at the beginning of the thirteenth century. The greatest number were borrowed, however, in the sixteenth century in the EModE period. Examples of Late ME borrowings include Middle Dutch (MDu) *marct* > ME *mart* 'market,' MDu *pekel* > ME *pikil* 'brine, vinegar,' MDu *spoele* > ME *spole* 'spool,' MDu *sledde* >

ME *sledde* 'sleigh,' MDu *boje ~ boei* > ME *bōye* 'buoy,' and Middle Low German *doten* > ME *dōten* 'to be foolish, dote.'

EModE Vocabulary

We cannot accurately tell the total number of words in the vocabulary of OE or ME or EModE. A rough count, however, of the headwords listed in *A Concise Anglo-Saxon Dictionary* by John R. Clark Hall, supplement by Herbert D. Meritt (Cambridge, 1960), shows a total of approximately 35,000 OE words. In comparison, Charles C. Fries has estimated that from 1475 to 1700 the vocabulary of English increased from about 45,000 items to about 125,000 items, a rise of approximately 275 per cent.[7] That sharp increase in vocabulary items may be attributed to the large influx of loanwords from Latin, French, Greek, and many other languages that entered English between 1475 and 1700.

Borrowings from Latin in the EModE period related primarily to science and the arts. Examples of such Latin loanwords include *fulcrum, pendulum, data, pharynx, vertebra, appendix, quarto, folio,* and *caesura.* Also from Latin (and French) have come such ModE prefixes as *con-, de-, dis-, en-, ex-, in-, infra-, inter-, per-, pre-, pro-, trans-,* and such suffixes as *-able, -al, -ance, -ant, -ary, -ate, -ent, -ery, -ity, -ment, -ory.*

Loanwords from French include such examples as *commandant, gavotte, volley, rendezvous,* and *envoy.*[8]

From Greek were borrowed such prefixes as *anthro-* in EModE *anthropophague* 'man eaters,' *auto-* in *automaton, bio-* in *biography,* and *epi-* in *epigramme.* Loanwords from Greek also entered the language indirectly through Latin (*irony, drama*) and through French (*ode, machine*).

Numerous words were also adopted into English in the EModE period from languages other than Latin, French, and Greek. Some examples indicative of the wide range of such borrowings include German *zinc,* Italian *piano,* Spanish *tornado,* Portuguese *flamingo,* Arabic *sofa,* Persian *jasmin,* Dravidian *calico,* Javanese *bantam,* Japanese *kimono,* Malayan *bamboo,* and so on.

Latin-English Controversy

As the wave of the Renaissance rolled westward and north over Europe from Italy, scholarly interest in classical literature strengthened the old opinion that Latin was the best idiom for all fields of learning. Scholars associated literary and rhetorical excellence with the Latin classics. Moreover, Latin was the standard educated language of Europe.[9] Consequently, scholars violently criticized the emerging vernaculars of French, Italian, and Spanish as lacking the purity and extensive vocabulary of Latin.

English also came under attack in the sixteenth century by various writers who called the language 'uneloquent' in such terms as *base, simple, rude, gross, barbarous,* and *vile.* They said that because English lacked an adequate vocabulary to express abstract ideas and treat a variety of disciplines, serious compositions about theology, medicine, philosophy, law, and the like should be written in Latin.

A typical complaint was that of Roger Ascham in *Toxophilus* (1545):

> As for ye Latin or greke tongue, euery thing is so excellentlie done in them, that none can do better: In the Englysh tongue contrary, euery thinge in a manner so meanly, both for the matter and handelynge, that no man can do worse.

Thomas Elyot, in *The Boke named the Gouernour* (1531), even went so far as to advise that:

> hit shall be expedient that a noble mannco conne, in his infancie, haue with hym continually onely such as may accustome hym by litle and litle to speake pure and elegant latin. Semblably the nourishcs [nurses] and other women about hym, if it be possible, to do the same.

But not all Englishmen shared the purists' views. Richard Mulcaster declared in *The First Part of the Elementarie* (1582):

> I take this present period of our English tung to be the verie height therof, bycause I find it so excellentlie well fined [refined], both for the bodie of the tung it self, and for the customarie writing thereof, as either foren workmanship can giue it glosse, or as homewrought hanling can giue it grace ... and whatsoeuer shall becom of the English state, the English tung cannot proue fairer, then it is at this daie, if it maie please our learned sort to esteme so of it, and to bestow their trauell [labor] vpon such a subiect, so capable of ornament, so proper to themselues, and the more to be honored bycause it is their own.

English Translations

The Latin-English controversy was so intense that some Englishmen, who altruistically wanted their untutored countrymen to share the heritage of the ancients, felt compelled to apologize in print for having "Englyshed" works from Latin and Greek. Other English writers, however, such as John Caius, wrote "one boke in Englishe onely for Englishemen not learned, one other in latine for men of learninge more at large."[10]

At any rate, in the late sixteenth century the arguments against the legitimacy of English were drowned out by the public demand for English translations of foreign-language works. In the sixteenth and seventeenth centuries, for example, there appeared translations of such ancients as Aristotle, Plato, Thucydides, Marcus Aurelius, Xenophon, Caesar, Cato, Cicero, Livy, Plutarch, Seneca, Terence, and Tacitus; such medieval writers as Augustine, Boethius, and Kempis; and such contemporaries as Calvin, Erasmus, and Luther. In addition, there were a number of translations of Latin, French, German, Italian, and Spanish works dealing with warfare, medicine, navigation, astronomy, surgery, foreign travel, religion, education, and government.

Bible Translations

The Church also contributed indirectly to the support of English through various translations of the Greek-Latin Bible. For example, in the EModE period there were such Protestant versions as the William Tyndale Bible (1525–34), the Miles Coverdale Bible (1535), the Great Bible (1539), the Geneva Bible (1560), the Bishops' Bible (1568), and the King James Bible or Authorized Version (1611). For Roman Catholics the vernacular Rheims-Douay version (1582–1610) was based on the Vulgate or Latin version by St. Jerome and others in the fourth century.

Inkhorn Terms

Another dispute among scholars in the EModE period concerned the copious introduction into English of loanwords from

Latin and other languages, as well as archaic words from the earlier periods of English. Because such neologisms and resurrected terms came primarily from scholarly and learned sources, they were regarded as obscure, affected, and ornate. They were derisively labeled *inkhorn* terms.

Thomas Wilson, in *The Arte of Rhetorique* (1560) complained:

> Some farre iourneyed gentlemen at their returne home, like as they loue to goe in forraine apparell, so thei wil pouder their talke with ouersea language. He that commeth lately out of Fraunce, will talke French English and neuer blush at the matter. An other chops in with English Italienated, and applieth the Italian phrase to our English speaking . . . The fine courtier wil talke nothing but Chaucer. The misticall wiseman and Poeticall Clerkes, will speake nothing but quaint Prouerbes, and blinde Allegories, delighting much in their owne darkenesse, especially, when none can tell what they doe say. The vnlearned or foolish phantasticall, that smelles but of learning (such fellowes as haue seen learned men in their daies) wil so Latin their tongues, that the simple can not but wonder at their talke, and thinke surely they speake by some reuelation. I know them that thinke Rhetorique to stande wholie vpon darke wordes, and hee that can catch an ynke horne terme by the taile, him they coumpt [count] to be a fine Englisheman, and a good Rhetorician.

Wilson complained of such inkhorn terms as EModE *splendente, spendidious, adnichilate, continguate, collaude, obtestate,* and *fatigate.* Fortunately or unfortunately, such words have long since gone to their grave, but other EModE inkhorn terms such as *expending, celebrate, extol, clemencie, relinquish, contemplate,* and *dexteritie,* to which Wilson also objected, remain in use.[11]

George Puttenham, in *The Arte of English Poesie* (1589), also complained of:

> Many inkhorne termes so ill affected brought in by men of learning as preachers and schoolemasters: and many straunge termes of other languages by Secretaries and Marchaunts and trauailours, and many darke wordes . . . dayly spoken in Court.

Puttenham, however, was "not vnwilling to acknowledge his owne fault" in regard to use of such inkhorn terms as EModE *scientificke, Maior-domo, Idiome, Politien, Conduict, Methode, significatiue, placation, function, assubtiling, refining, compendious, prolixe, numerositee, sauage,* and *harmonicall.*

Despite his complaint, Puttenham recognized the impoverishment of the English vocabulary in relation to the "artes of Grammer, Logike, Rhetoricke, Arithmeticke, Astronomie, Geographie, etc." Thus, he said:

> I cannot see how we may spare them, whatsoeuer fault wee finde with Ink-horne termes: for our speach wanteth wordes to such sence so well to be vsed.

Spelling Reform

By about 1600 the controversy concerning inkhorn terms had largely subsided, although opposition to borrowed words continued for a long time afterwards. As the semantic debate waned, scholarly attention shifted to the growing interest in spelling reform.

We can make the generalization that English spelling in Late ME was relatively phonetic, for there was a fair measure of correlation between spelling and pronunciation. But in the early portion of the EModE period spelling became quite fluid and largely a matter of individual preference. For example, in Caxton's works the following variants for 'French' occur: *ffrensh, frensh, frenssh, frenshe, frensshe, ffrensshe, ffrenshe, Frensshe, Frenshe.*

Scholarly reaction to such disorder prompted various proposals for the reform of English spelling. There ensued a verbal conflict between the conservatives and the advocates of change.

Richard Mulcaster lamented in *The First Part of the Elementarie* (1582):

> Whereby it commeth to passe, that we both write vnproperlie, not answering the sound of that, which we saie, and ar neuer like our selues, in anie our writing, but still varie according vnto the writers humor, without anie certain direction. Whereupon forenners and strangers do wonder at vs, both for the vncertaintie in our writing, and the inconstancie in our letters.

As a remedy for the orthographic confusion in the EModE period, advocates of reform in the last half of the sixteenth century and the first half of the seventeenth century proposed that English spelling be remodeled along phonetic lines to reflect more accurately contemporary pronunciation.[12] They proposed, for example, such spellings as *bras* 'brass,' *sutl* 'subtle,' *biznes* 'business,' *eest* 'east,' *prisner* 'prisoner,' *supt* 'supped,' *telst* 'tellest,' and *kuriozite* 'curiosity.'

In the face of such proposed spellings the scholar Mulcaster voiced a conservative opinion. He favored elimination of the defects in the English spelling system, but not the adoption of a totally new system of spelling, as urged by some writers. He also believed that spelling reform should be based on the authority of popular usage, and that spelling should no more than approximate pronunciation because, "When the age of peple, which now vse the tung so well, is dead and departed there will another succede, and with the peple the tung will alter and change."

Edmund Coote, in the *English Schoole-Master* (1597), also opposed the reform of spelling. Said Coote, "Because it lyeth not in vs to reforme, I wish you rather to obserue the best, and follow that which wee haue, than to labour for innouation, which we cannot effect."

Etymological Spellings

The sound advice of Mulcaster and Coote did not deter scholars from remodeling some English words to make them conform to the spelling of their etyma, or earlier forms. For example, the etymological remodelers, as they may be called, succeeded in adding *b* to *debt* (ME *dot ~ dette*) in order to make it conform to Latin *debitum*, from which the English word was derived through Old French *dette ~ debte*. These are some other examples of scholarly additions of graphemes:

p in *receipt* (ME *receite* from OFr *recete*), to conform to Middle Latin *recepta*, fem. past. part. of *recipere*.

s in *island* (ME *īlond ~ eilōnd*), to conform by analogy with unrelated *isle* (ME *yle*, OFr *isle ~ ile*) from Late Latin *iscle* < Latin *insula*.

c in *indict* (ME *endīten ~ indīte ~ indight*, OFr *enditer*), to conform with Latin *in+dictāre*.[13]

Fixation of Spelling

Although such etymological spellings remain in English, most of the other changes advocated by EModE scholars in the spelling reform movement (c. 1550–c. 1650) did not come into general use. The majority of spelling changes that actually were adopted were determined by correctors, that is proofreaders and editors, who sought to spell the same word more or less uniformly in texts produced from their presses. As a result of their conservative efforts, influenced mainly by Late ME SEMid forms, there emerged by c. 1650 a system of English spelling which became standardized, with relatively few exceptions, in the following century through the additional regulatory influence of dictionaries. Since that time English spelling has been more or less fixed. Thus, the discrepancies between the way we currently pronounce and spell words may be attributed, in large measure, to the fact that our spelling, mostly inherited from Late ME, has remained more or less fixed since c. 1650, unlike the pronunciation of those Late ME words. For example, we spell *knight* just as it was spelled in the Late ME period, but today we pronounce it [náɪt] instead of [kníxt], as in the ME period.

AmE Vocabulary

When the emigrants from Britain settled along the Atlantic Coast of America in the colonial period, the situations confronting them were in many ways different from those in the Old World. The topography of the land was different, as were the animals and plants. Under these new conditions, the colonists changed the meanings of some words and coined others. For example, they altered the meaning of *creek* from 'small arm of the sea' to 'small stream' and the meaning of *pond* from 'artificial pool' to 'small natural lake.' They also created words, such as *lot* 'plot of ground,' from the practice of drawing lots to apportion land.[14]

Indian Loanwords

Over the years the pioneers, as they moved westward, borrowed a large number of Indian words, including such animal names as *opossum, raccoon, skunk*; topographical names such as *Massachusetts, Ohio, Mississippi, Connecticut*; plant names such as *squash, hickory, tamarack, pecan*; and a variety of other Indian words such as *papoose, moccasin, wigwam, succotash.*

Other Loanwords

AmE also includes many loanwords adopted from various ethnic groups who settled in the New World. From Swedish, for example, is derived *smorgasbord*; from Pennsylvania German, *hex* 'to bewitch' and *schnitz and knep*, 'quartered apples and dumplings with ham.' Other examples are from Dutch, *coleslaw, cruller, boss, Santa Claus*; from Spanish, *adobe, bronco, mustang, vamoose, stampede*; from Yiddish, *schlemiel, schmaltz, mazuma*; from German, *kindergarten, pumpernickel, schnapps, sauerkraut, zwieback*; from French, *prairie, bateau, levee*, and *sashay*. AmE also includes such Africanisms as *voodoo, hoodoo, goober* 'peanut,' and *cooter* 'turtle.' Many more loanwords from other ethnic groups could be added to our brief list.

Frontier Americanisms

AmE also includes a large number of Americanisms associated with life on the frontier. Some examples are *Conestoga wagon, log cabin, homestead, six shooter, derringer, 49er*, and *pony express*. Reflective also of an earlier way of life are *bushwacker, batter bread, johnny cake, Bowie knife, showboat, shanghai, jayhawker, high muckamuck*, and *mercantile store*, the last now shortened to *merc* in the West.

Trade Names and Inventions

In addition to Indian loanwords, loanwords from ethnic groups, and Americanisms associated with the frontier, the word stock of AmE contains vocabulary items drawn from trade names and inventions. For example, AmE words adopted from trade names include *kodak, Stetson*, and *Eskimo pie*. Words developed from inventions include *typewriter, hydrant, steamboat, soda fountain*, and *basketball*.

Modern Americanisms, including slang, are numerous. For example, we may have watched a *rookie warm up* in the *bullpen*, and following the *double header* we may have gone to the *country club*, where we discussed the merits of the *bonus baby* or the *Thousand Island dressing* on our salad.

As Americans, we freely refer to *motels, hardware stores, mail-order stores*, and *funeral homes*. We buy *overcoats*, and perhaps have illegally *hitchhiked*. Sometimes we drive on the *super-highway* to get to a *supermarket*.

If we have a pocket full of *dough*, we may be inclined to *goldbrick* because things are *O.K.* But, being *up-and-coming* individuals with *horsesense*, who are *on the ball* and *on the up and up*, but not *uppity*, we keep our noses to the *grindstone* because *that's how the cookie crumbles*.

As you can see there are thousands of Americanisms, and we have no more than scratched the surface with our few examples. Our heritage, therefore, not only includes all those words that have come down to us from OE times, but the hundreds of new words that have entered the language from new inventions, scientific discoveries, and a continually changing way of life. One could, after all, easily think of many words that Abraham Lincoln did not know, and it is reasonable to expect that our great-grandchildren will use many additional words that we shall never know.

Words

In concluding this chapter, we offer a brief general discussion about changes in words, their formation, and their meanings.

You have learned that words become archaic and fade from use, as ME *palfrey* 'woman's saddle horse.' You also have learned that words enter the language through borrowings, such as the loanword *noodle* from German *nudel* and the loanword *igloo* from Eskimo *igdlu*. In addition, you have learned that words are formed by compounding, such as *super+high+way* and *cow+boy*, or are derived from other words through the use of prefixes (PBs) and derivational suffixes (PoBs), as in *un+holy* and *kind+ness*.

Words are also formed in other ways. For example, some words are shortenings, such as *auto* from *automobile* and *piano* from *pianoforte*. Some vocabulary items are formed through back formation, such as *edit* from *editor* and *burgle* from *burglar*. Acronyms are created from combining the initial letters or syllables of several words, such as FBI from Federal Bureau of Investigation, and *radar* from *r*adio *d*etecting *a*nd *r*anging. A portmanteau word is one in which the form and the meaning of two words are blended, such as *brunch* from *br*eakfast+l*unch*, and *smog* from *sm*oke+f*og*. Sometimes words are remodeled through folk etymology to conform to an incorrect notion of their origin and meaning, such as *Welsh rarebit* from *Welsh rabbit* and *cold slaw* from *cole slaw*. Also, new words may be substituted for older words, such as *hi-fi* for older *phonograph*, which in turn was substituted for earlier *victrola*.

The meanings of words not only differ from country to country, such as *bonnet* BrE in one sense 'hood of an automobile' in contrast to AmE 'woman's hat,' but words change in meaning over the course of the centuries. For example, the meaning of *professor*, once restricted to 'teacher,' one who professes something, has been expanded in meaning to include 'any person assumed or claiming to be skilled in some art or sport,' as *Professor Za Za*, the Hungarian tattoo artist. On the other hand, a word may become restricted in meaning. *Deer*, for example, used by Shakespeare to mean 'animals,' now is popularly restricted in meaning to the hoofed, usually antlered kind.

Words that once had a "pleasant" meaning sometimes acquire an "unpleasant" one. The word *knave*, for example, which once meant 'youth, male servant,' now means 'dishonest person, rogue, rascal.' On the other hand, words that once had an "unpleasant" meaning sometimes acquire a "pleasant" one, as in the case of *fond*, earlier 'foolish, idiotic, foolishly naive,' but now meaning 'tender, loving, cherishing with great affection.'

In view of the complex changes that words undergo, it is a fallacy to speak of the earlier meaning of a word as its true or real meaning in contrast to its current meaning. Words have whatever meaning people give them. Words, after all, are only arbitrarily selected bundles of sounds to which a culture attaches various meanings. For example, in English we call a 'tree' a *tree*, but in French the word is *arbre* and in German *baum*. Furthermore, because the trees in Africa differ from those in the Pacific Northwest or Maine, what the Bantu thinks of as a 'tree' may not be the same as what we think of as a 'tree.' Finally, as we stated in an earlier chapter, some cultures may have many words for snow, and other cultures have none. Words and their meanings are culturally conditioned.

SUMMARY

OE — Germanic stock, Latin and Celtic loanwords.

ME — French, Latin, Nordic, and Low Germanic loanwords, OFr dialects.

EModE — Latin, Greek, French loanwords and those from many other languages, Latin-English controversy, English translations, Bible versions, Inkhorn terms, spelling reform, etymological spellings, fixation of spelling (c. 1650).

AmE — Indian loanwords and those from ethnic groups, frontier Americanisms, those from trade names and inventions, and modern Americanisms.

Changes in words, their formation and their meanings.

NOTES

[1] A loanword is a word borrowed from another language, such as Modern English *coffee* from Italian *caffé*.

[2] See Harold Whitehall, "The English Language," in *Webster's New World Dictionary of the American Language*, College Edition (Cleveland, 1960), p. xxviii.

[3] There were about 180 Latin loanwords borrowed on the Continent by the Germanic peoples and about 360 Latin borrowings by the Anglo-Saxons during the period c. 450–1066. See Mary S. Serjeantson, *A History of Foreign Words in English* (London, 1935), Appendix A, pp. 271–288.

[4] Albert C. Baugh, *A History of the English Language* (New York, 1957), pp. 214–215.

[5] For example, French loanwords borrowed since the late seventeenth century include such examples as *boulevard, cigarette, champagne, de luxe, etiquette, menu, restaurant, souvenir,* and others.

[6] William the Conqueror's wife was Matilda of Flanders, and there were Flemings in William's retinue.

[7] *Linguistics and Reading* (New York, 1962), p. 168. Whitehall, "English Language," p. xxxii, offers a higher estimate of 50,000–60,000 OE items and 100,000–125,000 ME items.

[8] Many of the phonological developments that characterize Modern French occurred by about 1500. Thus, some modern borrowings from French differ in form from those of an earlier period. For example, [č] occurs in the ME borrowing *chēēf* 'chief,' but French [č] later became [š], as in the LModE borrowing *chef*. Similarly, [ǰ] occurs in the ME loanword *juge* 'judge,' but [ǰ] later became [ž] in French, as in the LModE borrowing *garage*.

[9] Richard Mulcaster, *The First Part of the Elementarie* (1582), ed. E. T. Campagnac (London, 1925), p. 268: "There be two speciall considerations, which kepe the Latin, & other learned tungs, tho chefelie the *Latin*, in great countenance among vs, the one thereof is the knowledge, which is registered in them, the other is the conference, which the learned of *Europe*, do commonlie vse by them, both in speaking and writing."

[10] *A boke, or counseill against the disease commonly called the sweate*, 1552, dedication. Quoted in Jones, *Triumph*, p. 39.

[11] Roger Ascham said earlier, in *Toxophilus* (London, 1545), dedication: "He that wyll wryte well in any tongue, must folowe thys councel of Aristotle, to speake as the common people do ... Many English writers haue not done so, but vsinge straunge wordes as latin, french, and Italian, do make all thinges dark and harde."

[12] The principal spelling reformers and their chief works include John Cheke's letter to Sir Thomas Hoby (1557), in the latter's *The Courtyer of count Baldessar Castillo* (1561); Thomas Smith's *De recta et emendata linguae anglicae scriptione* (1568); John Hart's *An Orthographie* (1569) and *A Methode or comfortable beginning for all vnlearned* (1570); Robert Laneham's *A Letter* (1575); William Bullokar's *Bullokars Booke at large, for the Amendment of Orthographie for English speech* (1580) and *Pamphlet for Grammar* (1586); Richard Mulcaster's *The First Part of the Elementarie VVhich entreateth chefelie of the right writing of our English tung* (1582); Alexander Gil's *Logonomia Anglica* (1619, 1621); Charls Butler's *The English Grammar* (1633, 1634); and Richard Hodges' *A Special Help to Orthographie* (1643).

[13] In the EModE period many of the earliest printers came from Holland. They introduced *gh* in such words as *ghossip*, *ghospel*, and *ghost*. Subsequently *h* was dropped in *gossip* and *gospel*, but not in *ghost*. See Stuart Robertson and Frederic G. Cassidy, *The Development of Modern English* (Englewood Cliffs, 1954), pp. 332–333.

[14] See Albert H. Marckwardt, *American English* (New York, 1958); Thomas Pyles, *Words and Ways of American English* (New York, 1952); Mitford M. Mathews, *A Dictionary of Americanisms*. 2 vols. (Chicago, 1951); William A. Craigie and James R. Hulbert, eds., *A Dictionary of American English on Historical Principles*. 4 vols. (Chicago, 1938–44).

English Dictionaries

The English dictionary that we regard as a commonplace and take so much for granted did not always exist. Actually, the dictionary as we know it today is a modern product that dates from the early eighteenth century. Its roots, however, go back in time to the OE period. In this chapter we shall examine the history and development of the English dictionary from its origins to the present period.

Dictionary

The word *dictionary* is derived from Middle Latin *dictionarium ~ dictionarius* 'a collection of phrases and words (*dictiones*).' It dates from at least c. 1220, when the Englishman John of Garland used *Dictionarius* as the title for his Latin prose tract with interlinear English glosses.

OE Period

English lexicography originated in the OE period from the schoolboy practice of writing word cribs in Latin texts. Then, as sometimes now, above a difficult Latin word a student wrote its English equivalent, or added a more familiar Latin synonym in the space between the lines of the text as an aid in translation.

Such words of explanation are called interlinear glosses. The word or phrase over which a gloss is written is called a lemma. For example, OE *alle* 'all' is the gloss for the Latin lemma *omnia* 'all' in one OE work. Another example is the OE gloss *duerg* 'dwarf' and the Latin gloss *pumilio* 'dwarf' for the Latin lemma *nanus* 'dwarf.'

OE Glossaries

Eventually such OE and Latin glosses and their lemmas were collected from various texts and made into compact study lists or glossaries for students. The earliest extant manuscript of an English glossary of the type we have described is that of the *Corpus Glossary*, which has come down to us in an eighth- or ninth-century manuscript. Other early Latin-Latin and Latin-OE glossaries from the OE period include the *Leiden*, *Epinal*, and *Erfurt* glossaries.

Most of the words in these OE glossaries relate to the Scriptures, the basic reading materials of OE schoolboys in monastic schools. The entries are arranged in alphabetical order as in modern dictionaries. In some other OE glossaries, however, words are arranged by subject.[1]

ME, EModE Periods

The use of glossaries as aids in the study of Latin, and later French, continued throughout the ME period and the transition period to EModE. One trilingual word list is Alexander Neckham's Latin French-English *De nominibus utensilium* (c. 1200). English-Latin and Latin-English works include the *Promptorium parvulorum sive clericorum* (c. 1440), the *[H]Ortus vocabulorum* (printed 1500), and the *Catholicon Anglicum* (c. 1483).

Following the introduction of printing to England, there appeared on the market various bilingual English-Latin and Latin-English vocabulary lists and spelling books. They include John Stanbridge's *Vocabula* (1496) and *Vulgaria* (1508), the *Dictionary of Syr Thomas Eliot* (1538), Richard Huloet's *A B Cedarium Anglo-Latinum* (1552), John Withal's *A Short Dictionarie for Yonge Begynners* (1553), Thomas Cooper's *Thesaurus linguae Romanae & Britannicae* (1565), Thomas Thomas' *Dictionarium linguae Latinae et Anglicanae* (1587), and John Rider's *Bibliotheca scholastica* (1589). A trilingual work is John Baret's *An Alvearie or Triple Dictionarie in English, Latin, and French* (1573).[2]

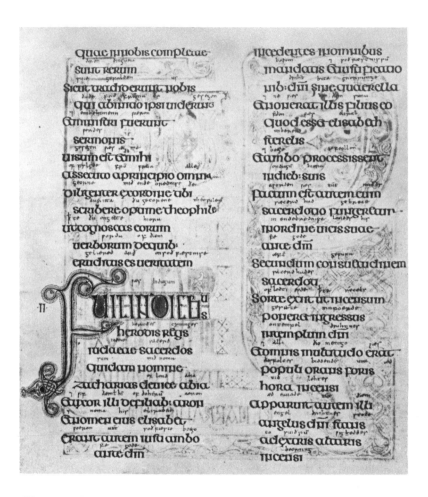

Plate 16. From OE *Lindisfarne Gospels* (B.M. MS. Cotton Nero D. IV, fol. 139v) with interlinear glosses. Copyright of the Trustees of the British Museum; reproduced by permission.

Of special historical note are two sixteenth-century publications. The first is the anonymous *Abc for chyldren* (1551–58), the first English spelling book.[3] The second is Peter Levin's English-Latin *Manipulus vocabulorum* (1570), the first English rhyming dictionary.[4]

Edmund Coote

By the late sixteenth century, writers used so many inkhorn terms that the general reading public needed explanatory lists of these difficult words. Such a list was published in Edmund Coote's *The English Schoole-Master* (1597), a seventy-nine page miscellany of chronology, syllabification, numbers, spelling, catechism, psalms, grammar, and table of difficult words with glosses. Although not itself a dictionary, Coote's work contains a vocabulary of about 1,500 difficult words that occupies about eighteen double-columned pages.

First English Dictionary

In point of time, Coote's *Schoole-Master* was the predecessor of the first true English dictionary, Robert Cawdrey's *A Table Alphabeticall . . . of hard vsuall English wordes* (1604).[5] That work was the first volume in English devoted entirely to a listing of difficult English words explained by other English words, rather than by those from another language, such as Latin.

Cawdrey's dictionary contains approximately 2,500 words, the entries ranging alphabetically from *abandon* to *Zodiack*. Some examples from it are *furniture* 'all things necessary to use,' *obnubilate* 'to make dark,' *pole* 'the end of the axeltree whereon the astronomers saine the heauens to be turned,' *lumber* 'old stuffe,' and *crocodile* 'kind of beast.' Apparently a popular reference work, Cawdrey's dictionary went through a fourth edition (1617).

Hard-Word Dictionaries

The *Table Alphabeticall*, which initiated the "hard-word" stage of the English dictionary, was followed by several works

A

Table Alphabeticall, conteyning and teaching the true vvriting, and vnderstanding of hard vsuall English wordes, borrowed from the Hebrew, Greeke, Latine, or French. &c.

With the interpretation thereof by *plaine English words, gathered for the benefit & helpe of Ladies, Gentlewomen, or any other vnskilfull persons.*

Whereby they may the more easilie and better vnderstand many hard English wordes, vvhich they shall heare or read in Scriptures, Sermons, or elswhere, and also be made able to vse the same aptly themselues.

Legere, et non intelligere, neglegere est.
As good not read, as not to vnderstand.

AT LONDON,
Printed by I. R. for Edmund Weauer, & are to be sold at his shop at the great North doore of Paules Church.
1 6 0 4.

Plate 17. Title page of Robert Cawdrey's *A Table Alphabeticall* (Bod. Lib. Malone 754, T.P.). Copyright of Bodleian Library; reproduced by permission.

of a similar nature throughout the seventeenth century. They include John Bullokar's *An English Expositor: Teaching the Interpretation of the hardest words vsed in our Language* (1616); Henry Cockeram's *The English Dictionarie: or An Interpreter of Hard English Words* (1623); Thomas Blount's *Glossographia: or a Dictionary Interpreting all such Hard Words . . . as are now used in our refined English Tongue* (1656); Edward Phillips' *The New World of English Words . . . Containing the Interpretations of . . . hard words* (1658); and Elisha Coles' *An English Dictionary . . . containing Many Thousands of Hard Words* (1676).[6]

Nathan Bailey

The father of the so-called "modern" dictionary was Nathan Bailey. IIis *An Universal Etymological English Dictionary* (1721), gave increased attention to etymology. Bailey's supplementary volume in two parts, *Containing I. An additional Collection* and *II. An orthographical dictionary shewing both the orthography and orthoepia of the English Tongue*, appeared in 1727. It included the accentuation of words "by Accents placed on each Word, directing to their . . . Pronunciation," a feature that we likewise associate with modern dictionaries. Also, the work offered a large portion of the English vocabulary, including many specialized terms, whereas many earlier dictionaries were confined to lists of "hard words," particularly Latin and Greek loanwords. In addition, the 1727 volume included various illustrations or "engraven Schemes" as an instructive device, although woodcuts had appeared in earlier dictionaries, notably the anonymous *Glossographia Anglicana Nova* (1707).

Bailey had his hand in one other dictionary. It was the *Dictionarium Britannicum: or, a more compleat universal etymological English dictionary than any extant* (1730), compiled by Bailey and others. That work included some 48,000 vocabulary items and five hundred woodcut illustrations "for Giving a clearer Idea of those Figures, not so well apprehended by verbal Description."

Thus, in Bailey's works we find amplified etymologies, accentuation, pictorial illustrations, and a comprehensive listing of English words and their spellings. All things considered, dic-

An Univerſal Etymological
Engliſh Dictionary:

COMPREHENDING

The Derivations of the Generality of Words in the *Engliſh* Tongue, either Antient or Modern, from the Antient *Britiſh*, *Saxon*, *Daniſh*, *Norman* and Modern *French*, *Teutonic*, *Dutch*, *Spaniſh*, *Italian*, *Latin*, *Greek*, and *Hebrew* Languages, each in their Proper Characters.

AND ALSO

A Brief and clear Explication of all difficult Words derived from any of the aforeſaid Languages; and Terms of Art relating to Anatomy, Botany, Phyſick, Pharmacy, Surgery, Chymiſtry, Philoſophy, Divinity, Mathematicks, Grammar, Logick, Rhetorick, Muſick, Heraldry, Maritime Affairs, Military Diſcipline, Horſemanſhip, Hunting, Hawking, Fowling, Fiſhing, Gardening, Husbandry, Handicrafts, Confectionary, Carving, Cookery, &c.

Together with

A Large Collection and Explication of Words and Phraſes us'd in our Antient Statutes, Charters, Writs, Old Records, and Proceſſes at Law; and the Etymology and Interpretation of the Proper Names of Men, Women, and Remarkable Places in *Great Britain*: Alſo the Dialects of our different Counties.

Containing many Thouſand Words more than either *Harris*, *Philips*, *Kerſey*, or any *Engliſh* Dictionary before Extant.

To which is Added a Collection of our moſt Common Proverbs, with their Explication and Illuſtration.

The wholeWORK compil'd andMethodically digeſted, as well for the Entertainment of the Curious, as the Information of the Ignorant, and for the Benefit of young Students, Artificers, Tradeſmen and Foreigners, who are deſirous thorowly to underſtand what they Speak, Read, or Write.

By N. BAILEY, Φιλολόγ⊙.

LONDON:

Printed for E. BELL, J. DARBY, A. BETTESWORTH, F. FAYRAM, J. PEMBERTON, J. HOOKE, C. RIVINGTON, F. CLAY, J. BATLEY, and E. SYMON. 1721.

Plate 18. Title page of Nathan Bailey's *An Universal Etymological English Dictionary* (B.M. MS. 12984 bbb16 fol. 1). Copyright of the Trustees of the British Museum; reproduced by permission.

tionaries published since Bailey's differ from them only in amplification of material and features. It is generally acknowledged, therefore, that the modern English dictionary began with Bailey's supplementary or 1727 volume of his *Universal Etymological English Dictionary*.

Samuel Johnson

Another milestone in the field of English lexicography was Samuel Johnson's two-volume *Dictionary of the English Language* (1755).[7] A work of almost 2,300 pages, in bulk it was about two and a half times as large as the 950 pages of Bailey's dictionary of 1721.

Johnson's influential work virtually dominated the field of English lexicography for at least a century after its publication. For one thing, Johnson's dictionary provided more lengthy definitions and more elaborate etymologies than previous dictionaries. It also introduced the feature of illustrative quotations to indicate current usage and gave judgments about the propriety of certain words. Thus, Johnson labeled *excepting* "an improper word" and *fun* "a low cant word." Furthermore, Johnson's dictionary helped "fix" the spelling of some questionable words. For example, Johnson rejected the spelling *intire* in favor of *entire*, and that is the way we spell it today.

Mutability

Johnson's preface to his dictionary is perhaps as significant as the work itself, because it illustrates a basic linguistic principle which many people today refuse to accept — that language is subject to change in the course of time.

In keeping with the eighteenth-century prescriptive temper, Johnson said he studiously endeavored to collect examples and authorities from before the Restoration whose works he regarded as "the wells of English undefiled, as the pure sources of genuine diction."[8] He added:

> Those who have been persuaded to think well of my design, require that it should fix our language, and put a stop to those alterations which time and change have hitherto been suffered to make in it without opposition.

However, said Johnson:

> With this consequence I will confess that I flattered myself for a while, but now begin to fear that I have indulged expectation which neither reason nor experience can justify. When we see men grow old and die at a certain time one after another, from century to century, we laugh at the elixir that promises to prolong life to a thousand years; and with equal justice may the lexicographer be derided, who being able to produce no example of a nation that has preserved their words and phrases from mutability, shall imagine that his dictionary can embalm his language, and secure it from corruption and decay, that it is in his power to change sublunary nature, or clear the world at once from folly, vanity, and affectation.

In short, Johnson said it is impossible to prevent language from changing so long as it is spoken.

Despite the truth of Johnson's conclusion, it went virtually unheeded in the eighteenth century. Men of "reason" continued to clamor for the linguistic regulation of English. Zealously, they called for the removal of linguistic impurities from the language.

Pronouncing Dictionaries

One manifestation of that prescriptive temper was the inclusion by some English lexicographers of the "correct" pronunciations of words in their works. Three such publications were Benjamin Martin's *Lingua Britannica Reformata . . . Directing the True Pronunciation of Words by Single and Double Accents* (1749); Thomas Sheridan's *A General Dictionary of the English Language. One main Object of which, is, to establish a plain and permanent Standard of Pronunciation* (1780); and John Walker's *A Critical Pronouncing Dictionary and Expositor of the English Language* (1791).

The general prescriptive tenor of these works may be illustrated by the following statement by Sheridan in his *Dictionary:*

> There was a time, and that at no very distant period, which may be called the Augustan age of England, I mean during the reign of Queen Anne, when English was the language spoken at court; and when the same attention was paid to propriety of pronunciation, as that of French at the Court of Versailles. This produced a uniformity in that article in all the polite circles; and a gentleman or lady would have been as much ashamed of a wrong pronunciation then, as persons of a liberal education would be now

of mis-spelling words . . . From that time the regard formerly paid to pronunciation has been gradually declining; so that now the greatest improprieties in that point are to be found among people of fashion; many pronunciations, which thirty or forty years ago were confined to the vulgar, are gradually gaining ground; and if something be not done to stop this growing evil, and fix a general standard at present, the English is likely to become a mere jargon, which every one may pronounce as he pleases. It is to be wished, that such a standard had been established at the period before mentioned, as it is probable, that English was then spoken in its highest state of perfection.

Sheridan's suggestion that a permanent standard of English pronunciation be established is as mistaken as the linguistic error from which Johnson escaped. As this text illustrates, the pronunciation of English has undergone many changes over the centuries. Furthermore, English, so long as it is spoken, undoubtedly will undergo additional changes in pronunciation. It is wishful thinking, therefore, to attempt to establish a permanent standard of English pronunciation. Even if one could be agreed upon, it would be impossible to enforce.

OED

Without doubt the most important British dictionary published since the period of Johnson, Sheridan, and Walker is the monumental *Oxford English Dictionary* (*OED*), earlier known as *A New English Dictionary on Historical Principles* (*NED*). Edited by J. A. H. Murray *et al.* in twelve volumes (Oxford, 1884–1928), with a supplement (1933), the work is unquestionably the most ambitious historical dictionary of any language in the world, aimed at listing every English word in use from c. 1100. A new supplement is in progress.

American Dictionaries

The first dictionary published in America was *A School Dictionary* (?1798) by Samuel Johnson, Jr.[9] He was not the son of the Samuel Johnson who compiled the *Dictionary* of 1755, but the son of Samuel Johnson, first president of King's College, forerunner of Columbia University. An unoriginal work of almost two hundred pages, the *School Dictionary* contains less than five thousand words.

Two years later in 1800, Johnson, Jr., together with John Elliott, published *A Selected, Pronouncing and Accented Dictionary*, which aimed at eliminating "the indiscriminate use of vulgar and indecent words." In 1800 also appeared Caleb Alexander's *The Columbian Dictionary of the English Language*, in which for the first time were listed in an American dictionary "Many NEW WORDS, peculiar to the United States."

A number of early American dictionaries, like those of Walker and Sheridan, were pronouncing dictionaries. Some others, in addition to the Johnson-Elliot volume mentioned above, were Richard S. Coxe's *New Critical Pronouncing Dictionary of the English Language* (1813); Burgiss Allison's *The American Standard of Orthography and Pronunciation and Improved Dictionary of the English Language* (1815); and Joseph E. Worcester's *Comprehensive Pronouncing and Explanatory Dictionary of the English Language* (1830).

The first dictionary of Americanisms was John Pickering's *A Vocabulary, or Collection of Words and Phrases which have been supposed to be peculiar to the United States of America* (1816). It was later followed by John R. Bartlett's *Dictionary of Americanisms, a Glossary of Words and Phrases usually regarded as peculiar to the United States* (1848).

More recent collections of Americanisms are the four-volume *A Dictionary of American English on Historical Principles* (Chicago, 1938–44), edited by William A. Craigie and James R. Hulbert; Henry L. Mencken's *The American Language* (New York, 1936), Supplement I (1945), II (1948);[10] and Mitford M. Mathews' two-volume *A Dictionary of Americanisms* (Chicago, 1951).

Spelling Reform

Closely associated with the development of American dictionaries is the American spelling-reform movement. One early reformer was Benjamin Franklin, who in *A Scheme for a New Alphabet and Reformed Mode of Spelling* (1768), suggested that the spelling of words be remodeled along phonetic lines.[11] Some of his remodeled spellings, for example, were *gilti, kalm, az, alfabet, siriin* 'serene,' *hi* 'he,' and *feer* 'fair.'

Other works which also treated the subject of spelling reform in America were Joseph Neff's *Sketch of a plan and method of Education* (1808), James Ewing's *Columbian Alphabet* (1798), and William Pelham's *System of Notation* (1808).

Noah Webster

The name most widely associated with American spelling reform and the American dictionary, however, is that of Noah Webster (1758–1843).

Inspired by Franklin's *Scheme*, Webster in 1783 published Part I of *A Grammatical Institute of the English Language.* Called *The American Spelling Book* in subsequent editions, this popular blue-back speller, a compendium of spelling, pronunciation, reading, and short introduction to grammar, is estimated to have sold a hundred million copies.[12] Thus, its influence in America was enormous.

A zealous advocate of spelling reform, in editions of his *Spelling Book* Webster urged such changes as *music* for *musick, honor* for *honour, center* for *centre*, as well as *enrol, sley,* and *turky*. In his *Collection of Essays and Fugitive Writings* (1790), Webster also proposed such remodeled spellings as *karacter, reezon, ahuv, reeder, rong, helth,* and *tung,* but under the pressure of mounting public criticism, Webster abandoned his extreme reforms and generally retained more conservative spellings in the later editions of his *Spelling Book*.

Webster's Dictionaries

Webster also became progressively more conservative about spelling in the various editions of his several dictionaries.

His first work was the 28,000–word *A Compendious Dictionary of the English Language* (1806). It was followed by the shorter *A Dictionary of the English Language compiled for the use of common schools in the United States* (1807), and the 70,000-word *An American Dictionary of the English Language* (1828) in two volumes.

In the 1807 edition Webster advocated such spellings as *fether, wimmen, examin, ake, chesnut,* but in the 1828 edition

A

Compendious Dictionary

OF THE

English Language.

In which FIVE THOUSAND Words are added
to the number found in the BEST ENGLISH COMPENDS ;

The ORTHOGRAPHY is, in some instances, corrected ;

The PRONUNCIATION marked by an Accent or other suitable Direction ;

And the DEFINITIONS of many Words amended and improved.

TO WHICH ARE ADDED FOR THE BENEFIT OF THE

MERCHANT, the STUDENT and the TRAVELLER,

I.——TABLES of the MONEYS of most of the commercial Nations in the world, with the value expressed in Sterling and Cents.

II.——TABLES of WEIGHTS and MEASURES, ancient and modern, with the proportion between the several weights used in the principal cities of Europe.

III.——The DIVISIONS of TIME among the Jews, Greeks and Romans, with a Table exhibiting the Roman manner of dating.

IV.——An official List of the POST-OFFICES in the UNITED STATES, with the States and Counties in which they are respectively situated, and the distance of each from the seat of Government.

V.——The NUMBER of INHABITANTS in the United States, with the amount of EXPORTS.

IV.——New and Interesting CHRONOLOGICAL TABLES of remarkable Events and Discoveries.

By NOAH WEBSTER, Esq.

From Sidney's Press.

FOR HUDSON & GOODWIN, BOOK-SELLERS, HARTFORD, AND INCREASE COOKE & CO.

BOOK-SELLERS, NEW-HAVEN.

1806.

Plate 19. Title page of Noah Webster's *A Compendious Dictionary of the English Language.* Courtesy of G. and C. Merriam Co., publishers of the Merriam-Webster dictionaries.

he gave preference to *feather, women, examine, ache,* and *chestnut.* In his 1828 edition, however, Webster tried reformed spelling again, unsuccessfully, with *bild, furlow, parsnep, ribin.* Thus, Webster was only partially victorious in his attempts to reform American spelling. Yet as a result of those attempts, our spelling differs somewhat from that of the British.

Merriam-Webster

On the death of Webster in 1843, the publishing rights of his 1828 dictionary were purchased by George and Charles Merriam. In 1847 they produced the first Merriam-Webster unabridged dictionary, subsequent editions of which appeared in 1864, 1890, 1909, 1934, and 1961. The last or sixth edition, entitled *Webster's Third International Dictionary,* is indicative of the gigantic undertaking that dictionary publishing has become in America.

For example, according to the preface in the *Third* by Editor-in-Chief Philip B. Gove, the 1961 edition cost more than three and a half million dollars, and the work was in preparation for more than ten years. Based on a file of more than six million examples of recorded usage, *Webster's Third* contains a vocabulary of more than 450,000 words.

The Future

The English language continues to change. As a result of the expansion of mass media and rapid current developments in technology, the arts, and the sciences, new words continue to enter the language, old words change in meaning, and some words die. In the face of such changes, and of new developments in lexicography and linguistic studies, Editor Gove estimates that a new English dictionary will be required about once every generation, or every twenty-five years.[13] Thus, producing reliable English dictionaries appears to be a task without end.

Webster's Rivals

Although we have confined our discussion of the development of American dictionaries largely to those published by Webster and Merriam-Webster, various other large dictionaries have been published in America. Among several large works published in the late nineteenth century were the six-volume *Century Dictionary* (1889–91); the ten-volume *Century Dictionary and Cyclopedia* (1889–97); and the two-volume *Standard Dictionary* (1893–94).

Later publications include Richard H. Thornton's *An American Glossary*, issued in two volumes in 1912; *A Pronouncing Dictionary of American English* (1949) by John S. Kenyon and Thomas A. Knott; and the *Dictionary of American Slang* by Harold Wentworth and Stuart B. Flexner (1960), as well as others.

SUMMARY

Three stages may be noted in the development of the English dictionary: the bilingual and later multilingual stage, of which the *Corpus Glossary* (8th–9th cent.) is an early representative; the hard-word stage initiated by Robert Cawdrey's *A Table Alphabeticall* (1604), and the modern stage, as initiated by the supplementary volume (1727) of Nathan Bailey's *An Universal Etymological English Dictionary*. In America, Noah Webster's *A Compendious Dictionary of the English Language* appeared in 1806. His larger dictionary in two volumes, *An American Dictionary of the English Language*, was published in 1828.

NOTES

[1] See Thomas Wright and Richard Wülcker, *Anglo-Saxon and Old English Vocabularies*. 2 vols. (London, 1884).

[2] Another factor that contributed to the growth of vocabulary studies in England was the rise in the sixteenth century of international trade, which aroused interest in such modern languages as French, Spanish, and Italian. As a result, there emerged such dictionaries as William Salesbury's *Dictionary in Englyshe and Welshe* (1547); William Thomas' *Principal rules of the Italian grammar, with a dictionarie* (1550); William Stepney's English-Spanish *The Spanish Schoolemaster* (1591); Claudius Hollyband's *A Dictionarie French and English* (1593); John Florio's English-Italian *Florio his firste Fruites* (1578); and Randle Cotgrave's *A Dictionarie of the French and English Tongues* (1611).

Studies in the EModE period were also made of Germanic and the older stages of English. Franciscus Junius (1589–1677), for example, studied OE, Gothic, Frisian, German, Scandinavian, and Dutch. Publications of the time include Laurence Nowell's *Vocabularium Saxonicum* (1565); William Somner's *Dictionarium Saxonico-Latino-Anglicum* (1659); Thomas Benson's *Vocabularium Anglo-Saxonicum* (1701); George Hickes' *Grammar* (1689) of OE, Gothic, Icelandic, and his *Linguarum Veterum Septentrionalium Thesaurus* (1703–05); and Humfrey Wanley's *Antiquae Literaturae Septentrionalis Liber Alter* (1705).

3 See reprint by Ed Flügel, *Anglia*, XIII (1891), 461–467.

4 See reprint by Henry B. Wheatley, *EETS*, 27 (1867).

5 See edition with introduction by Robert A. Peters (Scholars' Facsimiles & Reprints: Gainesville, Fla., 1966).

6 Other dictionaries of "hard words" include John Kersey's *A New English Dictionary* (1702), Edward Cocker's *Cocker's English Dictionary* (1704), and John Wesley's *The Complete English Dictionary* (1753).

7 Examples of some of Johnson's definitions which now produce amusement are:
Network 'Any thing reticulated or decussated, at equal distances, with interstices between the intersections'
Cough 'A convulsion of the lungs, vellicated by some sharp serosity'
Oats 'A grain, which in England is generally given to horses, but in Scotland supports the people'
See further E. L. McAdam, Jr., and George Milne, *Johnson's Dictionary* (New York, 1963).

8 The Restoration refers to the re-establishment of the monarchy in England in 1660 with the reign of Charles II (1660–1685). Following the execution of Charles I (Charles Stuart) in 1649, England was ruled in the Commonwealth period (1649–1660) by Oliver Cromwell (1653–1658), his son Richard (1658–1659); and by parliament (1659–1660).

9 See Martha J. Gibson, "America's First Lexicographer Samuel Johnson, Jr., 1757–1836," *American Speech*, XI (1936), 283–292; XII (1937), 19–30.

10 An abridged and revised edition of Mencken's work (New York; 1963) was made by Raven I. McDavid, Jr., with the assistance of David W. Maurer.

11 See William Angus, "Poor Richard's Alphabet and His Pronunciation," *Speech Monographs*, II (1935), 60–70; Kemp Malone "Benjamin Franklin on Spelling Reform," *American Speech*, I (1925), 96–100.

12 See Harry R. Warfel's *Noah Webster, Schoolmaster to America* (New York, 1936). See also Warfel's reprint with introduction of Webster's *Dissertations on the English Language* (Scholars' Facsimiles & Reprints: Gainesville, Fla., 1951).

13 "Linguistic Advances and Lexicography," *Word Study*, XXXVII (The G. & C. Merriam Co., 1961), 3.

Development of English Punctuation

This chapter contains a brief outline of the history of English punctuation. We shall trace the development and use of certain marks of punctuation from the OE period to modern times.

System

The word *punctuation* is derived from Middle Latin *punctuatio*, which in turn is derived from Latin *punctus* 'point.'

Punctuation is a system of arbitrary and conventional graphic marks used in written and printed matter to separate structural units, and to clarify meaning in LModE. In earlier periods, the function of punctuation was different, as we shall later explain.

Nine Marks

Our discussion of the marks of punctuation in English and their development is restricted to those graphemes that function in LModE as morphemic signals or as structural markers for those furnished in speech by suprasegmental phonemes. The marks of punctuation have other graphemic uses in LModE, as summarized in the prescriptive "rules" of punctuation, but we shall not discuss those uses.

The marks of punctuation that we shall talk about are nine in number;

      1. Three end marks: <. ? !>
      2. Four internal marks: <, ; : —>
      3. Two morphemic marks: <' ->

We exclude from our discussion those marks of punctuation which do not function like the nine symbols above, namely, quotation marks <" ">, parentheses <( )>, and brackets <[ ]>.

End Marks

In LModE, the end marks — the period <.>, the question mark <?>, and the exclamation mark <!> — normally characterize, respectively, statements, questions, and exclamations, in which they indicate terminals. Some examples are *Coffee.* / ↘ /, *Coffee?* / ↗ /, and *Coffee!* / ↘ /. Thus, as a generalization, <.> = / ↘ /, <?> = / ↗ /, and <!> = / ↘ /. <?> also = / ↘ /, as in *Is that so?* / ↘ /.

Internal Marks

In LModE, the internal marks — the comma <,>, the semicolon <;>, the dash <—>, and the colon <:> — indicate level, rising, and falling terminals, as in these examples:

<,> = / → /	*Tom,* / → / *who was ill,* / → /, *did not go.*
<,> = / ↗ /	*One,* / ↗ /, *two,* / ↗ /, *three,* / ↗ /, *four.*
	Because it rained, / ↗ / *we left.*
	After the party, / ↗ / *Tom sang a song.*
<,> = / ↘ /	*One,* / ↘ /, *two,* / ↘ /, *three,* / ↘ /, *four.*
<;> = / ↘ /	*She bought a dog;* / ↘ / *later, she was sorry.*
<:> = / ↘ /	*Dear Abby:* / ↘ /
<—> = / ↘ /	*Heat and hard work —* / ↘ / *those things we knew.*
<—> = / ↗ /, / → /	*The men —* / ↗ / *tired, cold, hungry —* / → / *complained.*

Hence, in LModE the primary function of the end marks (in addition to differentiating statements, questions, and exclamations) and the internal marks is to set off structural units — the sentence, clause, phrase, and word, as the above examples illustrate.

Morphemic Marks

In LModE, the morphemic marks are the apostrophe $<'>$ and the hyphen $<->$.

The apostrophe indicates possessive case as in sg. *boy's* and pl. *boys'*.

The hyphen marks a compound word, specifically the superfix or stress pattern of a compound word. For example, the superfix of the compound *mân-èating* in *ă mân-èatĭng ánt* is / ˆ ˋ /. In contrast, the superfix of the noun+verb *mán êating* in *ă mán êatĭng fóod* is / ' ˆ /. The hyphen is also used in a word divided at the end of a line.

Origin

The origin of Western punctuation is found in ancient rhetorical theory, in which the terms *periodus, komma, kōlon* referred to segments of discourse. Each was a rhythmical unit as well as physiological unit of breath or pause. The *periodus* was a rhythmic rounding off that comprised a not-too-large portion of speech. It consisted of shorter physiological-rhythmical units or *kola* (Latin *membra*). They, in turn, consisted of short units or *kommata* (Latin *incisa*).[1]

By the third century B.C. a regular system of punctuation by points was developed for Greek in the schools of Alexandria. The invention of that system is credited to Aristophanes of Byzantium (260 B.C.).[2]

By the fourth century A.D. — seven centuries after Aristophanes — grammarians were using punctuation points at the end of units of discourse to indicate an opportunity for taking a breath or pause. Eventually the terms *period, comma,* and *colon* came to be attached to the punctuation points or marks, as well as to the units of discourse they set off. The *period* marked a full stop at the end of a sentence; the *comma* a brief, incomplete unit; and the *colon* a longer unit, but one less than a sentence.

Near the beginning of the seventh century, Isidore of Seville, in his *Etymologiae*, suggested that the marks of punctuation be used for setting off sense as well as rhythm.[3] Later in the medieval period, there was a tendency toward the use of punctuation points as markers of sense as well as markers of oratorical units associated with breathing. That drift marked a blending of the old classical use associated with physiological-rhythmical units and the medieval tendency toward association with sense.

OE, ME Periods

In the OE period, punctuation in manuscripts written in English was rare. In the earlier portion of that period a centered comma — one written level with the middle of a grapheme — was sometimes used, but until the late-tenth century the principal mark of punctuation was the dot $<.>$, frequently centered.[4] In the late tenth century two additional marks were used: the so-called semicolon $<;>$, and the mark $<!>$, later known as the *punctus elevatus* and the *punctus cum virgula*. Many twelfth-century manuscripts written in English have the dot as the only mark of punctuation, whereas those written in Latin have the dot, $<;>$, and $<!>$.

The marks $<.>$, $<;>$, and $<!>$ in the OE period did not constitute a coherent or meaningful system of punctuation in manuscripts written in English.[5] They appeared at the ends of sentences, and they also marked various prosodical and rhetorical divisions, but their use was unsystematic and frequently meaningless.

Variations of marks of punctuation in OE manuscripts include doubling of marks, and sometimes the addition of various ornamental symbols. One variation, for example, was a triangle of dots. Another was a triangle of dots above a comma. A third was a colon followed by one of various marks, such as a check mark or a figure approximating the number 7. Such elaborations appeared chiefly at the end of a chapter, a section, or a paragraph (See OE prose extract, page 230).

The question mark or *punctus interrogativus* $<\mathcal{C}>$ came into use in the late tenth century.[6] The hyphen, a horizontal line, appeared in manuscripts written in English shortly before the eleventh century. It was not a morphemic mark, however, but a marker at the end of a line to signal a divided word run over to the beginning of the next line below, where sometimes another hyphen appeared.

In the ME period, with few exceptions, the use of punctuation marks was the same as in the OE period. ME manuscripts show that punctuation was not only rare, but as chaotic, and frequently as meaningless as in the OE period. In short, by the end of the ME period a systematic use of punctuation had not yet developed in English.

EModE Period

By the end of the period of transition to EModE — that is, shortly before the onset of the sixteenth century — the use of punctuation in English works was little better than in the ME period. For example, the prologues and epilogues of Caxton's printed books (1475–91) provide a fair sample of the chaotic punctuation of his times.[7]

Liturgical Use

By the early sixteenth century, however, in liturgical works written in Latin, there is evident a rough but relatively more consistent use of marks of punctuation than in earlier times. For example, in the *Wolsey Gospel Book* (MS. Magdalene College, Oxford), written c. 1520, the marks used in relatively consistent fashion are the comma $<,>$, the period $<.>$, the colon $<:>$, the semicolon $<!>$, and the question mark $<?>$. The hyphen $<=>$ marked a word divided at the end of a line, and the apostrophe $<'>$ indicated the omission of a letter in an abbreviated word. The exclamation mark and the dash were not used.

English Development

In the late sixteenth and early seventeenth centuries, such liturgical practice spread to works written in English, and thereafter a system of English punctuation slowly evolved. That system approximated the classical-medieval association of marks of punctuation with physiological-rhetorical units and with units of meaning, such as the sentence.[8]

For example, Richard Mulcaster in the *Elementarie* (1582) speaks of the period, comma, and colon as "helps to our breathing, & the distinct vtterances of our speche." Mulcaster said that the comma "followeth som small branch of the sentence, & . . . warneth vs to rest there, and to help our breth a little." The colon "followeth som full branch, or half the sentence." The period "followeth a perfit sentence, and . . . warneth vs to rest there and to help our breth at full."[9]

By 1594 in the *Grammatica Anglicana* of P.G. ~ P.Gr. (?Paul Greaves), a growing use of marks of punctuation in English is evident. For example, P.G. uses the period <.>, colon <:>, comma <,>, semicolon <;>, and question mark <?>. The apostrophe indicated elision (*subdu'd*) but not the possessive case (*Hectors blood*). The hyphen <-> marked compound words (*shoe-horne*) and also words split at the end of a line (*sixe-teene*).

Charls Butler's *English Grammar* (1633) shows an even more expanded use of marks of punctuation. Butler not only lists all the punctuation marks that P.G. employed, but also the exclamation mark <!>, as well as parentheses <( )> and brackets <[ ]>.

Jonson

Despite the partial morphemic use of the hyphen in compound words, by the mid-seventeenth century marks of punctuation in English were still regarded essentially as markers of breath and pause, and to a degree as markers of units associated with meaning, such as the "perfect" and "imperfect" sentence. For example, Ben Jonson in *The English Grammar* (1640) said:[10]

All parts of *Syntaxe* have already beene declared.

There resteth one generall Affection of the whole, dispersed thorow every member thereof . . . and consisteth in the breathing, when we pronounce any *Sentence*; For, whereas our breath is by nature so short, that we cannot continue without a stay to speake long together; it was thought necessarie, as well for the speakers ease, as for the plainer deliverance of the things spoken, to invent this means, whereby men pausing a pretty while, the whole speech might never the worse be understood.

These Distinctions are, either of a *perfect*, or *imperfect* Sentence. The distinctions of an imperfect Sentence are two, a *sub-distinction*, and a *Comma*.

A *Sub-distinction* is a meane breathing, when the word serveth in-differently, both to the parts of the Sentence going before, and following after, and is marked thus (;)

A *Comma* is a distinction of an *imperfect* Sentence, wherein with somewhat a longer breath, the Sentence <going before is marked off from the Sentence> following; and is noted with this shorter semicircle (,).

... The Distinction of a perfect Sentence hath a more full stay, and doth rest the spirit, which is a *Pause*, or a *Period*.

A *Pause* is a Distinction of a Sentence, though perfect in itselfe, yet joyned to another, being marked with two pricks (:).

A *Period* is the Distinction of a Sentence, in all respects *perfect*, and is marked with one full prick, over against the lower part of the last letter, thus (.)

If a Sentence be with an *Interrogation*, we use this note (?)

... If it be pronounced with an *Admiration*, then thus (!)

... These Distinctions ... as they best agree with nature: so come they neerest to the ancient staies of Sentences among the *Romans*, and the *Grecians*.

The Apostrophe

As we have already illustrated, in the early portion of the EModE period the apostrophe was used to indicate omission or contraction.[11] Some additional EModE examples, taken from William Shakespeare's *The Tempest*, are *th'Mariners, too't, let's, I'le, turn'd, swallow'd, 'Tis, call'd*, and *saw'st*.[12] The apostrophe was not used in the early portion of the EModE period to mark the possessive case of nouns, as we use it today. For example, Ben Jonson in his *English Grammar* (1640) said, "there is ... a *Genitive Case*, made in the Singular number by putting to *s* ... the genitive plurall is made by adding *s* ... as Sing. *childe. childes*. Plur. *children. childrens*."

Examination of a random selection of prose texts shows that the apostrophe was not regularly used to mark the singular possessive-case forms of nouns until the late seventeenth century.[13] Chronological examples illustrating that development in the seventeenth century are *the Generals booke, the dukes sonne, Saint Pauls Church, the Kings Maiestie* (all 1602), and *King Arthurs age, his mothers name, Popes right foot*, and *Gods own kingdome* in 1637. A rare 1637 use is *a wealthy man's wife*. By 1640 the predominant forms remained *a mans wit* and *Virgils felicity*, with, occasionally, *Achiles's Armour* and *Heath's Epigrams*.

By 1666 about half of the singular possessive forms show an apostrophe: *Mans heart, Man's imbecillity, Gods patrimony, God's spirit, Christs professed enemy,* and *Christ's Prerogative.*

By 1692 about one third more forms appear with an apostrophe than without. Examples are *her Father's House, his Brother's Hands,* but also *St. Clements Church-yard* and *A Masons Daughter.*

The growing use of the apostrophe is confirmed in the 1692 revised edition of Jonson's *Grammar,* in which we learn that:

"To the *Genetive Cases* of all *Nouns* denoting a Possessor, is added 's with an *Apostrophe,* thereby to avoid the gross *Syntax* of the *Pronoun his* joining with a *Noun;* as *The Emperor's Court, The General's Valour;* not *The Emperor* his *Court,* & c."[14]

The complaint about the use of *his* was voiced earlier by Jonson in the 1640 edition of his *Grammar,* in which he labeled "monstrous Syntaxe . . . the *Pronoune, his,* joyning with a *Noune,* betokening a *Possessor;* as, the *Prince* his *house;* for, the *Princis house.*" In Greater-London English, for example, the possessive singular suffix of nouns was written *–es* and later *–is ~ –ys* as in, say, *kinges > kingis ~ kingys.* Thus, when a construction such as *the kingys sonne* was pronounced, apparently those who heard [ðə kɪŋɪz sʌn] confused the suffix [–ɪz] with the possessive-case pronoun *his* when pronounced as unstressed [ɪz]. As a result, they erroneously wrote *the kyng hys sonne.* In reality, however, genitive singular *s* in EModE was a development from OE *–es,* as in OE *cyninges >* ME *kinges >* EModE *kingis > kings > king's.*[15]

Nevertheless, by about 1700 the apostrophe was regularly used in English to mark the possessive-singular forms of nouns. Occasionally, however, forms without the apostrophe continued to appear in print until the last quarter of the eighteenth century. Whether or not they are typographical errors, we do not know. Some examples are *her Fathers Drawer* (1692), *the Lawyers English* (1703), *his Mothers Eve* (1711), *Authors Solidity* (1740), and *a Summers Day* (1787).[16]

Possessive Plural

After the apostrophe became regular in the possessive-singular forms of nouns, the apostrophe was gradually extended by analogy to the possessive-plural forms of nouns in the eighteenth century.

The grammarians offer conflicting evidence about the use of the apostrophe in the possessive plural. James Greenwood, for example, in *An Essay Towards a Practical English Grammar* (1711), listed *Men's Nature*, but as late as 1767 James Buchanon in *English Syntax* said, "We . . . have a Genitive Plural, though there has been no Mark to distinguish it . . . [as in pl.] warriors arms." The evidence of actual usage, however, shows that the apostrophe in the possessive-plural forms of nouns was relatively frequent from about 1740 and appears to have become more or less a regular feature by about 1770.

Modern System

Earlier, we made the generalization that by about 1650 English grammarians regarded punctuation basically as a device for marking breath, pause, and units associated with meaning. But for a few decades prior to 1650 there was a tendency toward use of marks of punctuation to set off structural units. We shall not enter into those details here except to say that in the pre-1650 period the use of marks of punctuation in English to set off syntactic units was in a formative stage.

Thereafter, from about 1650 onwards, English punctuation came to be used increasingly as a syntactic and morphemic device. In large measure that development was brought about by "correctors" and compositors in English printing houses who sought to provide a greater degree of punctuation uniformity in works issued from their presses. Another contributing factor toward regularity was the spread of education and the increased number of grammar books.

In time, there evolved in English a general code of punctuation usage. By 1700–1740, for example, punctuation marks were clearly used as structural and morphemic markers. If we accept c. 1770 as the date by which the apostrophe was more or less regularly used in the possessive-plural forms of nouns, then our modern system of punctuation dates from 1740–1770, or, as a convenient round number, c. 1750.

Rules

In the late eighteenth century and in the nineteenth century, English punctuation became thoroughly regularized and codified through numerous prescriptive "rules" of punctuation formulated by grammarians. A number of those "rules," however, are no longer found in English handbooks.

Since 1900, the general tendency has been to use less punctuation than in previous times. For example, in the current period of the twentieth century we tend to write short sentences that require less punctuation, as in newspaper style. In contrast, in the literature of the nineteenth century, we more frequently encounter long and relatively complex sentences containing many marks of punctuation, usually for clarity. Another factor contributing to the modern trend toward less punctuation in sentences is an aesthetic and artistic one, the desire to present fewer hindrances to the reader's eye.

SUMMARY

In ancient rhetorical theory the period, colon, and comma referred to segments of discourse that were both rhythmical units and physiological segments of breath or pause. In the Middle Ages there was a tendency toward use of the punctuation "points" as markers of sense as well. The system of English punctuation that developed by c. 1650 largely reflected classical-medieval use. By about 1750 punctuation became a syntactic and morphemic device, as it basically is today. Printing houses, grammarians, and schools helped promote and regulate eighteenth-century development. Prescriptive "rules" of punctuation were formulated in the late eighteenth century and in the nineteenth century. Since 1900 there has been a marked tendency toward less use of punctuation than in the preceding century.

NOTES

[1] See Donald L. Clark, *Rhetoric in Greco-Roman Education* (New York, 1957), pp. 97–98.

[2] Edward M. Thompson, *Handbook of Greek and Latin Palaeography* (New York, 1893), p. 70.

³ For this and other developments in the Middle Ages, see Walter J. Ong, "Historical Backgrounds of Elizabethan and Jacobean Punctuation Theory," *PMLA*, LIX (1944), 353, *passim*.

⁴ N. R. Ker, *Catalogue of Manuscripts Containing Anglo-Saxon* (Oxford, 1957), xxxiii–xxxvi.

⁵ John W. Clark, *A Study of Old and Middle English* (London, 1957), pp. 81–82.

⁶ A. Campbell, *Old English Grammar* (Oxford, 1959), p. 13.

⁷ See *The Prologues and Epilogues of William Caxton*, ed. W. J. B. Crotch, *EETS*, 176 (London, 1928).

⁸ See Ong, "Backgrounds," p. 353, *passim*; Charles C. Fries, "Shakesperian Punctuation," *Univ. of Mich. Publications in Lang. and Lit.*, I (1925), 67–86.

⁹ Six marks of punctuation occur in Thomas Wilson's *The Arte of Rhetorique* (1553): the period <.>, colon <:>, comma <,>, question mark <?>, exclamation mark <!>, and hyphen <=>. The last marked a word divided at the end of a line <re=maineth>.

¹⁰ C. H. Herford, Percy and Evelyn Simpson, *Ben Jonson*, VIII (Oxford, 1954), 551–553.

¹¹ Jonson, *English Grammar* (1640): "*Apostrophus* is the rejecting of a Vowell from the beginning, or ending of a Word. The note whereof, though it many times, through the negligence of Writers and Printers, is quite omitted, yet by right should, and of the learneder sort hath his signe and marke, which is such a Semicircle ᾿ placed in the top . . . as . . . *th᾿inward man*."

¹² See Helge Kökeritz and Charles T. Prouty, *Mr. William Shakespeares Comedies, Histories, & Tragedies* (New Haven, 1954).

¹³ Kökeritz and Prouty, *Shakespeares Comedies*; William Segar, *Honor, Military, and Ciuill* (London, 1602); William Camden, *Remaines Concerning Britain* (London, 1637); Ben Jonson, *Timber: or, Discoveries* (London, 1641); Richard Hooker, *Of the Lawes of Ecclesiastical Politie* (London, 1666); the 1690 English translation of Henry More's *Enchiridion Ethicum* (Facsimile Text Society: New York, 1930); Elkanan Settle, *The Notorious Imposter* (1692) and *Diego Redivivus* (1692), *Augustan Reprint Society*, 68 (1958); Helen C. White, Ruth C. Wallerstein, and Ricardo Quintana, *Seventeenth-Century Verse and Prose*, 2 vols. (New York, 1951–52).

¹⁴ Herford and Simpson, VIII, 511, n. 22–9.

¹⁵ Complain as he did about the use of *his*, Jonson himself was sometimes guilty of this. Two examples of such use by Jonson are *Sophocles his Ajax* and *Terrence his Comedies*. See Henry C. Wyld, *Colloquial English* (Oxford, 1936), pp. 315–316.

¹⁶ *James Thomson (1700–1748) Letters and Documents*, ed. Alan D. McKillop (Lawrence, Kansas, 1958); *G. W. Magazine, or Animadversions on the English Spelling* (1703), *ARS*, 70 (1958); William Wagstaffe, "A Comment Upon the History of Tom Thumb" (1711) in *Parodies of Ballad Criticisms (1711–1787)*, *ARS*, 63 (1957); Mateo Aleman, Dedication and "Preface

of The Life of Guzman d'Alfarache" (tr. 1708) in *Prefaces to Three Eighteenth-Century Novels (1708-1751-1797)*, *ARS*, 64 (1957); Jonathan Swift, *Gulliver's Travels, 1726*, ed. Herbert Davis (Oxford, 1959); *An Historical View of the . . . Political Writers in Great Britain* (1740), ed. Robert Haig, *ARS*, 69 (1958); Francis Coventry, Chapter 1 of Book 1 and Chapter 1 of Book 2 of *The History of Pompey the Little* (1751) and dedication of third edition (1752) in *Prefaces*, *ARS*, 64; Robert Lowth, *A Short Introduction to English Grammar* (London, 1763); George Canning, "The Knave of Hearts" (1787) in *Parodies*, *ARS*, 63.

British English

In this final chapter of our survey of the history of the English language, we shall examine some features that differentiate British English (BrE) from AmE. Our list is not complete, but it is suggestive of some features of pronunciation, stress, intonation, elision, spelling, vocabulary, and usage that differentiate BrE from AmE.

Dialect Surveys

BrE, as in the case of AmE, consists of several regional dialects. An examination of those dialects is currently being made through two surveys: the survey of Scottish dialects begun by Angus McIntosh and Kenneth Jackson, both of the University of Edinburgh, and the survey of English dialects, in connection with *A Linguistic Atlas of England*, under the direction of Harold Orton of the University of Leeds.

Two publications based on these surveys are the *Survey of English Dialects*, Introduction and Vol. I, parts 1–3 (Leeds, 1962), ed. Harold Orton and Wilfred J. Halliday; and *An Introduction to a Survey of Scottish Dialects* (Edinburgh, 1952), by Angus McIntosh. Related articles include Harold Orton and Eugen Dieth's "The New Survey of Dialectal English," *English Studies Today*, ed. C. L. Wrenn and G. Bullough (Oxford, 1951), pp. 63–73; and Eugen Dieth's "A Survey of English Dialects," *Essays and Studies*, XXXII (1947), 74–104.[1]

Pronunciation

Our illustration of some features of BrE pronunciation is based on the non-conservative general variety of that BrE dialect called Received Pronunciation (RP).

RP, which is primarily educated Southern BrE, continues to have great prestige in Britain, at least implicitly, as a socially accepted standard of pronunciation. It is also that form of BrE pronunciation used in British books dealing with the phonetics of BrE. In addition, RP is the form of BrE pronunciation adopted by the British Broadcasting Corporation (BBC) for its announcers.[2]

In the examples of BrE that follow, some Eastern and Southern speakers of AmE will find that British RP frequently parallels or approximates their own pronunciation. The reader's attention is also called to the loss in BrE RP of preconsonantal and postvocalic *r*-coloring in such words as *beard* and *father*.

	[ɪə̯]	*beard* [bíə̯d], *fierce* [fíə̯s]
	[ə̯]	*father* [fɑ́:ðə̯], *Worcester* [wʊ́stə̯]
	[ɑ:]	*laugh, pass, bath, clerk, aunt, vase*
	[ʌ]	*cut, much, tough*
	[ɔ:]	*war, four, born, door*
R-less	[ɜ:]	*church, earth, worse, bird, fur, her*
	[ɒ]	*dog, of, cough, was, cod, what, want*
	[əʊ]	*oak, rope, both*
	[ə:ʊ]	*home, road, go*
	[aɪə̯ ~ a:ə̯]	*fire, iron, choir*
	[aʊə̯ ~ ɑ:ə̯]	*flower, our*
	[ʊə̯]	*poor, cure*
	[ɛə̯]	*scarce*
	[ɛ:ə̯]	*pair, there*

Also note these differences between BrE and AmE:

	BrE	AmE
Letter *z*	[zɛ́d]	[zí]
schedule	[šɛd–]	[skɛd–]
futile	[fyútaɪl]	[fyútəl]

Stress

There are also some differences between BrE and AmE in the accentuation of words. A difference in the position of the primary accent sometimes also causes a difference in syllabic quality. Compare, for example, these illustrations:

	BrE	AmE
aluminium	[ælyəmíniəm]	[əlúmənəm]
primarily	[práɪmərəlɪ]	[praɪmɛ́rəli]
quinine	[kwɪnín]	[kwáɪnaɪn]
temporarily	[tɛ́mpərərlɪ]	[tɛmpərɛ́rəli]
lieutenant	[lɛfténənt]	[luténənt]

Intonation

BrE and AmE also differ in intonation — the melody, or rise and fall in pitch, of the voice in speech. Although many intonational variations occur because of differing characteristics of individual speakers, BrE RP speech tends to have more melodic rises and falls in pitch levels than AmE speech.

Because such intonation differences are more readily noticeable in relatively long stretches of speech, it is difficult to provide one or two short examples that illustrate differences in pitch levels between BrE RP and AmE speech. In BrE RP, however, one might hear *I think that's about all we can do* and *Can you let me have it tomorrow?* In contrast, AmE speech tends to be somewhat more monotonous, as in *I think that's about all we can do* and *Can you let me have it tomorrow?*

Elision

In rapid BrE speech whole syllables tend to be elided or omitted in pronunciation. On the other hand, AmE tends to be more deliberate, perhaps as a result of classroom drills to pronounce all syllables of a word in order to be "correct." Compare these examples:

	BrE	AmE
February	[fɛbrɪ]	[fɛbruɛri ~ fɛbrəwɛri ~ fɛbəwɛri]
difficult	[dítklt]	[dífəkəlt]
government	[gʌ́vmənt]	[gʌ́vərmənt ~ gʌ́vərnmənt]
police	[plíːs]	[pəlís]
literary	[lítrɪ]	[lítərɛri]
library	[láɪbrɪ]	[láɪbrɛri]

Spelling

Mainly as a result of reforms initiated by Noah Webster, some differences now distinguish BrE spelling from AmE spelling. A few examples illustrating the principal differences are these:

BrE	AmE
labour, valour, favour	*labor, valor, favor*
centre, (auto) *tyre, calibre*	*center, tire, caliber*
waggon, traveller, jewellery	*wagon, traveler, jewelry*
offence, defence, spelt	*offense, defense, spelled*
gaol, cheque, programme	*jail, check, program*

Vocabulary

A large number of BrE vocabulary items differ from those used in America. The following list is but a small sampling:

BrE	AmE
puncture	*flat* (tire)
chemist	*druggist*
lorry	*truck*
wireless	*radio*
petrol	*gasoline, gas*
tin	*can*
crisps	*potato chips*
flat	*apartment*
chips	*French fried potatoes*
packet	*pack, package*
biscuit	*cracker*
underground	*subway*
caravan	*trailer*
serviette	*table napkin*
telly	*TV*

Usage

Differences in usage between BrE and AmE are more difficult to establish than those in spelling and vocabulary. Here are a few examples of differences in usage:

BrE	AmE
There's nothing in it	*There's nothing to it*
one uses one's head	*one uses his head*
first trip for four years	*first trip in four years*
go on holiday	*take a vacation*
turned round	*turned around*
lives in High Street	*lives on High Street*

Influence of AmE on BrE

AmE, as we stated in an earlier chapter, developed from the EModE dialects brought to North America in the seventeenth century. Although by c. 1780, AmE had sufficiently changed to differ from BrE, yet until World War I (1914–18) BrE tended to influence AmE. Since that time, however, BrE has come under the influence of AmE through American motion pictures, novels, plays, musical comedies, and, subsequently, American tourists, troops, and television programs.

AmE influences on BrE appear to be restricted largely to vocabulary, and perhaps to some extent to usage; BrE phonology evidently is unchanged, and BrE and AmE morphology and syntax appear to be generally identical. All in all, it is not likely that BrE will be superseded by AmE.

SUMMARY

RP, differences in pronunciation, stress, intonation, elision, spelling, vocabulary, and usage.

NOTES

[1] See also W. W. Skeat, *English Dialects from the Eighth Century to the Present Day* (Cambridge, 1911), and Joseph Wright, *English Dialect Dictionary*, 6 vols. (London, 1898–1905).

[2] See Daniel Jones, *The Pronunciation of English* (Cambridge, 1956) and *An English Pronouncing Dictionary* (London, 1956); P. A. D. MacCarthy, *English Pronunciation* (Cambridge, 1952); A. C. Gimson, *An Introduction to the Pronunciation of English* (London, 1962).

Glossary

The selected glossary of linguistic terms that follows is intended as a handy table of short definitions for student reference. As stated in the text, some of the definitions are more narrow or more expanded than those that may be encountered in other linguistic works. Furthermore, some of the terms defy adequate definition at present for various reasons, including lack of agreement among linguists.

affix   A bound morpheme attached to the front or end of a base or to another affix.

affricate   A stop with fricative release.

allograph   One of the nondistinctive variants comprising a grapheme, all of which have the same reference, e. g., the allographs, *a*, *a*, *A* of the grapheme *A*.

allomorph   A class of phonemically and semantically identical morphs constituting one of the nondistinctive variants comprising a morpheme.

allophone   A class of identical phones constituting one of the nondistinctive variants comprising a phoneme.

alphabet   A system of graphemes (letters) that represent phonemes in a somewhat close, but imperfect, correspondence.

analogy   That linguistic process by which words become imitative of more familiar words and patterns without having undergone the same linguistic development themselves.

articulation   All of the movements of the speech organs and the alterations in the shapes of the air-passages and resonance cavities of the human vocal tract involved in producing a speech sound.

aspect   Of an English verb phrase, the status or category of action with reference to its continuation ('be'+present participle) or completion ('have'+past participle).

assimilation   That linguistic process by which a sound is partially or totally adapted to the position or articulation of an adjacent sound.

base   A morpheme whose allomorphs do not contain /+/.

case   One of the forms of an inflected word which indicates that word's syntactical relationship to another word in a grammatical construction.

class dialect   The dialect of a particular social class.

cognate   A word or a morpheme related to another word or morpheme by descent from the same linguistic ancestor.

complex nucleus   A syllabic nucleus characterized by a single continuous articulatory glide from the position for one nucleus to that for another within the same syllable.

concord   A grammatical correlation that exists between two or more words, namely a system of correspondence in regard to gender, number, case, or person.

consonant   A phoneme whose allophones normally pattern as syllabic margins in a language.

dialect   A class or regional variety of a language that differs linguistically in some measure from other varieties of the language.

diphthong   A vowel phoneme whose allophones normally pattern as complex nuclei in a language.

focal area   An area containing a major cultural center from which linguistic forms are spreading to adjacent areas.

form class   A class of words distinguished by form, namely by inflectional suffixes or by postbases or by the absence of inflectional suffixes and postbases.

fricative   A speech sound with audible turbulence or friction produced as a result of passage of the air stream through a relatively small opening.

function word In morphological terms, a form class marked by the absence of inflectional suffixes and postbases and with little or no lexical meaning; in syntactic terms, a set of words that functions to connect other words into syntactic structures.

glide A speech sound characterized by an uninterrupted articulatory movement from the position of one speech sound to that of another.

government The system by which one word controls the case or mood of another word.

grammar The phonology, morphology, and syntax of a language.

grapheme A graphic symbol (sign) in a writing system.

Grimm's Law A systematic series of correspondences between certain Germanic consonants, derived from Proto-Indo-European stops, and consonants in cognate words in other Indo-European languages, as stated in 1822 by Jacob Grimm.

immediate constituent One of the components into which a linguistic construction is cut in first analysis.

inflectional suffix A bound morpheme that conveys a grammatical signal (e. g., number, case, tense) and is attached, sequentially or nonsequentially, to a base, postbase, or another inflectional suffix.

intonation contour A suprasegmental morpheme, consisting of a meaningful pattern of pitches and a terminal, accompanying syntactic structures as phrases and sentences.

isogloss A postulated line on a dialect map marking the boundary between linguistic features.

language An arbitrary system of articulated sounds used by humans to carry on the social affairs of their society.

lateral A speech sound in which the air stream passes laterally over one or both sides of the tongue.

logography A system of writing in which the graphemes (logograms) represent words (e. g., *&* = *and*).

mood A distinction signaled by a modal auxiliary or an inflectional form of a verb, whose selection depends either on stylistic convention or on whether the action or state which the verb denotes is regarded as fact or in some other manner.

morph Any sequence of one or more phonemes that has meaning.

morpheme A class of semantically identical allomorphs in complementary distribution or free variation, comprising the smallest linguistic unit that has meaning in a language or period of a language.

morphology The study of the form and structure of words, namely the arrangement and interrelationship of their component morphemes.

nasal A speech sound characterized by passage of the air stream through the nasal passage.

nonstandard usage The usage of speakers of a language or dialect, whose usage differs from that of standard speakers of the language or dialect and may not be socially acceptable to them.

paradigm A listing of all the forms of a form class word marked by inflectional suffixes or postbases.

part of speech A form class of lexical words marked by a set of inflectional suffixes or postbases.

passive voice A form of an English verb phrase, consisting of 'be' plus a past participle of a transitive verb, which signals that the subject of the verb undergoes or receives rather than performs the action expressed by the verb.

phone Any single speech sound, namely a unique minimal segment of speech.

phoneme A class of phonetically similar allophones in complementary distribution or free variation, comprising the smallest contrastive sound class that functions to distinguish utterances from one another in a language or period of a language.

phonetic alphabet A set of symbols used to represent phonetypes in a one-to-one correspondence of symbol to phonetype.

phone-type A class of identical phones.

phonology The study of the components and structure of the sound system of a language or dialect, namely the phonetic and phonemic system of a language or dialect.

phrase A linguistic construction — either morphological or syntactic — consisting of more than one base.

point of articulation The position of juncture or near juncture between a movable speech organ (articulator) and a relatively stationary part of the vocal tract, or between two articulators.

prebase A bound morpheme attached to the front of a base or to another prebase.

prestige dialect A class dialect having prestige over others.

Proto-Germanic The hypothetical reconstructed linguistic ancestor of the Germanic languages.

Proto-Indo-European The hypothetical reconstructed linguistic ancestor of the Indo-European languages.

regional dialect A dialect characteristic of a particular geographical area.

relic area A dialect area in geographic or cultural isolation, usually lacking a major cultural center, where linguistic forms occur which are lost elsewhere.

rune A grapheme in the ancient Germanic runic alphabet or *futhark*.

segmental morpheme A morpheme (e. g., base, prebase, postbase, inflectional suffix) that is a segment of a linear sequence.

segmental phoneme A phoneme (e. g., vowel, consonant) that is a segment of a linear sequence.

sentence A grammatically self-contained unit of speech marked by at least one superfix and intonation contour, which unit is bounded initially either by silence or another intonation contour; in Transformational grammar, S → NP+VP.

sibilant A groove or [s]-like fricative formed by the air stream passing through a groove-like opening along the center length of the tongue.

standard usage The usage of speakers of a language or dialect, which is a socially acceptable standard because its speakers have authority and status.

stem That part of a morphological construction to which an inflectional suffix is added.

stop   A speech sound in which there is complete stoppage and then release of the air stream.

strong adjective   One of a class of Germanic adjectives characterized by a paradigm of vocalic inflections.

strong verb   One of a class of Germanic verbs whose past tense is signaled by internal change of the syllabic nucleus.

superfix   A suprasegmental morpheme whose allomorphs consist of stress phonemes with or without /+/.

suprasegmental morpheme   A morpheme (e. g., superfix, intonation contour) that occurs simultaneously with one or more segmental morphemes.

suprasegmental phoneme   A phoneme (e. g., pitch, stress, open transition, terminal) that occurs simultaneously with one or more segmental phonemes.

syllabary   A system of graphemes (syllabograms) that represent syllables (e. g., *I C U = I see you*).

syllabic margin   A speech segment, not under the domain of stress, that forms the boundary or margin of a syllable.

syllabic nucleus   That most prominent part of a syllable which is the domain of stress.

syllable   A unit of speech, uttered in a single vocal impulse, containing a syllabic nucleus alone or with one or more syllabic margins.

syntax   The arrangement and interrelationship of words in phrases and sentences.

transition area   An area lacking sharply defined linguistic features of its own and which shares the features of adjacent areas.

trill   A speech sound produced by the rapid vibration of an articulator.

ultimate constituent   One of the components of a linguistic construction on its last or lowest level of analysis.

usage   The customary use in a language of sounds, words, and grammatical structures by a group or class of speakers of that language

Verner's Law   A statement by Karl Verner in 1876, explaining certain exceptions to Grimm's formulation on the basis of the position of the principal stress accent in words in Proto-Germanic.

voice   That vocal quality of a speech sound resulting from the modulation of the air stream by the quasi-periodic opening and closing of the vocal cords.

voiced sound   A speech sound characterized by voice.

voiceless (unvoiced) sound   A speech sound not characterized by voice.

vowel   A phoneme whose allophones normally pattern as syllabic nuclei in a language.

weak adjective   One of a class of Germanic adjectives characterized by a paradigm of *−n* inflections.

weak verb   One of a class of Germanic verbs whose past tense is signaled by a dental suffix.

word   Morphemically, a linguistic free form consisting of a superfix and either a morphological phrase or a base with or without one or more affixes.

writing   One of various systems of conventional graphic signs used by humans as a form of communication.

zero allomorph   An allomorph without phonemic content postulated to indicate a zero variant in a paradigm, e. g. LModE plural *sheep* = /šip/ + /Ø/, wherein the zero allomorph is /Ø/.

Selected Bibliography

Abbott, O. L. "The Preterit and Past Participle of Strong Verbs in Seven-teenth-Century American English," *American Speech*, XXXII (1957), 31–42.

————. "Verbal Endings in Seventeenth-Century American English," *American Speech*, XXXIII (1958), 185–194.

Allen, Harold B. "Minor Dialect Areas of the Upper Midwest," *Publication of the American Dialect Society*, 30 (1958), 3–16.

————. *Readings in Applied English Linguistics.* 2nd ed. New York: Appleton-Century-Crofts, 1964.

Alston, R. C. *English Grammars Written in English and English Grammars Written in Latin by Native Speakers.* Leeds: E. J. Arnold & Son, 1965.

————. *The English Dictionary.* Leeds: E. J. Arnold & Son, 1966.

Anderson, George K. *The Literature of the Anglo-Saxons.* Princeton: Princeton University Press, 1949.

Anderson, Majorie and Blanche C. Williams. *Old English Handbook.* Cambridge, Mass.: Houghton Mifflin, 1935.

Andrews, Charles M. *Our Earliest Colonial Settlements.* New York: New York University Press, 1933.

Angus, William. "Poor Richard's Alphabet and His Pronunciation," *Speech Monographs*, II (1935), 60–70.

Atwood, E. Bagby. *A Survey of Verb Forms in the Eastern United States.* Ann Arbor: University of Michigan Press, 1953.

Babcock, C. Merton. *The Ordeal of American English.* Boston: Houghton Mifflin, 1961.

Bach, Emmon. *An Introduction to Transformational Grammars.* New York: Holt, Rinehart and Winston, 1964.

Baldwin, T. W. *William Shakespere's Small Latine & Lesse Greeke.* Urbana: University of Illinois Press, 1944.

Bambas, Rudolph C. "Verb Forms in –S and –TH in Early Modern English Prose," *Journal of English and Germanic Philology*, XLVI (1947), 183–187.

Baugh, Albert C. *A History of the English Language.* 2nd ed. New York: Appleton-Century-Crofts, 1957.

Bede. *A History of the English Church and People.* Translated by Leo Sherley-Price. Harmondsworth, Eng.: Penguin Books, 1955.

Bennett, H. S. *English Books & Readers, 1475 to 1557.* Cambridge, Eng.: Cambridge University Press, 1952.

Bense, J. F. *A Dictionary of the Low-Dutch Element in the English Vocabulary.* Parts I–V. London: H. Milford, 1926–1939.

Berrey, Lester V. "Southern Mountain Dialect," *American Speech,* XV (1940), 45–54.

Bigelow, Gordon E. "More Evidence of Early Loss of [R] in Eastern American Speech," *American Speech,* XXX (1955), 154–156.

Blair, Peter H. *An Introduction to Anglo-Saxon England.* Cambridge, Eng.: Cambridge University Press, 1956.

———. *Roman Britain and Early England, 55 B.C.–A.D. 871.* Edinburgh: Thomas Nelson and Sons, 1963.

Bloomfield, Leonard. *Language.* New York: Henry Holt and Co., 1933.

Bloomfield, Morton W. and Leonard Newmark. *A Linguistic Introduction to the History of English.* New York: Alfred A. Knopf, 1963.

Bolinger, Dwight L. "Contrastive Accent and Contrastive Stress," *Language,* 37 (1961), 83–96.

———. *Generality, Gradience, and the All-or-None.* s-Gravenhage: Mouton and Co., 1961.

Bosworth, Joseph and T. Northcote Toller. *An Anglo-Saxon Dictionary.* London: Oxford University Press, 1898; reprinted 1954. *Supplement* by Toller, London: Oxford University Press, 1921; reprinted 1955.

Bradley, Henry. *The Making of English.* New York: Macmillan, 1904.

Bronstein, Arthur J *The Pronunciation of American English: An Introduction to Phonetics.* New York: Appleton-Century-Crofts, 1960.

Brook, G. L. *A History of the English Language.* London: Andre Deutsch, 1958.

Brunner, Karl. *An Outline of Middle English Grammar.* Translated by Grahame Johnston. Oxford: Basil Blackwell, 1963.

Bryan, W. F. "The Midland Present Plural Indicative Ending –e(n)," *Modern Philology,* XVIII (1921), 457–473.

Bryant, Margaret M. *Modern English and Its Heritage.* 2nd ed. New York: Macmillan, 1962.

Butterworth, Charles C. *English Primers, 1529–1545.* Philadelphia: University of Pennsylvania Press, 1953.

Campbell, A. *Old English Grammar.* Oxford: Oxford University Press, 1959.

Carpenter, Charles. *History of American Schoolbooks.* Philadelphia: University of Pennsylvania Press, 1963.

Carroll, John B. *The Study of Language.* Cambridge, Mass.: Harvard University Press, 1953.

Cawdrey, Robert. *A Table Alphabeticall of Hard Usual English Words.* Facsimile edition with introduction by Robert A. Peters. Gainesville, Fla.: Scholars' Facsimiles & Reprints, 1966.

Chambers, R. W. and Marjorie Daunt. *A Book of London English; 1384–1425.* Oxford: Oxford University Press, 1931.

Chitwood, Oliver P. *A History of Colonial America.* 3rd ed. New York: Harper & Row, 1948.

Chomsky, Noam. *Syntactic Structures.* The Hague: Mouton and Co., 1962.

Clark, John W. *Early English.* London: Andre Deutsch, 1957.

Collingwood, R. G. and J. N. L. Myres. *Roman Britain and the English Settlements.* 2nd ed. Oxford: Oxford University Press, 1937.

Craigie, William A. and James R. Hulbert, eds. *A Dictionary of American English on Historical Principles.* 4 vols. Chicago: University of Chicago Press, 1938–1944.

Crotch, W. J. B., ed. *The Prologues and Epilogues of William Caxton.* Early English Text Society, O.S. 176. London, 1928; reprinted 1956.

Davies, Constance. *English Pronunciation from the Fifteenth to the Eighteenth Century.* London: Dent, 1934.

DeCamp, David. "The Genesis of the Old English Dialects: A New Hypothesis," *Language,* 34 (1958), 232–244.

Denholm-Young, N. *Handwriting in England and Wales.* Cardiff: University of Wales Press, 1954.

Dickins, Bruce and R. M. Wilson, eds. *Early Middle English Texts.* New York: Norton, 1951.

Dobson, E. J. *English Pronunciation 1500–1700.* 2 vols. Oxford: Oxford University Press, 1957.

Ekwall, Eilert. *The Concise Oxford Dictionary of English Place-Names.* 4th ed. Oxford: Oxford University Press, 1960.

Eliason, Norman E. "Old English Vowel Lengthening and Vowel Shortening Before Consonant Groups," *Studies in Philology,* XLV (1948), 1–20.

Elliott, Ralph W. V. *Runes; An Introduction.* Manchester: Manchester University Press, 1959; reprinted 1963.

Emerson, Oliver F. *The History of the English Language.* New York: Macmillan, 1935.

———. *A Middle English Reader.* New and revised edition. New York: Macmillan, 1915; reprinted 1960.

Ewert, Alfred. *The French Language.* Revised edition. London: Faber & Faber, 1956.

First Texas Conference on Problems of Linguistic Analysis in English, April 27–30, 1956. Austin: The University of Texas, 1962.

Flower, R. and A. H. Smith, eds. *The Parker Chronicle and Laws; A Facsimile.* Early English Text Society, O.S., 208. London, 1941.

Francis, W. Nelson. *The English Language: An Introduction.* New York: Norton, 1965.

————. *The Structure of American English* with a chapter on American English dialects by Raven I. McDavid, Jr. New York: Ronald Press, 1958.

Friedrich, Johannes. *Extinct Languages.* Translated by Frank Gaynor. New York: Philosophical Library, 1957.

Fries, Charles C. *Linguistics and Reading.* New York: Holt, Rinehart and Winston, 1963.

————. "The Rules of Common School Grammars," *Publications of the Modern Language Association,* XLII (1927), 221–237.

————. *The Structure of English: An Introduction to the Construction of English Sentences.* New York: Harcourt Brace, 1952.

————. *The Teaching of English.* Ann Arbor: George Wahr, 1949.

Gelb, I. J. *A Study of Writing.* Revised edition. Chicago: University of Chicago Press, 1963.

Gimson, A. C. *An Introduction to the Pronunciation of English.* London: Edward Arnold, 1962.

Gleason, H. A. Jr. *An Introduction to Descriptive Linguistics.* Revised edition. New York: Holt, Rinehart and Winston, 1961.

————. *Linguistics and English Grammar.* New York: Holt, Rinehart and Winston, 1965.

Godfrey, John. *The Church in Anglo-Saxon England.* Cambridge: Cambridge University Press, 1962.

Gordon, E. V. *An Introduction to Old Norse.* 2nd ed. Revised by A. R. Taylor. Oxford: Oxford University Press, 1957.

Graham, Ian C. C. *Colonists from Scotland: Emigration to North America, 1707–1783.* Ithaca: Cornell University Press, 1956.

Grandgent, Charles H. "From Franklin to Lowell," *Publications of the Modern Language Association,* XIV (1899), 211–212.

————. *Old and New.* Cambridge, Mass.: Harvard University Press, 1920.

Grattan, J. H. G. and Charles Singer. *Anglo-Saxon Magic and Medicine.* London: Oxford University Press, 1952.

Gray, G. W. and C. M. Wise. *The Bases of Speech.* 3rd ed. New York: Harper & Brothers, 1959.

Gray, Louis H. *Foundations of Language.* New York: Macmillan, 1939.

Hall, John R. C. *A Concise Anglo-Saxon Dictionary.* 4th ed. with supplement by Herbert D. Meritt. Cambridge: Cambridge University Press, 1960.

Hall, Robert A. Jr. *Introductory Linguistics.* Philadelphia: Chilton, 1964.

Hansen, Marcus L. *The Atlantic Migration, 1607–1860.* Cambridge, Mass.: Harvard University Press, 1940.

Harmer, F. E. *Anglo-Saxon Writs*. Manchester: Manchester University Press, 1952.

Hawkes, Christopher and Jacquetta. *Prehistoric Britain*. Harmondsworth, Eng.: Penguin Books, 1943; reprinted 1952.

Heffner, R. M. S. *General Phonetics*. Madison: University of Wisconsin Press, 1950; reprinted 1964.

Hill, Archibald A. *Introduction to Linguistic Structures: From Sound to Sentence in English*. New York: Harcourt Brace, 1958.

Hockett, Charles F. *A Course in Modern Linguistics*. New York: Macmillan, 1958.

————. "The Origin of Speech," *Scientific American*, 203 (1960), 89–96.

————. "The Stressed Syllabics of Old English," *Language*, 35 (1959), 575–597.

Hodgkin, R. H. *A History of the Anglo-Saxons*. 2 vols. 3rd ed. New York: Oxford University Press, 1953.

Howard, Edwin J. "The Printer and Elizabethan Punctuation," *Studies in Philology*, XXVIII (1930), 220–229.

Hubbell, Allan F. *The Pronunciation of English in New York City*. New York: King's Crown Press, 1950.

Hughes, John P. *The Science of Language: An Introduction to Linguistics*. New York: Random House, 1962.

Jackson, Kenneth. *Language and History in Early Britain*. Cambridge, Mass.: Harvard University Press, 1954.

Jenkinson, C. H. and C. Johnson. *Court Hand*. 2 vols. Oxford: Oxford University Press, 1915.

Jenkinson, Hilary. "Notes on the Study of English Punctuation of the Sixteenth Century," *Review of English Studies*, II (1926), 152–158.

Jespersen, Otto. *A Modern English Grammar on Historical Principles*. 7 vols. Copenhagen: Einar Munksgaard, 1909–1949.

————. *Growth and Structure of the English Language*. 9th ed. Oxford: Basil Blackwell, 1962.

Jones, Daniel. *An Outline of English Phonetics*. 8th ed. Cambridge: W. Heffer & Sons, 1957.

————. *The Pronunciation of English*. 4th ed. Cambridge: Cambridge University Press, 1956.

Jones, Richard F. *The Triumph of the English Language*. Stanford: Stanford University Press, 1953.

Kantner, Claude B. and Robert West. *Phonetics*. Revised edition. New York: Harper & Brothers, 1960.

Kennedy, Arthur G. *Bibliography of Writings on the English Language from the Beginning of Printing to the End of 1922*. Cambridge, Mass.: Harvard University Press, 1927.

Kenyon, John S. *American Pronunciation*. 10th ed. Ann Arbor: George Wahr, 1961.

———— and Thomas A. Knott. *A Pronouncing Dictionary of American English*. Springfield, Mass.: G. & C. Merriam Co., 1953.

Ker, N. R. *Catalogue of Manuscripts Containing Anglo-Saxon*. Oxford: Oxford University Press, 1957.

————. *English Manuscripts in the Century after the Norman Conquest*. Oxford: Oxford University Press, 1960.

Kökeritz, Helge. *A Guide to Chaucer's Pronunciation*. New York: Holt, Rinehart and Winston, 1962.

————. *Shakespeare's Pronunciation*. New Haven: Yale University Press, 1953.

———— and Charles T. Prouty. *Mr. William Shakespeares Comedies, Histories, & Tragedies*. New Haven: Yale University Press, 1954.

Krapp, George P. *The English Language in America*. 2 vols. 2nd ed. New York: Frederick Ungar, 1960.

Krause, Wolfgang. *Abriss der altwestnordischen Grammatik*. Halle (Salle): Max Niemeyer, 1948.

Kuhn, Sherman M. "On the Syllabic Phonemes of Old English," *Language*, 37 (1961), 522–538.

———— and Randolph Quirk. "Some Recent Interpretations of Old English Digraph Spellings," *Language*, 29 (1953), 143–156.

————. "The Old English Digraphs: A Reply," *Language*, 31 (1955), 390–401.

Kurath, Hans. *A Phonology and Prosody of Modern English*. Ann Arbor: University of Michigan Press, 1964.

————. *A Word Geography of the Eastern United States*. Ann Arbor: University of Michigan Press, 1949.

————. "The Binary Interpretation of English Vowels," *Language*, 33 (1957), 111–122.

————. "The Origin of the Dialectal Differences in Spoken American English," *Modern Philology*, XXV (1928), 385–395.

———— and Sherman M. Kuhn, eds. *Middle English Dictionary*. Ann Arbor: University of Michigan Press, 1952 —. In progress.

———— and Raven I. McDavid, Jr. *The Pronunciation of English in the Atlantic States*. Ann Arbor: University of Michigan Press, 1961.

———— et al. *Handbook of the Linguistic Geography of New England*. Washington, D. C.: American Council of Learned Societies, 1939.

———— et al. *Linguistic Atlas of New England*. 3 vols. in 6. Providence: Brown University, 1939–1943.

Laird, Charlton and Robert M. Gorrell. *English As Language; Backgrounds, Development, Usage*. New York: Harcourt, Brace & World, 1961.

Lees, Robert B. *The Grammar of English Nominalizations*. Bloomington: Indiana University Research Center in Anthropology, Folklore, and Linguistics, 1960.

Lehmann, Winifred P. *Historical Linguistics: an Introduction.* New York: Holt, Rinehart and Winston, 1962.

Leonard, Sterling A. *The Doctrine of Correctness in English Usage, 1700–1800.* University of Wisconsin Studies in Language and Literature, 25. Madison, 1929.

Lindblad, Karl-Erik. *Noah Webster's Pronunciation and Modern New England Speech.* Essays and Studies on American Language and Literature, XI. Upsala: A.-B. Lundequistska Bokhandeln, 1954.

Lindsay, W. M. *The Corpus Glossary.* Publications of the Philological Society, VIII. Oxford, 1921.

Littlehales, Henry, ed. *The Medieval Records of a London City Church.* 2 vols. Early English Text Society, O.S. 125, 128. London, 1904–1905.

Llewellyn, E. C. *The Influence of Low Dutch on the English Vocabulary.* Oxford: Milford, 1936.

Lloyd, Donald J. and Harry R. Warfel. *American English in Its Cultural Setting.* New York: Alfred A. Knopf, 1957.

Lowe, E. A. *English Uncial.* Oxford: Oxford University Press, 1960.

Lyman, Rollo L. "English Grammar in American Schools Before 1850," *U. S. Office of Education Bulletin,* XII. Washington, D. C.: 1921.

MacCarthy, Peter A. D. *English Pronunciation.* 4th ed. Cambridge, Eng.: W. Heffer & Sons, 1950.

Malmstrom, Jean and Annabel Ashley. *Dialects — U. S. A.* Champaign, Ill.: National Council of Teachers of English, 1963.

Malone, Kemp. "Benjamin Franklin on Spelling Reform," *American Speech,* I (1925), 96–100.

———. "When Did Middle English Begin?" *Curme Volume of Linguistic Studies,* Language Monograph, 7. Baltimore: Waverly Press, 1930, 110–117.

Marckwardt, Albert H. *American English.* New York: Oxford University Press, 1958.

———. "Origin and Extension of the Voiceless Irregular Weak Verb Conjugation," *University of Michigan Publications in Language and Literature,* XII (1943), 151–328.

———. "Principal and Subsidiary Dialect Areas in the North-Central States," *Publication of the American Dialect Society,* 27 (1957), 3–15.

———. "Verb Inflections in Late Old English," *Philologica: The Kemp Malone Anniversary Series.* Baltimore: Johns Hopkins Press, 1949, pp. 79–88.

Mathews, Mitford M., ed. *A Dictionary of Americanisms on Historical Principles.* 2 vols. Chicago: University of Chicago Press, 1951. Third impression, 1956.

———. *The Beginnings of American English.* Chicago: University of Chicago Press, 1931.

McAdam, E. L. Jr. and George Milne. *Johnson's Dictionary.* New York: Pantheon Books, 1963.

McDavid, Raven I. Jr. "Grammatical Differences in the North-Central States," *American Speech*, XXXV (1960), 5–19.

———. "Postvocalic /–r/ in South Carolina," *American Speech*, XXIII (1948), 194–203.

McIntosh, Angus. *An Introduction to a Survey of Scottish Dialects*. Edinburgh: Thomas Nelson and Sons, 1961.

Mencken, H. L. *The American Language*. 4th ed. and two supplements abridged, with annotations and new material, by Raven I. McDavid, Jr., with the assistance of David W. Maurer. New York: Alfred A. Knopf, 1963.

Miller, Virginia R. "Present-Day Use of the Broad A in Eastern Massachusetts: A Social Analysis," *Speech Monographs*, XX (1953), 235–246.

Moore, Samuel. "Earliest Morphological Changes in Middle English," *Language*, 4 (1928), 238–266.

———. "Grammatical and Natural Gender in Middle English," *Publications of the Modern Language Association*, XXXVI (1921), 79–103.

———. *Historical Outlines of English Sounds and Inflections*. Revised by Albert H. Marckwardt. Ann Arbor: George Wahr, 1957.

———. "Loss of Final *n* in Inflectional Syllables of Middle English," *Language*, 3 (1927), 232–259.

———, Sanford B. Meech, and Harold Whitehall. "Middle English Dialect Characteristics and Dialect Boundaries." *Essays and Studies in English and Comparative Literature*, University of Michigan Publications in Language and Literature, XIII. Ann Arbor: University of Michigan Press, 1935, 1–60.

——— and T. A. Knott. *The Elements of Old English*. Revised by James R. Hulbert. 10th ed. Ann Arbor: George Wahr, 1955.

Mossé, Fernand. *A Handbook of Middle English*. Translated by James A. Walker. Baltimore: Johns Hopkins Press, 1952.

Moulton, William G. "The Stops and Spirants of Early Germanic," *Language*, 30 (1954), 1–42.

Muller, Siegfried H. *The World's Living Languages*. New York: Frederick Ungar, 1964.

Murray, J. A. H. et al., eds. *Oxford English Dictionary*. 12 vols. Oxford: Oxford University Press, 1884–1928. *Supplement*, 1933.

Nietz, John A. *Old Textbooks*. Pittsburgh: University of Pittsburgh Press, 1961.

Orton, Harold and Eugen Dieth. *Survey of English Dialects*. Leeds: E. J. Arnold & Son, 1962.

Partridge, Eric and John W. Clark. *British and American English Since 1900*. London: Andrew Dakers, 1951.

Pedersen, Holger. *Linguistic Science in the Nineteenth Century*. Translated by John Spargo. Cambridge, Mass.: Harvard University Press, 1931.

Peters, Robert A. "Case-Number Morphs of Old English Nouns," *Linguistics*, 14 (1965), 41–51.

———. "Linguistic Differences Between Early and Late Modern English," *Studia Neophilologica*, XXXVII (1965), 134–138.

———. "Morphemic Differentiation of Old English Adverb Subsets," *The Canadian Journal of Linguistics*, 13 (forthcoming).

———. "Phonic and Phonemic Long Consonants in Old English," *Studies in Linguistics*, 19 (forthcoming).

Pike, Kenneth L. *Phonemics: A Technique for Reducing Languages to Writing*. Ann Arbor: University of Michigan Press, 1947.

———. *The Intonation of American English*. Ann Arbor: University of Michigan Press, 1945.

Platt, Joan. "The Development of English Colloquial Idiom During the Eighteenth Century," *Review of English Studies*, II (1926), 72–73, 196.

Plummer, Charles. *Two of the Saxon Chronicles Parallel*. Oxford: Oxford University Press, 1892–1899. Reprinted 1952 with additions by Dorothy Whitelock.

Poole, Austin L. *Medieval England*. 2 vols. Revised ed. Oxford: Oxford University Press, 1958.

Pooley, Robert C. *Teaching English Grammar*. New York: Appleton-Century-Crofts, 1957.

Pope, M. K. *From Latin to French with Especial Consideration of Anglo-Norman*. Manchester: Manchester University Press, 1934; reprinted 1956.

Price, H. T. *Foreign Influences on Middle English*, University of Michigan Contributions in Modern Philology, X. Ann Arbor, 1947.

Prokosch, Eduard. *A Comparative Germanic Grammar*. Philadelphia: Linguistic Society of America for Yale University, 1939.

Pulgram, Ernst. *Introduction to the Spectrography of Speech*. 's-Gravenhage: Mouton and Co., 1959.

Pyles, Thomas. *The Origins and Development of the English Language*. New York: Harcourt, Brace & World, 1964.

———. *Words and Ways of American English*. New York: Random House, 1952.

Quirk, Randolph and C. L. Wrenn. *An Old English Grammar*. New York: Henry Holt and Co., 1957.

Reaney, P. H. *The Origin of English Place-Names*. London: Routledge and Kegan Paul, 1960.

Reed, Carroll E. "The Pronunciation of English in the Pacific Northwest," *Language*, 37 (1961), 559–564.

Reed, David W. "The History of Inflectional *n* in English Verbs before 1500," *University of California Publications in English*, VII (1950), 157–328.

Roberts, Paul. *English Sentences*. New York: Harcourt, Brace & World, 1962.

———. *English Syntax*. Alternate edition. New York: Harcourt, Brace & World, 1964.

Robertson, Stuart. *The Development of Modern English.* 2nd ed. Revised by Frederic G. Cassidy. Englewood Cliffs, N. J.: Prentice-Hall, 1954.

Robins, R. H. *Ancient and Medieval Grammatical Theory in Europe.* London: Bell, 1951.

————. *General Linguistics: An Introductory Survey.* Bloomington: Indiana University Press, 1964.

Second Texas Conference on Problems of Linguistic Analysis in English, April 26–29, 1957. Austin: The University of Texas, 1962.

Serjeantson, Mary S. *A History of Foreign Words in English.* London: Routledge and Kegan Paul, 1935; second impression 1961.

Shannon, Ann. *A Descriptive Syntax of the Parker Manuscript of the Anglo-Saxon Chronicle from 734 to 891.* The Hague: Mouton and Co., 1964.

Sievers, Eduard. *Altenglische Grammatik nach der angelsächsischen Grammatik.* 2nd ed. Revised by Karl Brunner. Halle (Salle): Max Niemeyer, 1951.

Simpson, Percy. *Proof-Reading in the Sixteenth, Seventeenth, and Eighteenth Centuries.* London: Oxford University Press, 1935.

Sisam, Kenneth, ed. *Fourteenth Century Verse & Prose.* Oxford: Oxford University Press, 1924; reprinted 1950.

Skeat, W. W. *The Gospel According to Saint Matthew.* Cambridge: Cambridge University Press, 1912.

Sledd, James. *A Short Introduction to English Grammar.* Chicago: Scott, Foresman and Co., 1959.

———— and Wilma R. Ebbitt. *Dictionaries and That Dictionary.* Chicago: Scott, Foresman and Co., 1962.

Smith, A. H. *English Place-Name Elements.* 2 vols. Cambridge: Cambridge University Press, 1956.

Starnes, DeWitt T. *Renaissance Dictionaries English-Latin and Latin-English.* Austin: University of Texas Press, 1954.

———— and Gertrude E. Noyes. *The English Dictionary from Cawdrey to Johnson 1604–1755.* Chapel Hill: University of North Carolina Press, 1946.

Stenton, Frank M. *Anglo-Saxon England.* 2nd ed. Oxford: Oxford University Press, 1947.

Stidson, Russell O. *The Use of Ye in the Function of Thou.* Revised by Arthur G. Kennedy. Stanford: Leland Stanford Jr. University, 1917.

Stratmann, F. H. *A Middle English Dictionary.* Revised by Henry Bradley. Oxford: Oxford University Press, 1891.

Sturtevant, E. H. *The Pronunciation of Greek and Latin.* 2nd ed. Philadelphia: Linguistic Society of America, 1940.

Suggett, Helen. "The Use of French in England in the Later Middle Ages," *Transactions of the Royal Historical Society*, 4th Series, XXVIII (1946), 61–83.

Tacitus. *On Britain and Germany.* Translated by H. Mattingly. Harmondsworth, Eng.: Penguin Books, 1948; reprinted 1954.

Thieme, Paul. "The Indo-European Language," *Scientific American*, (October, 1958), 63–74.

Third Texas Conference on Problems of Linguistic Analysis in English, May 9–12, 1958. Austin: The University of Texas, 1962.

Thomas, Charles K. *An Introduction to the Phonetics of American English.* 2nd ed. New York: Ronald Press, 1958.

———. "The Dialectal Significance of the Non-Phonemic Low-Back Vowel Variants before R," *Studies in Speech and Drama in Honor of Alexander M. Drummond* (Ithaca, 1944), pp. 244–254.

Trager, George L. and Henry L. Smith, Jr. *An Outline of English Structure.* Fifth printing. Washington, D. C.: American Council of Learned Societies, 1962.

Tucker, Susie I. *English Examined.* Cambridge: Cambridge University Press, 1961.

Warfel, Harry R. *Noah Webster, Schoolmaster to America.* New York: Macmillan, 1936.

Waterman, John T. *Perspectives in Linguistics.* Chicago: University of Chicago Press, 1963.

Webster's Third New International Dictionary of the English Language. Springfield, Mass.: G. & C. Merriam Co., 1961.

Wetmore, Thomas H. *The Low-central and Low-back Vowels in the English of the Eastern United States,* Publication of the American Dialect Society, 32. University: University of Alabama Press, 1959.

Whitehall, Harold. "The English Language" in *Webster's New World Dictionary of the American Language.* College Edition. Cleveland: World Publishing Co., 1960.

Whitelock, Dorothy, ed. *English Historical Documents c. 500–1042.* London: Eyre & Spottiswoode, 1955.

Wilson, R. M. "English and French in England 1100–1300," *History*, N. S., XXVIII (1943), 37–60.

Wright, C. E. *English Vernacular Hands from the Twelfth to the Fifteenth Centuries.* Oxford: Oxford University Press, 1960.

Wright, Joseph. *English Dialect Dictionary.* 6 vols. London: H. Frowde, 1898–1905.

——— and Elizabeth M. *An Elementary Historical New English Grammar.* Oxford: Oxford University Press, 1924; reprinted 1954.

———. *An Elementary Middle English Grammar.* 2nd ed. London: Oxford University Press, 1923.

———. *Old English Grammar.* 3rd ed. Oxford: Oxford University Press, 1925; reprinted 1954.

Wright, Louis B. *The Cultural Life of the American Colonies 1607–1763.* New York: Harper & Brothers, 1957.

———— and Virginia A. La Mar, eds. *Life and Letters in Tudor and Stuart England.* Ithaca: Cornell University Press, 1962.

Wyld, Henry C. *A History of Modern Colloquial English.* 3rd ed. Oxford: Basil Blackwell, 1936; reprinted 1956.

————. *A Short History of English.* 3rd ed. New York: John Murray, 1927; reprinted 1963.

————. "South-Eastern and South-East Midland Dialects in Middle English," *Essays and Studies*, VI (1920), 112–145.

Index

352